WHAT WORKS

WHAT WORKS

Gender Equality by Design

Iris Bohnet

THE BELKNAP PRESS OF
HARVARD UNIVERSITY PRESS

Cambridge, Massachusetts
London, England

First Harvard University Press paperback edition, 2018
Second printing

Many of the designations used by manufacturers and sellers to distinguish
their products are claimed as trademarks. Where those designations appear
in this book and Harvard University Press was aware of a trademark claim,
then the designations have been printed in initial capital letters.

Library of Congress Cataloging-in-Publication Data

Names: Bohnet, Iris, author.
Title: What works : gender equality by design / Iris Bohnet.
Description: Cambridge, Massachusetts : The Belknap Press of Harvard
University Press, 2016. | Includes bibliographical references and index.
Identifiers: LCCN 2015039199 | ISBN 9780674089037 (cloth : alk. paper) |
ISBN 9780674986565 (pbk.)
Subjects: LCSH: Sex discrimination in employment. | Gender mainstreaming. |
Organizational behavior.
Classification: LCC HD6060 .B64 2016 | DDC 331.4/133—dc23 LC record
available at http://lccn.loc.gov/2015039199

To Michael, Dominik, and Luca
and
Ruth, Paul, and Brigitte
ILY

Contents

Part Two

HOW TO DESIGN TALENT MANAGEMENT

Part Three

HOW TO DESIGN SCHOOL AND WORK

Part Four

HOW TO DESIGN DIVERSITY

Designing Change   285

We can do this; the DESIGN mnemonic; effortless and energy-saving design for lights in hotel rooms; behavioral insights teams across the globe; a leader is a behavioral designer; overcoming the tension between "want" and "should"; creating a global movement

WHAT WORKS

The Promise of Behavioral Design

As late as 1970, only 5 percent of musicians performing in the top five orchestras in the United States were women. Today, women compose more than 35 percent of the most acclaimed orchestras, and they play great music. This did not happen by chance. Rather, it required the introduction of blind auditions. The Boston Symphony Orchestra was the first to ask musicians to audition behind a screen, and in the 1970s and 1980s most other major orchestras followed suit. When they did so, usually in preliminary rounds, it raised the likelihood that a female musician would advance by 50 percent and substantially increased the proportion of women hired.[1]

In theory, an orchestra director cares about the sounds coming out of the bassoon, the flute, and the trumpet, not the ethnicity or sex of the person playing the instrument. In practice, the Vienna Philharmonic, for example, admitted its first female player in 1997. Not so long ago. Orchestra directors and selection committees were quite comfortable with all-male, all-white orchestras and likely not aware of their biases. To change this, no great technological feat was required, just awareness, a curtain, and a decision. Or, more precisely, a design decision. A simple curtain doubled the talent pool, creating amazing music and transforming what orchestras look like. But why did it take so long?

Consider the following image and compare squares A and B. What do you see?

Checkershadow illusion, part 1.

Most people see square B as being lighter than square A. It turns out that this is an illusion. Your mind made sense of the pattern it saw, a checkerboard. You put squares into categories, dark and light, and put them in order: light squares next to dark squares. You may also have taken the shadow into account and made sure it did not trick you into not seeing a pattern that you knew had to be there.

Consider the same checkerboard now, with square B isolated. Note that squares A and B in fact have the same color. They are both dark. By blocking some of the checkerboard, we allowed your mind to see square B for what it is—another dark square. It no longer had to be in a certain category and obey certain rules. It was liberated from the patterns we expect, just as curtains liberated orchestra selection committees. Professional musicians typically are quite shocked when they learn how much they are influenced by visual cues. A recent series of experiments showed that competition judges consciously value sound as central to their decision. Only the experimental evidence shows them that, in fact, they are instead relying heavily on visual cues.[2]

Checkershadow illusion, part 2.

Consider another, quite different example. A study examining the parole rulings of Israeli judges found that they ruled far more leniently right after meal breaks. Differing degrees of leniency were the unintended consequence of hunger, fatigue, the depletion of cognitive resources—and design. Just prior to taking a break, the judges reverted to the easy solution: the status quo. After a break, they were more deliberative. The timing and number of breaks the judges took—the design—had unintentional consequences. Bad designs, whether consciously or unconsciously chosen, lead to bad outcomes. Bias is built into our practices and procedures, not just into our minds. Here is our opportunity.[3]

This book's goal is to offer good designs to you; designs that make it easier for our biased minds to get things right. Based on research evidence, we can change the environments in which we live, learn, and work. My principal focus here is the stubborn, costly problem of gender inequality, but the recommendations I make stem from a wealth of research about decisions and behavior that go well beyond gender. The book takes as a given that people make mistakes; they make them often and (sometimes) unknowingly. As a consequence, these mistakes reduce everyone's well-being. The solutions I recommend come from the field of behavioral economics—putting up screens, timing breaks well, and dozens of more and less complicated interventions—all building on insights into how our minds work. My invitation to you is to become a behavioral designer—because it works, because it often is rather easy and inexpensive, and because it will start to level the playing field and give everyone greater opportunity to thrive.

Much like interior designers or landscape architects, behavioral designers create environments to help us better achieve our goals. They do not define goals, but they help us get there. Referred to as "choice architecture" in Richard Thaler and Cass Sunstein's path-breaking book *Nudge,* behavioral design goes beyond law, regulation, or incentives, although it acknowledges that these are and will remain important. But they do not always work. Based on 41 million observations for the population of Denmark, for example, research shows that tax subsidies have only a tiny impact on savings. Such incentives require people to take action and respond—which 85 percent of Danes fail to do. In contrast, behavioral designs that do not rely on people reacting to incentives but instead employ automatic mechanisms—such as automatic employer contributions to retirement accounts—do much better. They substantially increased the amount of money retirees have available. We do not always do what is best for ourselves, for our organizations, or for the world—and sometimes, a little nudge can help.[4]

A simple curtain transformed what orchestras look like and doubled the talent pool. Benefiting from 100 percent talent is good business for orchestras and just about every other organization. Careful timing of breaks allows judges to make decisions more accurately and fairly. To the business case, then, we must add the moral case: behavioral design is the right thing to do.

There is no design-free world. Organizations have to decide how to search for and select future employees. How they advertise open positions, where they post the job openings, how they evaluate applicants, how they create a short list, how they interview candidates, and how they make their final selections are all part of choice architecture. Why not design a bit more thoughtfully, increasing the chances that the best people are hired?

This book will show you how. Our research suggests, for example, that asking hiring managers to explicitly compare a given candidate with real alternatives makes evaluators focus on individual performance instead of stereotypes. Comparing two or more job candidates helps evaluators calibrate their judgments—without having to rely on an internal stereotype as a measuring rod. As academic dean of the Kennedy School of Government, I introduced this and other insights shared in this book to the faculty hiring and promotion procedures at Harvard University.

It bears repeating that design is everywhere. We constantly make choices about how to present information, structure interviews, or create teams, and we live day in, day out with the consequences of those choices. Whether or not employees are asked to "opt in" or "opt out" of a pension plan might well determine whether or not they have enough money to enjoy retirement. How your company hires and promotes might well determine bottom-line performance. By changing the design, we change the outcome: good design can lead to positive outcomes—nudge by nudge. We begin by uncovering the root causes for certain behaviors and designing interventions accordingly. These root causes include one difficult truth: no one is immune from biases.

A few years ago I entered a day-care center at my workplace, Harvard University. I had our young son in my arms. Like millions of parents who have taken their child to a caregiver for the first time, I was extremely anxious. One of the first teachers I saw was—a man. I wanted to turn around and run. How could I entrust this *man* with the most precious thing in my life? He did not conform to my expectation of what a loving, caring, and nurturing preschool teacher looked like. My reaction was not based on a conscious thought process, but rather on something deep in my gut. Was I being sexist? I fear the answer is yes.

Thankfully, I overcame my biased snap judgment, the teacher proved great, and he became a trusted caregiver. But to this day my gut reaction bothers me. Only about 10 to 20 percent of the elementary school teachers in the United States and many other countries are male. These men face an uphill battle. Just as in orchestras, there is likely an untapped talent pool of elementary school teachers. What is more, society's failure to draw on that pool of talent matters. A 2015 study by the Organisation for Economic Co-operation and Development (OECD) finds that at age fifteen, boys are 50 percent more likely than girls to lack basic proficiency in reading, mathematics, and science. The presence of male role models can impact what boys believe possible and important for themselves: seeing is believing.

Stereotypes serve as heuristics—rules of thumb—that allow us to process information more easily, but they are often inaccurate. What is worse, stereotypes describing how we believe the world to be often turn into prescriptions for what the world should be. Much psychological research shows that we cannot help but put people (and other observations) into categories. It rarely is a conscious thought process that informs our thinking about demographic groups. Rather, when we learn the sex of a person, gender biases are automatically activated, leading to unintentional and implicit discrimination.[5]

Through behavioral design we can move the needle toward creating equal opportunities for female musicians, for male teachers, and for everyone else. Good design often harvests low-hanging fruit, left on the tree not so much because of bad intentions but rather because of the mind bugs that affect our judgment. Behavioral design offers an additional instrument for our collective toolbox to promote change; it complements other approaches focusing, for example, on equal rights, education, health, agency, or on policies making work and family compatible.

Much has been written about the "business case" for gender equality, and research continues to accumulate. One clear insight is that the answer to what degree closing gender gaps yields economic returns is difficult to determine if outcomes are based on flawed decision processes. Take the example of orchestras. I presume that orchestras benefited from the introduction of blind auditions because curtains allowed evaluators to choose the best performers and build the best team—which also increased the fraction of women.

It is a trivial point but one largely overlooked in the literature. Whether or not the share of women and men in groups, say, corporate boards, is related to company performance does not depend only on the percentage of each gender on the board but also on how the board members, women and men, are chosen, how the boards are organized, and what the rules of engagement and decision making are. Gender equality is not just a numbers game. Numbers matter, but how those numbers came to be and how they work with each other is quite possibly even more important.

Still, we have learned a lot about the business case for gender equality. A recent study measuring the impact of an increase in the talent pool on the US economy between 1960 and 2008 found that aggregate output per worker had grown by 15 to 20 percent due to an improved allocation of talent. For example, while in 1960 the effective talent pool for doctors and lawyers consisted of white men—94 percent of all doctors and lawyers in the United States were white men—this had changed dramatically by 2008, when the fraction of white male doctors and lawyers had decreased to 62 percent. Casting the net more widely, including women and African, Asian, Hispanic, and Native Americans, had paid off.[6]

Leveling the playing field to include more women in the labor force is of vital economic importance for various countries. Consider Japan. The OECD estimates that if it does nothing to increase the labor force participation rates of its women, and these remain at their 2011 levels of 63 percent for women and 84 percent for men, the country's labor force will shrink by more than 10 percent during the next twenty years. In contrast, if Japan achieved gender parity in its labor force, its gross domestic product (GDP) would increase by almost 20 percent over the next twenty years. High returns as a result of women's economic inclusion is not just a Japanese phenomenon but generally shared by countries with low fertility rates, including Germany, Italy, Singapore, South Korea, and Spain, among others.[7]

A simulation assuming that women are completely excluded from the labor force found that this would lead to income per capita losses of almost 40 percent. Using labor market data for 126 countries from the International Labor Organization (ILO) to calculate the actual gender gaps in workforce participation (as well as in self-employment and pay if available) in various regions of the world, the total income losses are largest (27 percent) in the Middle East and North Africa. In addition, for an increasing number of countries, the talent argument has gained importance as the gender gap in education has reversed and more women than men graduate from college. In the United States, for example, more than half of bachelor's degrees have been held by women since the mid-1980s, and by the early twenty-first century, almost 60 percent of bachelor's degree holders were female.

While economists still debate the exact magnitude of the impact of increasing women's labor-force participation on GDP, we can safely agree with Christine Lagarde, managing director of the International Monetary Fund (IMF), that "excluding women simply makes no economic sense—and including women can be a tremendous boon to the 21st century global economy."[8]

On a micro-level, women have been found to put money to more productive use than men in several cases. In Ivory Coast, for example, there are "male" and "female" crops. Men grow coffee, cocoa, and pineapple; women grow plantains, bananas, coconuts, and vegetables. In years where the men's crops have high yields, research shows, households spend more money on alcohol and tobacco. When the women have good harvests, in contrast, more money is spent on food. In the United States, interesting micro-evidence on the relevance of women's inclusion stems from laboratory experiments measuring a group's "collective intelligence" across a variety of tasks. Gender-diverse teams scored more highly on collective intelligence than all-male or all-female teams. Importantly, a group's collective intelligence was only moderately related to members' individual intelligence, suggesting that a gender diverse team can indeed be more than the sum of its parts.[9]

While the macro- and the micro-evidence hold the promise of a business case, gender equality is not a magic bullet automatically leading to economic progress. This is why, at the end of the day, the case of gender equality must rest on a moral argument. It just is the right thing to do. Full stop.[10]

We cannot afford to get it wrong. In the most extreme case, getting it wrong is a matter of life and death. The United Nations estimates up to 200 million women and girls are missing worldwide as a result of sex-selective abortion, infanticide, neglect during the first five years, gendered violence, and discrimination later in life. This selective killing of members of a particular sex, referred to as "gendercide," might well be the greatest human rights tragedy in history. If the same number of females were "missing" in the United States, America would be a men-only country. Nick Kristof and Sheryl WuDunn remind us that this number exceeds all the men killed on the battlefield in all twentieth-century wars.

While horrendous by itself, gendercide has further consequences. In January 2010, the Chinese Academy of Social Sciences calculated that in 2020, one in five Chinese men would not be able to find a bride. The Academy expects a surplus of about 30 to 40 million young men without marriage prospects in 2020—which corresponds to nearly the whole young male population in the United States. A low female-to-male ratio has been shown to lead to an expansion of the marriage market by decreasing the age of brides, hampering their educational attainment and economic opportunities. It has also been linked to an increase in trafficking of girls, domestic violence, honor killings, and other crime.[11]

A problem that many fear too big to even start addressing inspired an amazing experiment by Rob Jensen, a former colleague and now professor at the Wharton School of the University of Pennsylvania. He examined what impact seeing economic opportunities for women in rural India had on how parents treated their daughters. Jensen exploited the fact that the business process outsourcing industry grew rapidly in India during the 1990s and created a significant number of new jobs, in particular for women. With the help of a recruitment firm, he provided three years of recruitment services to women in randomly selected rural villages. He then compared whether these women were more likely to work than their counterparts in control villages. Jensen also investigated whether this translated into a change in how parents treated their daughters. Indeed, the recruitment services significantly increased employment among women (without affecting men). In addition, in the villages chosen to receive recruitment services, girls aged five to fifteen experienced a substantial improvement in health and were significantly more likely to be in school.

Seeing women work in call centers allowed parents to imagine a different future for their own daughters. While the number of women newly working in call centers was relatively small (an increase of 2.4 percentage points), even this small possibility challenged parents' beliefs and their stereotypes about what women could accomplish.[12]

Behavioral design can affect faculty hiring in Cambridge, Massachusetts, and create counterstereotypical role models in rural villages outside of New Delhi, India. These are just two of the places where these insights are helping people get it right for themselves, their organizations, and the world. A tall order, you might think. I do not deny conflicts of interest or trade-offs in this book. Some games are zero-sum, and your gain will indeed be my loss. But not every game ends with a winner and a loser. Many games are positive sum, and here behavioral design is less like playing chess and more like dancing. We can improve girls' health, education, and opportunities in India without harming those of boys. And we can select job candidates in organizations across the world based on individual performance rather than group stereotypes, increasing both efficiency and equality.

How can we know that a particular design is effective? We can try different strategies and measure their impact. We can examine the effectiveness of behavioral design much like we evaluate the impact of a new drug, running a clinical trial in which people, schools, or even villages are randomly assigned to treatment or control groups. The goal of random assignment is to create groups that are as identical as possible, so that any change in behavior can be attributed to the "treatment." Indeed, much of the evidence discussed in this book will be based on such randomized controlled trials, allowing us to create a causal pathway from the design intervention to the outcome.

Thankfully, experimentation is becoming increasingly popular. More and more governments are designing policy interventions in collaboration with social science researchers, allowing them to evaluate their impact. Corporations are using advanced technologies and social media to test different marketing strategies and human resource practices. And nongovernmental organizations are running scientifically valid experiments to explore how to decrease homelessness or recidivism most effectively. Still, we should do more. At all levels, we need to create learning environments where people are encouraged to try out something new, possibly fail, and then learn from it.

This fear of trying new things and failing is a real constraint. It is also the one that I had underestimated most. Learning is my business and, naively, I expected everyone to be keen on uncovering past mistakes and improving their decision making. However, in some organizations, acknowledging past errors is risky. Thus, while the CEO or the president might be enthusiastic about discovering mistakes and piloting a new idea, managers at all levels might well feel threatened. To circumvent this, governments and corporations must create safe spaces for experimentation where mistakes are taken as an opportunity to learn.

In this book, I offer dozens of opportunities to try something new. These interventions mostly relate to gender, but sometimes I draw on research examining how to promote equality for other traditionally disadvantaged groups. Some of the same design features that level the playing field between men and women can also inform our thinking about other groups. But while we should learn from each other, from research on race in the United States or castes in India, we need to be mindful that findings do not automatically generalize. Rather, evidence from one field should serve as an invitation to experiment with similar design features in another.

Despite media attention paid to general issues of race and gender, we still know relatively little about the intersection between different social categories—for example, to what degree evidence on white women also applies to African, Asian, Hispanic, or Native American women. Similarly, the research on faltering academic achievement among boys and men, and what to do about it, is relatively young. A series on gender, education, and work in the *Economist* in the spring of 2015 highlights the challenges poorly educated men in the United States and elsewhere face. They are falling behind not only in school but also in work and society more generally. The series calls for a "change in cultural attitudes": "Men need to understand that traditional manual jobs are not coming back, and that they can be nurses or hairdressers without losing their masculinity."[13]

Bias hurts counterstereotypical individuals across gender, race, class, ethnicity, nationality, or caste. Consider this. Simulations show that even a tiny bias in performance evaluations can lead to huge disparities in representation at the highest levels. Assuming the typical corporate pyramid structure where only a few make it to the top, and holding everything else constant, one simulation found that a bias accounting for only 1 percent of the variance in evaluation scores led to only 35 percent of the discriminated-against group being represented at the top. Without the bias, each group would have held 50 percent of these seats.[14]

Going with your gut can have real effects. The first part of the book explores this further. It helps us better understand the problem—why gender bias is so prevalent and why it is hard to overcome by training alone. It explores approaches focused on de-biasing mindsets through diversity training and on helping women navigate the system, compete more effectively, negotiate more assertively, and lead more strategically. Women need to know how and when to "lean in" as Sheryl Sandberg eloquently described in her book. But a review of women's empowerment initiatives suggests that women will not be able to do it alone.[15]

The remainder of the book focuses on the solutions behavioral design offers. The second part introduces new designs for talent management. It is devoted to the importance of evidence, continuing the theme of experimentation but also arguing for improved data collection by gender and the use of big data. One of the more recent applications of big data has been in the area of *people analytics*. Generally, people analytics argues that we can learn more about, say, a given job applicant's likelihood of leaving the firm within the first year by analyzing the characteristics of current leavers and stayers than by clever tests or intricate interviews with the candidate. Replacing intuition, informal networks, and traditional rules of thumb with quantifiable data and rigorous analysis is a first step toward overcoming gender bias. Successful for-profit and not-for-profit organizations such as Credit Suisse, Goldman Sachs, Google, LinkedIn, Microsoft, and Teach for America increasingly run their HR departments like they run their finance or marketing departments, based on evidence. Some now refer to them as "people analytics departments."[16]

We also need to scrutinize the messages we send to people who consider joining our organizations. Do we attract the right or the wrong ones? Who opts in and who opts out? Is there gender bias in how we advertise job openings and describe the qualifications and characteristics we look for in a future employee? Do schools and universities encourage a broad set of applications or do we, consciously or unconsciously, send messages that deter certain groups of people from applying? Insights into gender differences in preferences for, say, competition or uncertainty, and self-stereotypes regarding aptitude for certain subjects, disciplines, or jobs help shape the signals we send, increasing the chances that people perceive the opening as an invitation to apply.

Much more can be done. The third part of the book dissects the environments in which people live, learn, and work for unintended biases. Are the portraits that hang in the hallways of your organizations only of past male leaders? Know that this is impacting what employees or students believe possible for themselves. Stereotypes can be activated by the most subtle cues, including whether or not test-takers are asked to check off boxes indicating their sex or race before taking a test. Stereotypes prescribing that Asians outperform whites in math, and girls do better than boys in reading and writing can become self-fulfilling prophecies—unless we de-bias how we do things.

Finally, in addition to redesigning how we manage talent and craft school and work environments, we can also apply behavioral insights to make diversity work better. The fourth part of the book shows that contact with other social groups can change stereotypical beliefs and help people collaborate across groups. But not all groups are created equally. Having a "critical mass" of every subgroup represented in a team has been shown to be crucial to team success. Success is also promoted by the use of specific design principles defining the rules of engagement or decision-

making. By choosing the "right numbers" and the "right procedures," you can help teams perform better.

These are some of the tools and techniques, often low-hanging
fruit, behavioral design offers to improve our classrooms and boardrooms, tests and performance evaluations, hiring and promotions, and policy- and decision-making. Based on evidence from
experimental studies in most cases, this book shows that small
changes can have surprising effects. Big data improves our understanding of what is broken and needs fixing, blind or comparative
evaluation procedures help us hire the best instead of those who
look the part, and role models shape what people think is possible.
Building on what works, behavioral design creates better and fairer
organizations and societies. It will not solve all our gender-related
problems, but it will move the needle, and often at shockingly low
cost and high speed.

Part One

THE PROBLEM

1

Unconscious Bias Is Everywhere

Meet Howard Roizen, a venture capitalist, former entrepreneur, and proficient networker. A case study taught at many business schools describes how he became a power player in Silicon Valley. He co-founded a very successful tech company, then became an executive at Apple, subsequently turning his attention to venture capitalism. Most recently, he became a member of the boards of directors of several prestigious companies. He is a friend of Bill Gates and was close to Steve Jobs. He maintains one of the most extensive networks in Silicon Valley.

After studying the case, students were asked to evaluate Howard's performance. They rated him as highly competent and effective. They also said that they liked him and would be willing to hire him or work with him.

But Howard does not actually exist. His real name is Heidi. He is a woman. And when studying the absolutely identical case with the protagonist being female, students find Heidi as competent and effective as Howard, but they no longer like or want to work with this successful entrepreneur and venture capitalist.

My friend Kathleen McGinn of Harvard Business School originally wrote the case study about Heidi Roizen in 2000 to highlight the steps taken by one successful entrepreneur to build and leverage personal and professional networks. A few years later, I encountered it again in a research seminar. Two professors had given half of their students McGinn's original case, which accurately identified Heidi, and the other half the same case, but with "Howard" swapped in for Heidi. This allowed them to compare how students felt about Heidi and Howard.[1]

Many business schools have since run the experiment, using it as a pedagogical tool to help their MBA students experience gender bias. Afterward, the students realize that the prototypical leader in their minds is male. Heidi does not look or act the part: she cannot be competent *and* likable at the same time. What is celebrated as entrepreneurship, self-confidence, and vision in a man is perceived as arrogance and self-promotion in a woman.

Women can't win. If they conform to the feminine stereotype of nurture and care for others, they tend to be liked but not respected. Dozens of studies have now demonstrated that women face a trade-off between competence and likability. Women in stereotypically male domains encounter backlash at every juncture: when getting hired, compensated, and promoted. Psychologists believe that these negative reactions are due to a clash between our stereotypical perceptions of what women are or should be like (their gender roles), and the qualities we think are necessary to perform a typically male job. If women like Heidi demonstrate that they can do a "man's job," they no longer fit our mental model of the "ideal woman." They violate norms, and people do not find norm violators appealing. Put differently, women who violate norms pay a social price.[2]

Most studies on the topic have been run with white men and women, mostly in the United States. We know little about whether the same dynamics apply to other races and ethnicities. What we do know is typically based on small samples, for the experiments have not been replicated widely. Thus we need to interpret them with care. While there exists no comprehensive study of whether the *agency penalty* established for white, female Americans also applies to African, Asian, Hispanic, and Native Americans, Robert Livingston and colleagues examined the question for African Americans. They found that black women are considered neither prototypical women nor prototypical blacks. Does this buffer them from some of the gender stereotypes white women experience? Indeed, experimental evidence showed that black women did not experience the same kind of backlash as white women when they expressed dominance rather than communality. In contrast, dominant African American men were penalized while white American men were not. If African American men are perceived as nonthreatening, they benefit. Physical features expressing warmth and deference have been shown to be an advantage for black male CEOs, but these same attributes hurt white male CEOs in the United States.

These findings are in contrast to models of *double jeopardy,* assuming that people with multiple "subordinate identities," for example, African American women, are subject to more prejudice than those with only one—African American men or white women. Identities appear to be not only additive but intersecting in ways that current research is starting to uncover. Erica Hall and collaborators suggest that a person's gender profile is composed of the "genders" of a person's sex and race and that we should take this gender profile into account to better understand gendered perceptions of occupational "fit."[3]

Gender stereotypes appear to generalize to some degree across cultures. For example, many societies differentiate warmth from competence when judging social groups; high-status groups are stereotypically perceived as competent but lacking in warmth, and the male stereotype is associated with the cultural ideal. The pervasiveness of these stereotypes has real effects on how people are evaluated.[4]

Again and again, the pattern that has emerged from experiments assessing women who are performing stereotypically male jobs—an aircraft company's assistant vice president for sales, for example—looks like this:

- When performance is observable, successful women are rated as less likable than men.
- When performance is ambiguous, successful women are rated as less competent than men.

In the latter case, when evaluators cannot easily measure quality, they fill in the blanks with stereotypes. In one recent study, Katy Milkman, Modupe Akinola, and Dolly Chugh sent thousands of professors at academic institutions across the United States an email from a phantom student requesting a ten-minute meeting the following week to learn more about a doctoral program the professor was involved in. The name of the student, however, varied: some were self-evidently male, others female; each sounded either white, African American, Hispanic, Indian, or Chinese. Almost 70 percent of the professors responded, and most agreed to meet with the student. However, they were significantly less likely to respond to a student who was not a white male than to a white male student. The bias was most pronounced in the field of business administration, with 87 percent of white men but only about 62 percent of all the women and students of color combined receiving a response. The professor's own demographic characteristics generally did not matter—Hispanic female professors were as likely to favor white male students as white male professors were (the one exception being Chinese students who requested a meeting with a Chinese professor). Did the professors, likely unconsciously, perceive the white men as more competent or more deserving of their attention?[5]

Another field experiment is illuminating. A man and a woman applied for a laboratory manager position at a university. They were otherwise identical and had the same qualifications. Science faculty rated the male candidate as significantly more competent than the female candidate and were more likely to hire him. The faculty's pre-existing bias against women affected their evaluation. In a further exploration of gender biases associated with STEM fields (science, technology, engineering, and mathematics), researchers had people hire candidates to perform a specific job: a well-defined arithmetic task on which both genders perform equally well. When the evaluators knew nothing except the candidates' gender, men were about twice as likely to be hired as women. The bias was barely affected, however, when the candidates were allowed to provide information on their qualifications. In keeping with other findings, when the male candidates did so they tended to boast, and when the female candidates did so they tended to under-report how good they were, behaviors evaluators did not take into account. Only information about how well the candidates had done on the task in an earlier round helped reduce the bias. But even this precise information was unable to eliminate it completely.[6]

How about men? What if men are evaluated for a counterstereotypical job, such as the assistant vice president of Human Resources? While this question has been studied less, it appears as if men in counterstereotypical roles experience some of the same bias-informed dynamics as women do—with one important exception: their likability is not affected. Male human resources managers may well be evaluated as less competent, but holding a stereotypically female position does not make them less likable. Women, thus, are in a double bind that men are not. They are perceived as either likable or competent but not both.

Biases about whether or not a person fits matter. Being disliked, in addition to being extremely unpleasant, can injure, even derail your career. Mothers might be even more affected than women without children. Much evidence suggests that stereotypical perceptions of warmth work against mothers in the labor market. Unlikable individuals have been shown to receive worse performance ratings and be deemed less worthy of salary increases or promotions than their more likable counterparts. This appears to be true for both men and women. But while colleagues have lots of reasons to dislike someone, from dishonesty to arrogance, "it is only women, not men, for whom a unique propensity toward dislike is created by success in nontraditional work." This quote, from Madeline Heilman, one of the leading researchers in this field, can be rephrased more bluntly. Because of our biases, we tend to react to successful women much like we react to dishonest men: we do not like them and do not want to work with them.[7]

Numerous additional field experiments have been conducted in which male and female candidates, otherwise equally qualified, have applied for the same jobs, and again and again bias has been found to influence outcomes. Whether applying to be waiters or

waitresses in the United States, or accountants, engineers, computer
programmers, or secretaries in the United Kingdom, or financial
analysts in France, sex-based discrimination has been influential. A
review of the evidence concludes that both women and men tend
to be discriminated against in jobs that are associated with and
dominated by the opposite sex. Men were discriminated against
when seeking jobs as secretaries and women discriminated against
when seeking jobs as engineers.[8]

While the evidence is still thin, there are some early signs that
we are starting to see a change in this trend. For a 2013 segment
of CNN's *Anderson Cooper 360°,* the Heidi-Howard study was
repeated at New York University's Stern School of Business.
The students still rated the successful female leader as less trust-
worthy than her male counterpart, but they no longer liked her
less. Indeed, they reported being more willing to work for her
than for the successful man. In 2015, a scientific study reporting a
reversal of this trend for entry-level jobs in academia appeared in
the *Proceedings of the National Academy of Sciences.* Wendy Williams
and Stephen Ceci found in five hiring experiments—in which
faculty evaluated profiles of hypothetical male and female candidates applying for jobs as assistant professors in biology, engineering, economics, and psychology—a substantial pro-female
bias in all disciplines but economics. Are we starting to harvest
the fruits of all the work that has been done to equalize the playing
field in science, technology, engineering, and math—at least at
the entry level?

As I write this book, it is too early to tell. Maybe faculty in
biology, engineering, and psychology are overcompensating for
past inequities in an effort to move the needle a bit more toward
gender equality in hiring. Perhaps STEM fields are catching up

with other areas where we have seen an increase in gender diversity at the entry level. Why this is happening in some fields but not in my own, economics, remains unclear.[9]

Another field where gender diversity at the entry level has dramatically increased is law. Analyzing panel data from more than 6,000 lawyers employed by one of the largest law firms in the world from 2003 to 2011, Ina Ganguli, Ricardo Hausmann, and Martina Viarengo found that an almost equal number of male and female lawyers entered at the associate level. However, this did not translate into closing the gender gap at the top, where only 23 percent of partners were female. Instead, the gender gap at the most highly ranked position, partner, was strongly related to a gender gap in promotions. In their book *Through the Labyrinth,* Alice Eagly and Linda Carli discuss how gender stereotypes constrain women's access to leadership roles. In particular, biases affected evaluations of women vying for the very top positions, or what is commonly known as the *glass ceiling effect.* In contrast to the entry level, there is no closure of the gender gap at the top in sight.[10]

Ganguli and colleagues' research shows why. The lawyers in their study worked for one firm in thirty-three different offices located in twenty-three countries on four continents. The three researchers had access to an almost unprecedented amount of individual-level data, including wages, bonuses, performance appraisals, educational background, employment status, career trajectory and leaves, as well as demographic characteristics. Promotion gaps persisted after controlling for all of these variables, including the fact that men and women left the firm at equal rates. But the degree of promotion gaps varied across countries—even though, at least in theory, the firm was guided by the same set of policies and practices. Female lawyers found it hardest to climb up the career ladder in countries where stereotypical thinking about gender roles was most pronounced, such as in the Russian Federation, Singapore, or Thailand, based on both survey data from the World Values Survey and the World Economic Forum Global Gender Gap Index as well as data concerning each country's gender gap in political representation. The playing field for female lawyers was more even in countries such as Belgium, the Netherlands, or Sweden.[11]

Another study examined the performance evaluation bias toward highly successful women in a number of contexts, including commanding officers in the US military. It turns out the evaluating officers gave female subordinates whose pay grades were close to their own lower performance scores than they gave to male subordinates. The authors identify this phenomenon as *gender hierarchy threat*. Female (but not male) subordinates whose objective performance was strong were punished by male (but not female) evaluators for violating gender norms.[12]

Let's take stock: the gender gap in leadership is real; its relationship to the gender gap in promotions is real; a connection exists between the promotion gap and the extent of stereotypical attitudes. These dynamics have been demonstrated in various contexts and countries, but too little is known to determine to what extent they generalize from whites to all other demographic groups. The stereotypes about "leadership fit"—or lack thereof—are hardly based on evidence. There simply are not enough women in positions of leadership to draw reliable inferences. Interestingly enough, when employees who prefer male leaders in theory are exposed to female leaders, they do not give them lower ratings, a large 2011 survey finds. The bias against female upper-level managers is in our heads—or, to quote from one of my favorite textbooks on organizational economics by two Stanford economists, Paul Milgrom and John Roberts: "even if the beliefs are completely groundless, no disconfirming evidence ever is generated because women never get a chance to prove the beliefs are wrong. Thus, the baseless beliefs survive, and with them, the unjustified discrimination."[13]

Our minds are not well equipped to deal with what is commonly known as *survivor bias*. We constantly make inferences based on biased samples. The archetypal example is a study of World War II bombers. With the hope of making them safer, the planes were examined for weaknesses *after* they returned from their bombing runs. But, of course, these were the wrong planes to examine. They were just the ones that made it back. To learn about weaknesses, one would have had to examine all the planes—or, as Abraham Wald, a mathematician at Columbia University, concluded at the time, the scientists should not have looked for the bullet holes the returning planes had, but for the bullet holes they did not have. It was these other "holes" that determined whether a plane made it back or not.[14]

This does not sound intuitive—and it is not. I regularly teach a case study at Harvard on sample bias based on the fatal launch of the shuttle *Challenger* in 1986. The students are asked to reach a decision structurally similar to what NASA's engineers faced, although in a different context where lives are not at stake. They are presented with the same data points on past successes and failures that the engineers focused on and encouraged to seek more information. Only very few do. Rather, they base their decision on a biased sample. In doing so they experience the bias that has been identified as one of the core mistakes that led to the launch of the shuttle *Challenger*.[15]

Although bias is prevalent, it is important to note that not all intuitive judgments automatically are inaccurate. Some intuitive judgments are based on accurate stereotypes that reflect the true distribution of a given group's characteristics. Consider the following story, a popular mental sleight of hand. A father and his son are in a car accident. The father does not survive, and the son is badly injured. An ambulance takes the son to the hospital, where the surgeon cries out: "I cannot operate because this boy is my son!"

For most of us, our intuitive reaction is, at first, confusion. Upon reflection, we realize that, of course, this is quite possible. The surgeon is the boy's mother.

About one third of all surgeons in the United States are female, so it is not that surprising that when we think of "surgeon" we also first think "man." Economists refer to this as *statistical discrimination*. People base their assessment of an individual person on group averages. They do this intuitively, as in the above example. They also do this to help them in situations where they do not have complete information about an individual's relevant characteristics.

In a field experiment demonstrating the existence of statistical discrimination, researchers sent in different buyers to negotiate with salespersons for a secondhand car. The sellers demanded a significantly higher initial price when the buyer was a woman or African American than when the buyer was a man or white. It appears that salespersons took advantage of the fact that on average female and African American car buyers have been found to be less well informed of the price of a car. Because sellers were aware of this, they statistically discriminated against these prospective buyers. The shadow statistical discrimination casts can be long and hard to escape. After being presented with the salesperson's initial price, even well-informed African Americans and women could not close the gap and reach the price the salesperson offered to white men in negotiations.[16]

There are obvious practical lessons to be learned from evidence of statistical discrimination. Unsurprisingly, I advise all of my students, but particularly women and people of color, to arrive extremely well prepared to any secondhand car dealerships (and, of course, to any negotiation!). Not only should they do their homework and know how much a car with certain attributes is worth, but they should also have an understanding of how to trade off fewer years against less mileage. And most importantly, they need to make sure the salesperson is aware of their knowledge and expertise before an initial price is presented to them.

We clearly use group characteristics all the time when judging individuals. These judgments have real consequences—no less real than those resulting from unconscious biases. For example, the labor market penalizes women but rewards men for having children. The *child salary penalty* is a well-known statistical fact for women, as is the *child salary premium* for men. Some of this is due to statistical discrimination, with employers expecting that mothers will be more likely than fathers to cut back on their hours and, maybe, leave the workforce altogether. Their assessment is accurate. In academia, for example, the large majority of faculty taking parental leave are female. In one study surveying married tenure-track parents of under-two-year-olds, 69 percent of the mothers and 12 percent of the fathers chose to take parental leave. Faculty who take leave have been found to be paid less. Accordingly, they tend to engage in bias avoidance by not taking parental leave if at all possible.[17]

Of course, statistical discrimination is not limited to gender. Racial profiling is hotly debated in the United States. Law enforcement has been reported to suspect an individual of breaking the law solely based on his or her race and ethnicity. To what degree a society wants to allow the use of demographic characteristics to prejudge people is a political, even a moral decision. As a society, we want our systems, laws, and organizational procedures to reflect our values. Accordingly, in many countries it is considered immoral and often illegal to base hiring decisions, for example, on information the employer has about the group a person belongs to. Equality, whether between men and women or between people of different racial, ethnic, national, or other demographic backgrounds, is a moral decision first.[18]

Consider, too, that much of what people believe to be statistical discrimination actually is not. Assessing the usefulness of a stereotype, say, in forming an opinion about a person's trustworthiness or future performance is a cognitively demanding task. Many stereotypes were never accurate to begin with, and some lost their accuracy over time. Most people still believe women to be worse at mathematics than men. However, the evidence is much more nuanced and varies by country and population. Indeed, in recent years, the gender gap in math has reversed in several countries, with girls outperforming boys in school on average. Stereotypes have not been nearly so quick to reverse.[19]

Evidence from behavioral decision research suggests that we do not update our stereotypes accordingly. In fact, when we think about a group, we do not even focus on the average, as suggested by statistical discrimination, but rather we recall the group's most distinctive types. We are influenced by salient representatives of a given category. Arguing this point, a recent article provides a helpful illustration: Pause now and think briefly of people living in Florida. Whom did you think of?

If you are like most others, you fell prey to the stereotype that most Florida residents are elderly. It turns out that this is not true at all. In 2013, 82 percent of Florida's residents were younger than sixty-five—only slightly fewer than in the overall population of the United States (where about 86 percent were under sixty-five). At the same time, it is true that among the country's older populations, more live in Florida than elsewhere in the United States. Thus, the relative frequency of the elderly living in Florida is higher than in the comparison group, the rest of the United States. Such stereotypes are based on representative characteristics of a group, not on its average ones. If you were among the majority and thought that most Florida residents were elderly, perhaps conjuring up a grandparent in Tampa, you succumbed to a known bias, the *representativeness heuristic.*[20]

When Florida calls to mind retirement communities and the aged, your System 1 is in control. In his 2011 masterpiece, *Thinking, Fast and Slow*, Daniel Kahneman, a psychologist and 2002 Nobel Laureate in Economics, helps us understand how this works. He introduces the reader to two modes of thinking, System 1 and System 2, a distinction often used in psychology. Our intuitive System 1 runs automatically, without much effort or control. It assesses information quickly. Some might say it makes snap judgments and employs a number of mechanisms to deal with life's complexity. It uses heuristics, or rules of thumb, to interpret the world and relies on categories represented by archetypes. The deliberative System 2, in contrast, is based on conscious reasoning, requires effort, and is controlled. It is slower than System 1 and capable of abstract analysis and rule-based thinking. When we think of nurses, teachers, and engineers, System 1 supplies a representation of a member of this category who qualifies as "normal" or "typical." We employ a stereotype when judging others. System 1 is satisfied by what it observes in the moment, a process that Kahneman dubs as WYSIATI, What You See Is All There Is. System 1 has a need for internal consistency and confirmation of previously held beliefs, and thus finds it hard to update and incorporate new information.

Much of the psychologist Susan Fiske's work has been devoted to better understanding how exactly this process works. She and her colleagues have developed a "continuum model of impression formation," a framework that helps us understand how we form impressions of people. Most of us form first impressions based on social categories, such as sex, race, age, or social class. We then work to confirm our initial category-based assessments, sometimes re-categorizing if the available information no longer fits. Eventually, we integrate a person's individual attributes if needed. She argues that "social categorization is a necessary, if unfortunate, byproduct of our cognitive makeup." Matching people to existing social categories helps us quickly make sense of the world, sizing up and classifying people based on our experiences. In short, we are economizing our cognitive effort.

Characteristics that manifest themselves in physical appearance tend to dominate nonvisual cues. The color of your skin and the cut of your hair, for example, matter more than your accent.

Among various visual cues, the one that stands out because of its surrounding environment is most likely to inform a category-based impression. Because the lone female director on a corporate board and the sole male elementary school teacher stand out, we more quickly place them in categories. But we do not need marked physical traits or outliers in their environments to convince us that someone belongs in a particular category. Even when people (or objects, for that matter) were arbitrarily given a random label (some individuals marked as in the "purple" group and others marked as in the "orange" group), observers started to see similarities among members of the "purple" group and among members of the "orange" group. They also observed differences between members of "purple" and "orange." In the most extreme case, people perceived some as the "ingroup," or similar to themselves, and others as an "outgroup," and treated each accordingly by allocating more rewards to ingroup members.

Depressingly, unlearning is basically impossible. Once an initial category-based assessment has been made, thereafter new information is interpreted in a biased way, favoring consistency with the initial impression, a process known as *confirmatory categorization*. My colleague Mike Norton of Harvard Business School and others show in a number of experiments with how much creativity our minds go about doing this. People were asked to evaluate job candidates for a stereotypically male job in a construction company. They were informed that both experience in the industry and educational background were important for the job. Among the top two candidates, one had more experience and the other more education. Given that it was a stereotypically male job, evaluators generally preferred male candidates. But what is more, they justified their decisions, made on biased social categories, by using information on experience and education selectively: when the male candidate had more experience but less education than the female candidate, they said that they valued experience more than education. When the male candidate had more education and less experience, they inflated the relative importance of education. Similar ex-post justifications have been demonstrated for race as well.[21]

A typical response to data like these is to conclude that they don't apply to you. Sure, participants in these studies demonstrated these biases and fell prey to confirmation categorization, but just as a majority of us are sure we're better than average drivers, many of us imagine we'd do better. To which I say: have a look at the task in the following illustration, and please name the color of the words out loud. Measure how long it takes to recite the whole list.

GRAY	BLACK	WHITE	WHITE	BLACK
GRAY	BLACK	GRAY	BLACK	WHITE
BLACK	GRAY	BLACK	BLACK	GRAY
WHITE	WHITE	GRAY	WHITE	GRAY
GRAY	BLACK	WHITE	WHITE	BLACK

The Stroop test, part 1

Now, name the color of the words out loud in the test that follows.

GRAY	BLACK	**WHITE**	**WHITE**	BLACK
GRAY	**BLACK**	**GRAY**	BLACK	**WHITE**
BLACK	**GRAY**	BLACK	**BLACK**	**GRAY**
WHITE	**WHITE**	GRAY	**WHITE**	**GRAY**
GRAY	**BLACK**	**WHITE**	**WHITE**	BLACK

The Stroop test, part 2

Undoubtedly, you will have noticed that it is much harder the second time around. When the name of the color does not match the color of the type, the brain stumbles over itself. The effect is even more pronounced with red, blue, green, and so on. Your mind cannot help but read the word first; then it automatically determines the semantic meaning of what it sees: when you read black, you think black. That's your System 1 at work, and it works very nicely in the first example. However, in the second example your System 2 has to come to System 1's aid to disentangle the letters from the colors. This is not a particularly demanding cognitive task, but it takes just a bit longer to make unusual associations than congruent ones. When the word is "gray," it should look gray. When it does not, our minds need to do some work.

I use this illustration, the Stroop test, with more colors than the print in this book allows whenever I teach about bias—and take pleasure in telling the audience that when my son was four years old he had no trouble beating them at this task. The explanation is simple: he knew his colors but could not yet read. Alas, we cannot leave de-biasing the world to four-year-olds.

The psychologists Mahzarin Banaji and Anthony Greenwald and their colleagues have arguably done the most to uncover the unconscious decision processes leading us to biased judgments about others and about ourselves. Much of that has been due to the IAT, the Implicit Association Test, which, building on the Stroop test, Greenwald created in 1994 as a new tool to measure what is going on in our minds.

The IAT asks people to make connections between words of different categories. System 1 makes such judgments automatically, using what Banaji and Greenwald, in their illuminating book *Blindspot*, refer to as "bits of knowledge about social groups." *Implicit bias* is measured by how quickly people make associations. For example, are they as fast to associate John with reading and writing or Susan with mathematics, or is it easier for people to connect John with mathematics and Susan with reading and writing? Literally hundreds of thousands of people have now taken the IAT online and have learned often uncomfortable truths about themselves—that they are implicitly sexist and racist and biased against people with certain looks, sizes, religions, and so on. You should take a moment and go online and test yourself at https:// implicit.harvard.edu/. You may find that Susan is more associated with reading and writing and John with mathematics, and perhaps some worse associations of which you were not aware.

People who make more gender-stereotypic associations on the IAT have been found to laugh more at sexist jokes. But laughing is not all. The racial bias measured by the IAT predicted discrimination in simulated hiring situations (preferring white applicants), physician behavior (being more likely to recommend the optimal treatment to whites), and voting (being more likely to vote for John McCain than Barack Obama in the US 2008 presidential elections), among others. In addition, in the STEM study discussed earlier in this chapter in which people were hired to perform an arithmetic task, the IAT accounted for evaluators' initial average bias against women by measuring their implicit stereotypes. What is more, the evaluators' performance on the IAT predicted the degree to which evaluators updated their beliefs when more information was made available to them. The more biased the evaluators, the less often they were able to take individual performance data into account.

It is crucial to appreciate that most of this happens unconsciously. This makes quite alarming a finding by Eric Kandel, a neuroscientist at Columbia University and the 2000 Nobel Laureate in Physiology or Medicine: Kandel guesses that 80 to 90 percent of the mind works unconsciously.

In addition to perceiving others in a stereotyped way, we also apply stereotypes to ourselves. Many women who take the IAT to explore gender biases experience the power of the unconscious mind. It is the truly rare woman who publicly subscribes to the belief that men are naturally superior at pursuing a career. But when women take the IAT, they are shocked to learn that they too instinctively associate careers with men and family with women. Such automatic gender stereotypes may lead to self-stereotyping that holds women back without their (conscious) knowledge.[22]

A fascinating experiment entitled "The Emergence of Male Leadership in Competitive Environments" supports the notion that stereotyping of the self and others interact in intricate ways.

A group of researchers showed that female MBA students at the University of Chicago Booth School of Business were selected as leaders much less often than their established skills warranted—because women as well as men conformed to what we expect of their genders. Male MBA students behaved in a more overconfident manner than their female classmates and were thus more likely to be chosen as leaders. In the experiment, before having to select a leader, everyone participated in a math task, learned about how well he or she did, and was paid based on his or her individual performance. Fifteen months later, the students were randomly assigned to groups, and each group selected a leader who would perform another math task on the group's behalf. His or her performance would determine every group member's earnings.

Group members had five minutes to consult each other and decide who would be their representative to compete with other group leaders on their behalf. People could talk freely but had to state and record on a piece of paper how well each of them thought they would perform in the upcoming math task. It turns out the men were more optimistic about their future performance than their female counterparts because they misremembered how well they had done in the past by a larger extent than women. Men had an inflated recollection of their past performance, overestimating it by about 30 percent; women also remembered their past performance as higher than it actually was, but by only about 14 percent. Based on these self-assessments, men were more likely to be chosen by their groups. Choosing the wrong leader had consequences. As you might expect, actual past performance was a much better predictor of future performance than the students' memories, most especially the male students' inflated recollection.[23]

What to do? If left unaddressed, we clearly have a problem. We do not take advantage of 100 percent of our talent pool nor do we match the right people with the right jobs and positions. But, of course, the problem is far greater than that. Most societies across the globe take pride in their belief that they provide equal opportunity for all. A wealth of research data stretching back decades proves this is not the case. That's the bad news.

The good news is that there is a fair amount we can do and can do quickly. We cannot rectify every aspect of gender inequality, but we can address many. Designing equality is feasible, practical and, as the orchestras evaluating musicians behind a screen demonstrate, already under way. But before we turn our attention to the problems on which we can make progress, we should acknowledge the limitations of behavioral design. It will not solve some of the very worst human rights violations women are the victims of, including sexual violence and human trafficking. Behavioral science does influence my thinking when serving on Harvard's Task Force on the Prevention of Sexual Assault, and I hope it helps us change gender relations on university campuses—but some atrocities require a hammer instead of a nudge. Nick Kristof and Sheryl WuDunn's important work *Half the Sky* provides guidance.[24]

There are certainly people who intentionally discriminate against women, some of them committing horrible crimes and some others deliberately treating women inequitably in the workplace. And they will likely keep doing so as long as the benefits outweigh the cost. They have a "taste for discrimination," a term coined by Gary Becker, the 1992 Nobel Laureate in Economics. Many societies have decided to make it costly for people to indulge their discriminatory tastes. There is also some empirical evidence in support of Becker's theory that competition can help.

Firms have been found to employ a larger share of women in more competitive environments than, for example, when they are protected. When a company can afford to discriminate against highly qualified but otherwise unwanted employees, namely women, many do.[25]

Unfortunately, perfect competition hardly exists, and relying on it to eliminate taste-based discrimination will not succeed. Other hammers will remain important, including laws giving everyone equal rights, protecting people from discrimination and exploitation, and deterring wrong-doers by making the cost of doing so greater than the benefits.

Because the stakes are high by every measure, let me be clear. Far from all gender inequities are the result of unconscious bias, which is only one of the culprits unjustly disadvantaging some and benefiting others. And behavioral interventions are one instrument in our collective toolbox to correct for these injustices. Biases are, however, a clear cause of inequality, and behavioral designs can accomplish things that hammers cannot. There is no better tool in that toolbox to harvest some of the lowest hanging fruit. Women should not have to choose between competence and likability, nor should organizations and society be deprived of their best talent. In an interview conducted after the case study she inspired gained attention, Heidi Roizen said, "there were certainly times when I would walk into a room or a situation where I did not feel particularly welcome. I don't think beating your head against those walls is a very effective approach. I think I learned that pretty quickly."[26]

No one should have to beat her head against the walls. Let's start redesigning them.

2

De-Biasing Minds Is Hard

Imagine that you are a plaintiff's trial attorney. Your client has been badly injured in a car accident that you allege was caused by the faulty repair work of her automobile dealership. Your client's injuries are quite serious—her recovery will take months and she will incur substantial medical bills—but you are unsure if you can prove the repair shop's liability. You file suit nevertheless, seeking $750,000 in damages. The automobile dealership's insurance company contacts you to see if a negotiated settlement can be reached, in the course of which you drop your original demand to $300,000 and the insurance company counters by offering you $25,000 in damages.

How should you advise your client? Obviously, that decision depends on how optimistic you are that you will win in court and how high you expect the award to be. You do your homework and come up with the following prediction: You expect that you have a 60 percent chance of winning and that the jury would award your client an estimated $260,000. Multiplying the two gives you the expected value of going to court (for simplicity we will not take other costs, such as legal fees, into consideration and assume that you and your client are risk neutral). It is $156,000. Thus, you should accept any settlement offer higher than $156,000 and go to court otherwise.

This is what my Harvard students conclude, on average, after reading a detailed fifteen-page case description. Or, at least, this is what the half of them tasked with representing the plaintiff decides. The other half represents the defendant. What do they decide to do?

The defendant, of course, has to decide what settlement amount to offer and when it is in their interest to go to court. My students representing the defendant, on average, predict that the plaintiff has about a 40 percent chance of winning a jury award of about $180,000. For them, the expected cost of going to court is $72,000. Put differently, a risk-neutral defendant should make settlement offers up to $72,000 and take the case to court otherwise.

How is it possible that the two parties come up with such vastly different estimates? In real life, you might conclude both sides have different pieces of information available to them. But in this exercise plaintiffs and defendants were given identical information as to the facts, witness statements, and the law. Any differences in their estimates must be based on how they interpreted the information provided.

In their differing conclusions you see their biased assessments of the same information. The plaintiff's attorneys paid particular attention to the information favoring their client's claims while the defendant's representatives focused on facts supporting their side. What is more, this biased assimilation of information affected their judgments despite the fact that they were asked explicitly to assume that they "were a *neutral* outside observer familiar only with the accident facts, witness statements and the law." They were unable to do so. Once they knew who they represented, they could no longer assess information objectively but fell prey to a *self-serving bias.*

Based on the numbers I gave you—the plaintiff seeking $156,000 to stay out of court, the defendant offering $72,000 to stay out of court—it is doubtful that the two parties will reach agreement. However, what I presented to you are average numbers, based on more than 900 students who have participated in this exercise. Over the years there have been less optimistic plaintiffs and more pessimistic defendants who managed to settle out of court. In fact, a bit more than half did so for an average settlement value of about $130,000. The real case the exercise is based on, by the way, settled out of court for $175,000 after twenty months of negotiations.[1]

The price of succumbing to self-serving bias can be high. It tends to prolong disputes, make the parties more hostile, and lead to impasses or costly resolutions in court. Wouldn't it be better if we could de-bias people before they begin negotiating and help them form more accurate judgments? What if we could assist people in overcoming unconscious biases, leaving stereotypical thinking behind and becoming less prejudiced? This isn't an original hope. Many organizations, and if you are employed, the odds are good your place of work is among them, run diversity training programs with exactly these objectives in mind. Sadly, there is little evidence to suggest that they work.

Two researchers at Carnegie Mellon University, Linda Babcock and George Loewenstein, were determined to find a cure for self-serving bias. They had observed Pennsylvania teachers' unions and school boards fall prey to such biases in salary negotiations. Ahead of negotiations, teachers and boards sought districts to compare themselves to—in a self-serving way. Babcock and Loewenstein's analysis showed that the teachers found substantially higher reference points than the school boards did. This inability to agree on appropriate comparable districts and salaries went hand in hand with increased strike activity. To test the impact of various interventions that might defuse such negotiations, the researchers turned to the laboratory.

In a series of experiments on legal disputes similar to the one that opens this chapter, Babcock and Loewenstein confirmed that self-serving biases were prevalent and, more sobering, found they are very hard to overcome. Typically, plaintiffs' predictions of awards were about twice as large as what the defendants expected, and they were substantially more optimistic about winning. What is more, self-serving biases did not go away with expertise. Lawyers and judges were as biased as the teachers, students, or inexperienced subjects tested in the lab—and nobody was aware of their biases. Indeed, much research suggests that experience alone is insufficient to correct biases.

To help people come up with more reasonable predictions, the researchers experimented with a number of de-biasing techniques. For example, before they formed a judgment, some participants were informed of the bias and its impact. There is evidence suggesting that bias awareness can help overcome the need to conform to stereotypes by triggering what psychologists refer to as *stereotype reactance*. Being made aware of the "leader = man" or "negotiator = man" stereotype, women have been found, for example, to do better in negotiations than when stereotypes are activated only implicitly. Alas, awareness did not affect people's own predictions in the legal case—they remained as biased as before. Interestingly, however, bias awareness did improve people's guesses about their opponent's predictions. Apparently, when informed of the bias, people assumed that their counterparts would be affected by it but believed they were capable of assessing the information objectively. It may be that bias awareness works when the bias can be attributed to others, similar to stereotype reactance where people respond to others' biases.[2]

People are quite ready to see biases in others, but they overlook the very same biases in themselves. In one study, participants were asked to rate the appearance, accent, and mannerisms of individuals introduced to them as math instructors. Before being rated, the instructors had to answer a number of questions. For the control group, the instructors answered the questions in a cold manner; the treatment group saw the same instructors answer the questions warmly. Accordingly, the study participants rated the "warm" instructors as more likable than the "cold" instructors. Finally, the participants were presented with three variables—appearance, mannerisms, and accent—and asked to rate the instructors based on them. Sure enough, they rated the "cold" instructor's accent, appearance, and mannerisms as more disturbing. The very same instructor was given higher ratings when he came across as likable. However, evaluators were not aware of being influenced by an instructor's likability. They did not state, "Because I liked him, I rated his appearance more positively." They simply asserted their impression of his appearance, believing inaccurately that whether or not they liked someone held no influence.

People routinely fall prey to the *halo effect*. A term coined by the psychologist Edward Thorndike, this effect occurs when an initial positive impression of a person impacts how favorably the person is subsequently perceived. In this experiment, participants were unaware that perceiving an instructor as likable affected how they interpreted his appearance, accent, and mannerisms, nor did they believe it affected their ratings. Halo effects are pervasive and, as we will see in later chapters, have been proven to distort our views in job interviews.

What is more, the halo effect did not go away when the evaluators were instructed to use introspection to make sure their judgments were unbiased. For example, when considering whether the instructor's warmth might be clouding the participants' judgment, say, of the math curriculum he planned to introduce, people were quick to come up with stories about why the new math curriculum was superior on its own merits. Instead of making people question their assumptions, introspection turns out to reassure people that they have been correct all along and that their conclusions are based on sound reasoning. When asked how susceptible they think they are to biases or stereotypical judgments, study participants conclude routinely that they are less biased than the average.[3]

It isn't just that being made aware of biases doesn't do the trick. It isn't just that urging introspection about whether your judgments might be biased doesn't work. It turns out that when research participants are asked not to give into their inclination to make stereotypical judgments, things can backfire.

In one experiment on unconscious bias, study participants taking an Implicit Association Test were instructed to suppress the tendency to be more favorable toward flowers than to insects and to whites as compared to blacks. They were unable to do so. A meta-analysis examining twenty-one studies aimed at reducing automatic stereotypes finds that suppression does not work. In extreme cases, instructions to resist stereotypes had the opposite effect, making stereotypes more salient and leading to an increase in biased judgments. For example, students evaluated older job applicants more negatively after watching a diversity training video asking them to suppress unfavorable attitudes toward the elderly. In addition, when trying to suppress racial bias and avoid referring to race in situations where it would have been natural to mention it, people perceive the suppressors as more racially biased.[4]

The same is true of *hindsight bias.* Sometimes referred to as the "knew-it-all-along effect," it says that people tend to see the present as more predictable than it really was. When the meteorologist predicts a 50 percent chance of rain, the drenched commuter declares he was 100 percent sure it was going to pour. Research on overcoming this bias has shown a similar pattern. People cannot help but fall prey to it, even after having been taught about the bias and being explicitly instructed to avoid it.

Baruch Fischhoff, an early contributor to this research, argued that for de-biasing to have any meaningful impact, it must involve at a minimum the following four steps: awareness of the possibility of bias; understanding of the direction of the bias; immediate feedback when falling prey to the bias, and a training program with regular feedback, analysis, and coaching.

This, of course, is a tall order. How many of us have our superego sit on our shoulders to regularly monitor our attitudes and behaviors, analyze them for their root causes, and then give feedback on what to do about them? Arguably none of us, and certainly not all the time. Often, we do not realize that we are biased, and even more often we do not receive feedback in time to link a specific decision or behavior to our bias. And even if we do, we may well not act on the information received. Put bluntly, changing behavior means work that the vast majority of us are not motivated to do.[5]

Yet the $8 billion US corporations alone spend annually on diversity training is spent largely ignorant of this fact. Such training sessions are unlikely to change attitudes, let alone behavior, if they set out only to make employees aware of their biases. Little is known about the effectiveness of diversity training programs, which differ widely yet are ubiquitous. Today, most US corporations offer some sort of diversity training. Some conduct workshops with trained instructors, others employ electronic formats and offer web seminars. Some focus on hiring and promotion and offer strategies to managers on how to avoid discrimination. Other programs are open to all employees and are geared toward fostering an inclusive culture and work environment. The strongest conclusion, drawn from one of the most comprehensive reviews of almost 1,000 studies, which was conducted by Elizabeth Levy Paluck of Princeton University and Donald Green of Yale University, was "the dearth of evidence" as to whether they work. "Entire genres of prejudice-reduction interventions, including moral education, organizational diversity training, advertising, and cultural competence in the health and law enforcement professions, have never been tested, as well as countless individual programs within the broad genre of educational interventions." Similarly, a 2005 review of about sixty studies examining cultural competence training for healthcare providers concluded that no inferences could be drawn about their impact due to the studies' lack of methodological rigor.[6]

The evidence from the few valid studies is sobering. One field experiment evaluated the effect of an anti-bias intervention in first- and second-grade classrooms in the United States where instructors led a series of sessions about sex, race, and body type in sixty-one randomly assigned classrooms over four weeks. The experiment, "designed to widen their circles of inclusion to include people who are different from themselves," involved 830 children. The program had no impact on the children's biases. Those receiving the training were equally unlikely to share or be happy about playing with others who were different from themselves after the intervention as those in a control group which had not been exposed to the instruction. The program ever so slightly improved the pupils' attitudes toward opposite-sex and opposite-race playmates, but it had no impact on their attitudes toward weight.[7]

One of the few studies to examine whether diversity training programs correlate with a diversifying workforce was aptly entitled "Best Practices or Best Guesses? Assessing the Efficacy of Corporate Affirmative Action and Diversity Policies." In this analysis of a national sample of more than 800 mid- to large-size US companies over three decades, between 1971 and 2002, my colleague Frank Dobbin of the Harvard Sociology Department and his co-authors found that diversity training has no relationship to the diversity of the workforce. In fact, in some cases diversity training programs were associated with a small drop in the likelihood that certain under-represented groups became managers.[8]

Dobbin and his colleagues are careful to point out that they do not have a good understanding of why the diversity of the workforce seems to have little to do with whether or not a firm had a diversity training program. But a different body of research suggests a possible answer: the slow, deliberative thinking undertaken by our brain's System 2 requires attention and effort. People who are already cognitively busy have been found to make more superficial judgments and use sexist language. It may be that people were too depleted to exert the self-control that is required to create a truly inclusive work environment. Pinning the efficacy of your diversity training on employees' over-tasked System 2 thinking might in fact open the door to unreflective, intuitive, and often biased System 1 thinking.

Diversity training programs may lead to *moral licensing,* where people respond to having done something good by doing more of something bad. A particularly noteworthy experiment illustrating this point was conducted in Taiwan. Some people were told that they had been given multivitamins while others were told they had received placebos. The people who thought they had taken the multivitamin were found to be more likely to smoke and less likely to exercise or choose healthy foods. In reality, everyone had been given a placebo—but the individuals who thought that they were enjoying the health benefits of dietary supplements granted themselves a moral license to smoke more cigarettes.[9]

Moral licensing, a relatively new field of inquiry, has been demonstrated in a number of domains, including bias. People who were given an opportunity to endorse Barack Obama in the 2008 US presidential election, for example, were later on more likely to discriminate against African Americans. The effect was particularly pronounced among people already racially prejudiced, raising the unsettling possibility that diversity programs aimed at influencing the worst offenders might backfire. A chauvinist manager who has undergone training might assume a moral license when conducting his next interview. Training designed to raise awareness about gender and race inequality may end up making gender and race more salient and thereby actually highlight differences. Indeed, according to Paluck and Green's meta-analysis mentioned earlier, interventions that discourage people from paying attention to social categories might be particularly effective in reducing automatic stereotypes.

At this point we have to conclude that diversity training either does not work or, at the very least, that we do not have enough evidence to know whether and under what conditions it does any good. Given the billions of dollars being spent globally on diversity training, this should give many companies pause. In part a response to these disappointing results, a few companies are trying different approaches, from implicit bias training to programs aimed at micro-inequalities, about whose impact we know even less. What, then, should the firm focused on achieving real results do?[10]

Babcock and Loewenstein's research on the effectiveness of various de-biasing techniques provides some hints. They tried two more interventions that had been shown to help in other contexts. You might have heard of *perspective-taking*. It is advice that you will get in almost any negotiation course. To negotiate more effectively, this advice runs, you should try to walk in your counterparts' shoes, take their perspective, understand where they are coming from. Although it turned out not to have a big impact in the legal dispute case that opened this chapter, perspective-taking has been shown to impact people's beliefs in other contexts. For example, "walking in an elderly person's shoes" by writing an essay from their perspective has been shown to reduce stereotypes about the elderly. Similarly, perspective-taking interventions that instructed people to focus on others' emotions, say by empathizing with African Americans when seeing or reading about discrimination, positively influenced attitudes and increased people's interest in interacting with them.

In another intervention, management students' bias against members of lower castes in India was attenuated through exposure to a reality TV show, *Satya Meva Jayate,* hosted by a famous Bollywood movie star. The program documented the atrocities and inequalities that lower-caste people often experience. Narrated using emotionally charged language, people from the lower castes shared their experiences of inhumane treatment, then a former justice of the Supreme Court reminded viewers of the values of equality, fraternity, liberty, and justice treasured in the Indian Constitution, followed by statistics of discrimination and observations narrated by a documentary filmmaker.

This arguably heavy-handed approach building on much psychological wisdom worked. It decreased implicit bias, measured by an IAT, and increased the likelihood that the students felt more favorably toward lower castes compared to a control group with no exposure to the TV program. Those results were evident three months later when another IAT was administered. The study's authors infer that "the emotionally charged nature of narrations was an important element in reduction in prejudice levels." Perhaps empathic perspective-taking will prove to be an important element of successful diversity training.[11]

Babcock and Loewenstein gave one last bias-removing technique a try. They experimented with what many perceive as the most general-purpose de-biasing strategy, namely a *consider-the-opposite* approach. This process encourages participants to play devil's advocate with themselves and come up with arguments for why their thinking, including their conclusions, might be wrong. In the experiment, plaintiffs and defendants were made aware of the self-serving bias and in addition were informed that "it could arise from the failure to think about the weaknesses in their own case." Then, they were instructed to write down their case's weaknesses. Thinking of holes in their arguments substantially decreased both parties' optimism, almost completely closing the gap in their assessments. While the impasse rate had been 35 percent in the control condition, it now decreased to only 4 percent, implying that almost all plaintiff-defendant pairings were able to settle out of court.

Calvin Lai and collaborators, running a contest on what interventions work to reduce racial bias, came to a similar conclusion. Exposing people to counterstereotypical images was one of the winners. A meta-analysis on automatic stereotype reduction suggests that a similar technique might also work for gender. Instructing individuals to "think counterstereotypical thoughts" about the social category or making counterstereotypes salient through exposure helped reduce automatic stereotypes, although the effect sizes were rather small, and it remained largely unknown how long the effects would last.[12]

Considering the opposite is part of *how to think* strategies that also include logical reasoning and statistical methods. Students with coursework in mathematics, economics, and statistics have been shown to apply basic principles from those disciplines to their decision making, reducing the likelihood that they make decision errors. For example, a series of laboratory experiments showed that training in statistical reasoning inhibited the formation of inaccurate stereotypes.[13]

Traditional diversity trainings could be augmented with instruction to help people think more clearly. One approach to increasing judgmental accuracy builds on the wisdom of crowds, showing that just taking the average of various forecasts outperforms more elaborate predictive procedures. It certainly trumps relying on the loudest voice in the room or the result of group discussions, which all too often fall prey to *groupthink*. A person's judgment can be improved even without outside forecasts by thinking up several forecasts, picking the average, and in effect benefiting from the crowd within.[14]

Here is how this works: Recall your role as an attorney for a client injured in a car accident. When asked to offer your best guess of the likelihood of winning in court and the jury award, write down your first answer. Then, take a moment to review the evidence you used for your prediction. In all likelihood, you will remember different pieces of evidence during this second, more deliberative round than during the first, more intuitive, round. Write down your second estimates. Then, repeat the process one more time. Force yourself to consider information you have disregarded the first two times around. Look in places where you might not normally look. Ask questions that you do not normally ask—and then, write down your third prediction. Finally, take the average of your three guesses and go with it. Research suggests that using this *crowd-within approach* significantly improves judgmental accuracy.[15]

Finally, there is evidence that there is a different sort of wisdom that arises from a crowd, wisdom that could prove useful to problems broader than employee diversity training. Consider the following experiment conducted in post-genocide Rwanda, a decade after 10 percent of the population, including 75 percent of the Tutsi ethnic minority population, had been killed in 1994. Together with the nongovernmental organization La Benevolencija, researchers ran a randomized field experiment using a yearlong "education entertainment" radio soap opera that aimed to help people overcome prejudice, violence, and trauma and learn to communicate and cooperate across ethnic groups. To listen to the radio—the most important form of mass media in Rwanda—people gathered in groups in their villages. Thus, the randomization took place at the community level with half of the communities assigned to the diversity and inclusion program, and the other half to a health program.

To the NGO's disappointment, the experiment had no impact on people's personal beliefs. At the same time, and somewhat surprisingly, it did affect behavior: listeners to the pro-diversity program became more empathic and open to intergroup marriage, and were more willing to openly dissent, talk about trauma, and cooperate. Individual behavior appeared to be more closely linked to changed perceptions of social norms than to personal attitudes. While this result was of utmost importance for reconciliation in Rwanda, it also has theoretical implications. Maybe the pathway to behavioral change is not a change in individual beliefs but instead a change in the socially shared definitions of appropriate behavior. While both mechanisms are likely relevant, norms are highly susceptible to behavioral design—opening the possibility for behaviorally designed training programs to deliver on the promise of increased diversity.[16]

Given all the evidence, what should an organization determined to run a diversity training program do? I urge companies to refocus the training on capacity building and adopt the framework *unfreeze-change-refreeze,* based on a method of one of the pioneers of applied social and organizational psychology, Kurt Lewin, and borrowed from my friend Max Bazerman, who together with Don Moore uses it in their wise book *Judgment in Managerial Decision Making.* You should not just focus on raising awareness, but also offer specific tools that help people make better decisions. Finally, think of ways you can refreeze the new insights gained and the new behaviors learned.[17]

Successful unfreezing happens when people start to question their current strategies and become curious about alternatives. Experiencing one's own biases, in an IAT for example, can be one such wake-up call. You should start your trainings with an unfreezing exercise. Unfreezing was also the goal of the previous chapter. By experiencing some of our own biases and learning that we are all in this together, we become curious about what went wrong, why, and what we might be able to do about it. The promise of behavioral design is that it offers an unobtrusive, low-cost way of changing behavior.

Once unfrozen, you might want to spend a bit of time on what your organization is currently doing—much like this chapter invites you to review current approaches and learn how to do better in the future. Successful training focuses on how to promote change, understanding that it is far from easy. Our thinking and behaviors are ingrained in personal rituals and organizational practices. Leaving the known, the status quo, for the unknown future bears risk. To make matters worse, a review of the status quo might reveal that past practices were inadequate and possibly counterproductive. Such learning can be painful, even threatening.

But you can do it, using the tools outlined in this book. Nobody has to adopt all of my recommendations, but your organization can pick and choose—and learn. Research suggests that people are much more willing to "unlearn" old procedures and try out new ones when they are involved, so be sure to collaborate with colleagues rather than blindly implement any new procedures. Coworkers are also more likely to accept unfavorable outcomes when they think the process was fair. Once you have agreed on a new procedure, you need to then test how it works.[18]

I cannot overstate the importance of testing and measuring what works and what does not. This chapter purposely is broad, learning from de-biasing techniques targeting gender, race, class, caste, ethnicity, appearance, and age as well as cognitive biases, in very different contexts and countries. These research-based examples should serve as inspiration but not relieve you from your own testing. We have not yet found the "one-size-fits-all" silver bullet. Perhaps we never will. Evan Apfelbaum of MIT and colleagues suggest, for example, that the relative share of the underrepresented group might inform which diversity approach to choose: "because racial minorities are generally represented in far fewer numbers than White women, focusing on notions of equality and fairness irrespective of social category differences may be particularly well-suited to address concerns among racial minorities, whereas explicitly recognizing differences and their benefits may be particularly well-suited to address concerns among White women."[19]

By the end of your program, you should think of ways to re-freeze the new insights gained. Reverting to past practices and bad habits is tempting. The final component of your program needs to focus on the organizational changes necessary to make it easier for our biased minds to get things right.

Consider the procedure that many hotels have introduced: guests have to insert a room key card to turn on their room's lights, and the lights turn off automatically when people take the card out to leave. The hotels realized that even well-intentioned and environmentally conscious guests often forget to turn off the lights. Hotels could just assume the costs of this, passing them on to guests in higher rates. They could remind guests when they check in to always remember to turn off their lights. They could post signs in rooms. Or they could solve the problem through a bit of technology and some smart design.

The refreezing technologies I recommend in this book are based on behavioral design practices and procedures. They rely neither on traditional compliance mechanisms inducing adoption by rewards and coercion nor on people internalizing a new set of values. Instead, as the Rwandan experiment demonstrated, these designs can change behavior even though participants' beliefs remain unchanged. Indeed, this is the very promise of behavioral design; it can change behavior by changing environments rather than mindsets. Soon, and I hope that means by the time you finish this book, the question will be not if individuals and organizations interested in diversity and inclusion have tried these designs, but why they haven't.

Designing Gender Equality—Change Practices and Procedures

- Stop simple diversity training focused on raising awareness.
- Follow an unfreeze-change-refreeze framework.
- Train people in more reasoned judgment strategies, such as consider-the-opposite or the crowd-within approach.

3

Doing It Yourself Is Risky

As academic dean at Harvard Kennedy School, one of my key responsibilities was faculty hiring and promotion, including negotiating compensation packages. This left me facing a dilemma. Having taught negotiation for many years before assuming this new role, I was not concerned with whether I was up to the challenge. In fact, my dilemma arose from knowing too much. The research of three of my closest professional friends, Linda Babcock, Hannah Riley Bowles, and Kathleen McGinn, had taught me that women were less likely to negotiate than men, and if they dared to negotiate, people in my role would like them less.

We discussed many of these insights at annual conferences on gender in negotiation I started to organize at Harvard in 2004. Hosted by the Women and Public Policy Program, a research center I direct at the Kennedy School, sometimes in collaboration with the Program on Negotiation at Harvard Law School and the Center for Gender in Organizations at the Simmons School of Management, we were a group of social scientists determined to unpack why it was that women did not seem to have a comfortable seat at the negotiating table and what to do about it. The conferences culminated in a special issue of *Negotiation Journal* summarizing the insights gained, for which Bowles and I served as guest editors in 2008. Much of this chapter draws on this research and the follow-up investigations it helped spur.[1]

Succinctly, a wealth of research now shows that deans and other people around the world responsible for personnel decisions feel women who ask for better compensation violate gender norms. It isn't just that we are biased to expect women to be collaborative, agreeable, and communal. It is that when we find certain women do not abide by these norms, we too often conclude we do not want to work with them. Much like the business school students who prefer working with Howard than Heidi, people prefer female employees who don't ask.

In a series of experiments, Bowles, Babcock, and Lei Lai found that managers were less likely to want to work with a female employee who had asked for a pay increase while a male employee asking for the same increase suffered hardly any penalty. Over a series of four experiments, their work explained women's disinclination to negotiate forcefully on their own behalf by showing that "asking" penalized women in a way it did not harm men. The first experiment focused on hiring and used undergraduate students role-playing a bank manager. The participants were presented with a request from a job candidate setting out a number of demands. The job candidate was given a gender-neutral name. The study found that participants' negative reactions to the demanding job candidate were much larger when referred to throughout as "she" than for the candidate referred to throughout as "he."

The second experiment focused on participants' willingness to work with a recently hired employee. College-educated adults role-playing as senior managers were made aware of what compensation the new employee had sought at the time of hire. Knowing that a job candidate identified as "he" had attempted to negotiate for higher compensation (either the "softer" ask, that he be paid "at the top of the pay range" and receive a performance bonus; or the "harder" ask, that he receive top pay and get a bonus equivalent to 25–50 percent of salary) had no significant effect on the participants' willingness to work with him. However, when the same candidate was identified as "she," their willingness to work with her was significantly reduced.

A third experiment replicated the second, but with videotaped interviews, with a male actor and a female actor performing as the job candidate and striving to approximate each other in manner and presentation. Both male and female participants were significantly less willing to work with demanding female candidates. Male participants proved willing to work with demanding male candidates. And, lastly, female participants were less willing to work with any demanding candidate, male or female. This experiment also revealed that male participants' disinclination to work with demanding female candidates was fully explained by their perception of whether or not a female candidate was "nice" or "demanding."

A fourth experiment asked participants to role-play as candidates for a job. They were tasked with choosing at the time of their "interview" to either ask for a top-range salary and a performance bonus or not. When the participant's evaluator was identified as "he," women were significantly less likely than men to ask force-fully for a higher salary and a bonus, but when the evaluator was identified as "she," men and women were equally unwilling to ask. Remarkably, candidates appear to have anticipated evaluators' behavior, expecting that male evaluators would give male candidates the benefit of the doubt but penalize women while female evaluators would penalize male and female candidates equally for asking, which in fact was what they did.

While most evidence on discrimination suggests that the sex of the evaluator is less important than the sex of the evaluated, it is not uncommon that lower-status individuals, in this case women, are more concerned about violating norms when confronted with a high-status individual, in this case a male evaluator. Bowles and Michele Gelfand found that the pattern applies not only to sex but also to race. In fact, it also applied when individuals were randomly assigned high or low status in an experiment. When judging deviant behavior, high-status evaluators were more inclined to punish low-status individuals than another fellow high-status individual. Low-status evaluators, on the other hand, were more inclined to treat high- and low-status individuals equally.[2]

Negotiating matters. In fact, it matters profoundly. People who are less likely to ask about better compensation are not just worse off than those who are willing to do so, but considerably so. Among master's degree students at Carnegie Mellon, almost all of the women, namely 93 percent, refrained from negotiating their employer's initial salary offer. Of the men, fewer than half, namely 43 percent, accepted the first offer, Babcock and Sara Laschever report in their path-breaking book *Women Don't Ask*. That alone is astounding. But there is more. The researchers report that men's starting salaries were $4,000, or almost 8 percent higher than women's. The rippling consequences hardly stop there. Willingness to negotiate also affects career advancement, as a former student of mine, Fiona Greig, found in a US investment bank. Women bankers again proved less likely to negotiate than their male peers. And those more willing to negotiate advanced more quickly in the firm than their less assertive colleagues. There is more. Greig demonstrated that a candidate's assertiveness had nothing to do with his or her performance, meaning the more assertive employee, but not necessary the best performer, was being promoted.[3]

Sadly, even when women negotiate, they tend to ask for less. Social science graduates in Sweden indicated on a survey whether their potential employer requested them to make an explicit wage bid, and if so how much they asked for. The survey also asked for the final wage offer. Otherwise equally qualified women applying for similar jobs as their male counterparts asked for and ended up with lower wages. Not only did employers counter women's already lower demands with more stingy counter-offers, they responded less positively when women tried to self-promote.

Women, it turns out, cannot even exercise the same strategies for advancement that men benefit from. I was also aware of the empirical research conducted in the UK academic labor market for economists. Not only did female economists not optimize their negotiation positions as frequently as men by seeking, for example, outside offers, but when they did, their improved positions did not translate into as many compensation goodies. To start with, holding productivity constant, female economists received fewer outside offers than their male colleagues did. And in contrast to the men, the outside offers women received hardly mattered for the counter-offers their current employers made. Sitting behind my new office door, I was all too aware of the fact that female academics cannot be blamed for seeking fewer outside offers than their male colleagues. Such offers were literally worth less to them.[4]

Thus, as academic dean I was left with a dilemma: if I represented the institution's interests and negotiated zealously on its behalf, I could take advantage of gender biases in negotiation. I would benefit from the fact that my female colleagues might not want to ask for perks and raises because of a reasonable fear of social backlash. However, if I tried to walk too much in their shoes, anticipate or even try to compensate for the biases I knew all too well skewed negotiations, I would not meet the expectations that came with the job. I had a limited budget available and had to use the money as wisely as possible.

Using it wisely meant, of course, attracting *and* retaining the most qualified individuals. Increasingly, managers are aware of the negotiation dilemma women face. And they do not want to lose disenchanted female employees who, after accepting a job and compensation package, find out that they were given a worse deal. Jennifer Lawrence, the Academy Award–winning actor, wrote about her dismay in October 2015 after a hack had revealed how much less she was paid than her male costars: "I would be lying if I didn't say there was an element of wanting to be liked that influenced my decision to close the deal without a real fight. I didn't want to seem 'difficult' or 'spoiled.' At the time, that seemed like a fine idea, until I saw the payroll on the Internet and realized every man I was working with definitely didn't worry about being 'difficult' or 'spoiled.'"[5]

Neither disregarding nor exploiting gender norms is wise, let alone fair. What then should managers do? Before telling you what strategy I followed, it is important for you to be broadly familiar with the evidence. One important research discovery by Bowles, Babcock, and McGinn is that transparency about negotiability is crucial. A survey of a set of MBA students in their first job revealed an average gender gap in pay of $6,000, controlled for appropriate variables. However, in fields with low ambiguity where applicants had good information about what to negotiate for, the gender gap almost vanished. In contrast, in fields with high ambiguity, men made about $10,000 more than women on average. Various experiments further corroborated this pattern. Gender effects appeared primarily when the situational cues regarding expected behavior were ambiguous. When, for example, cues about a position's typical wage range were clear, women were as good at negotiating as men.

In a field experiment, Andreas Leibbrandt and John List examined this further. They placed two different job advertisements for administrative assistant positions in nine major US cities. One ad made it clear that wages were negotiable; the other was ambiguous. An interesting gender pattern emerged among the 2,500 job seekers who responded to the postings: men were more likely to apply to jobs when it was left ambiguous if wages were negotiable than when the expectation of negotiation was made explicit. Did they know Bowles and collaborators' laboratory evidence documenting that ambiguity worked fine for men but not for women? Unlikely—but men clearly seem to be more comfortable with ambiguity and appear to expect to do better in a situation where negotiation is not expected. Indeed, the male job seekers were more likely to negotiate than their female counterparts when the ad did not indicate that wages were negotiable. The opposite was true for women. They were more willing to negotiate when the ambiguity was removed and the ad "invited" them to do so. Given the negotiation dilemma women face, external legitimization helps them overcome that hurdle.[6]

Consider the following anecdote. On December 19, 2014, President Barack Obama gave a press conference just before departing with his family for the holidays in Hawaii. It was business as usual but for one small difference, which instantly made the news: he called on female reporters only. What appeared to have been a deliberate move on the president's part was particularly remarkable given that the White House press corps has traditionally been dominated by men. Helen Thomas, the first woman to cover the president of the United States, was only admitted to their ranks in 1960.

Whether or not Obama was familiar with the relevant research, members of his administration certainly were. Victoria Budson of the Women and Public Policy Program had briefed the White House Council on Women and Girls on several occasions. One point she made more than once was that ever-increasing data show that women shy away from negotiation, do not speak up as often as their male colleagues do, and are less likely to be called upon.

Certainly, Google was aware of the evidence, as Laszlo Bock, head of People Operations at the company, describes in his fascinating book *Work Rules*. Analyzing their data, they had found a gender gap: women were less likely to nominate themselves for a promotion than their male counterparts. Survey evidence collected by Francesca Gino of Harvard Business School and her collaborators suggests that women find promotions less desirable and are less likely to pursue them because they expect stronger negative outcomes than men from promotion to a higher-level position (for example, stress or anxiety, difficult trade-offs or sacrifice, time constraints, burden of responsibility, or conflict with other life goals).

Bock and others at Google decided to try and do something about it. Accordingly, they sent out emails such as the one reproduced below to all technical Google employees: "I wanted to update everyone on our efforts to encourage women to self-nominate for promotion. This is an important issue, and something I feel passionately about. Any Googler who is ready for promotion should feel encouraged to self-nominate and managers play an important role in ensuring that they feel empowered to do so . . . We know that small biases—about ourselves and others—add up over time and overcoming them takes a conscious effort."[7]

Even after being given an explicit invitation to do so, women might still feel that self-promotion is too risky. It is important to realize this is not a matter of timidity, but of backlash. Bowles and Babcock discussed the social cost of asking with Sheryl Sandberg when they joined her on Katie Couric's television program to discuss Sandberg's illuminating book, *Lean In*. The research, they explained, was clear. We use different measuring rods to evaluate men's and women's behavior, or as Babcock said on the show, quoting Laura Liswood of the Council of Women World Leaders: "Women when they display anger come off as too aggressive. You know there's an old saying: men are too aggressive when they bomb countries, women are too aggressive when they put you on hold on the phone."[8]

Bowles and Babcock's research suggests that to lean in safely, women can invoke someone else, maybe a supervisor, to legitimize their decision to negotiate. The specific protocol they tested in their research had the negotiator say the following: "My team leader during the training program told me that I should talk with you about my compensation. It was not clear to us whether this salary offer represents the top of the pay range." It worked, making women's demands more acceptable. In addition, women might want to use more inclusive language and benefit from what the researchers refer to as "relational accounts." Women can improve their negotiation outcomes and mitigate the potential social consequences of asking by embedding their requests in a larger organizational context. Showing concern for the organization can legitimize requests made on their own behalf by arguing that in displaying their negotiation skills they are showing an asset that will benefit the organization.[9]

Such subtle changes can reap rewards. Sheryl Sandberg, for example, finds replacing "I" with "we" particularly powerful. We-language represents communal values and further embeds the individual's ask in the larger organizational context. Both attempts at legitimizing the ask can work for women, but neither the two researchers nor Sandberg were particularly excited about the message this sends. I can sympathize. Knowing in detail that biases are prevalent, skew the playing field, and require more of women seeking commensurate compensation than of men is dispiriting. I am always uneasy when I share these findings with my female students, but I also remind myself that just telling them to be patient and wait until we have fixed the system is an even worse answer.[10]

Without explicit invitations or external legitimization, it turns out even women in leadership positions speak up less than their male counterparts, and for good reason. In the Swedish parliament, the Riksdag, female members of parliament give significantly fewer speeches than their male colleagues, despite the fact that over 40 percent of the MPs are women. This is well above the average in Europe, where approximately 25 percent of parliamentarians are women, and in the United States, where below 20 percent of legislators are women. In the US Senate, power—measured by tenure, track record of legislation being passed, and leadership positions—is an excellent predictor of a senator's likelihood of speaking up on the floor—but only for men. For female senators, power does not translate into more speaking time.

Victoria Brescoll of Yale University examined why this might be the case. She asked a group of professional men and women to evaluate the competence of chief executives. The executives, male and female, differed in how much they spoke. Male executives who spoke up were rewarded with higher ratings of competence compared to their quieter peers. In contrast, both male and female evaluators punished women for speaking up and gave the female executives who spoke more than their peers substantially lower ratings. Women do not simply prefer saying less. Rather, in response to their environments, they understand that the "male way" might not work for them and so behave differently. This encapsulates the gender inequality bind that women find themselves in. The "male way" is the accepted way of advancement, but it not only doesn't work for women, women who adopt it are penalized for doing so. Women cannot break the ice on their own.[11]

Being called on by the president or a supervisor helps, but much more is required to level the playing field and allow organizations to benefit from everyone's contributions. In fact, the risks and rewards are even higher than just ensuring equal opportunities for everyone to contribute. Often, organizations are failing to hear from their best people. A former student of mine, Katie Baldiga Coffman, now at Ohio State, found in an experiment that it is particularly the very knowledgeable women who under-contribute.

But everyone, men and women, contributed too little in areas in which their gender was stereotypically considered to grant them less expertise. In Coffman's study, male and female participants were randomly put into groups of two. Groups were then presented questions and multiple choice answers in a number of areas, including gender stereotypical areas such as "Arts and Literature" and "Sports and Games." Participants had to decide whether or not to submit their answer as the group's answer, with the participant most willing to do so—measured by how quickly he or she decided—being chosen. Most people expect women to know more about, say, the arts and men more about, say, sports—which is correct. But the quiz-takers overestimated how much more the other gender knew and thus missed opportunities to contribute. This was even more remarkable because in Coffman's experiments people remained anonymous and consequently did not have to fear backlash. Everyone would have benefited if men and women, and in particular the top women, had offered their opinions more often. But even in the safety of anonymity, even the most informed women held back. They fell prey to self-stereotyping.[12]

So, on becoming dean, I decided to do a few things differently: first, I watched who asked. It was very tempting to infer from the act of asking that the person wanted something very badly and thus was also the most motivated to do the best job. Familiar with evidence refuting that assumption, I worked to keep it in check. Second, I kept track meticulously of what people asked for. It is very difficult to avoid being affected by the demands put on the table, and I did not want to respond to just these requests. Negotiation scholars call this *anchoring*. If men ask for more than women, then the typical negotiation dance in which the parties move closer to decrease the gap between demands and offers yields a gender gap in pay. Thus, rather than focusing on my counterpart's demands, I anchored myself at the going market rate and internal comparators. Third, I invited my counterparts to ask for what they wanted and needed—obviously, without promising that I could deliver. I tried to be as transparent as I possibly could about what was negotiable. Finally, I monitored the Kennedy School's compensation packages, promotion rates, pay raises and other relevant data by gender (and other characteristics) to make sure we did not inadvertently discriminate against a particular category of people.

I should now admit that when I was offered a job as assistant professor at Harvard in 1998, I did not ask—at all. I later learned that I could have and promised myself to handle things differently if ever given the chance to negotiate my salary and benefits again. The opportunity arose when I was granted tenure and needed to negotiate terms with the dean. Becoming a full professor with tenure is a big step for an academic, and it comes with sizable financial implications. So, being much more knowledgeable of the research on gender inequality and some of its causes in 2006 than I was in 1998, I did my homework, was lucky to have received an outside offer from a prestigious competitor, and was generally well prepared for my negotiation with the dean. Alas, I was also keenly aware of the evidence on social backlash. I wanted a nice salary, but I also wanted a good relationship. The strategy I chose may or may not be helpful to others, and I have never evaluated it systematically, but it felt right to me at the time: I shared with him what we have discussed in this chapter—and then asked.

He and I still have a good relationship. What is more, when I assumed the position of academic dean I learned about everyone's salaries. Consequently, I can attest that I was treated fairly in that negotiation. Maybe it was just him, maybe this only works in an academic environment where people care deeply about research-based evidence, or maybe it works in your circumstances as well. I have heard numerous stories of female executives who, after having participated in one of the Kennedy School's executive training programs, went back to their organizations to renegotiate their pay. They applied what they had learned, but also explained the broader context and the particular challenges women face. It did not always lead to a pay raise, but in many cases it opened the door to a meaningful discussion.

One additional and important piece of evidence I always leave my students with is that in many negotiations we negotiate on behalf of others. For me, this is one of the most empowering research findings. The negotiation dilemma completely disappears when women negotiate for someone else. This has no influence on men, but it gives women a great boost. Think of attorneys defending their clients, doctors advocating for their patients, professors sponsoring their students. There is no gender role conflict in these situations as women are expected to care about the people they represent and fight hard to advance their interests. A meta-analysis including more than 10,000 subjects (students as well as executives) confirmed the importance of representation and transparency.[13]

Indeed, many women (and men) negotiate their pay not just for themselves but on behalf of their families. An early study showed that this gives negotiators a justification to keep more for "their group" than they would have claimed for themselves, in particular, when the outcomes were public. While empowering on the one hand, the impact of household dynamics on external negotiation is a topic that social scientists have only recently started to unpack. Many internal negotiations take place within the household—on how time is allocated, income generated, care given, money spent, children raised, and so on. Bowles and McGinn offer a two-level negotiation as framework for analysis. In it, the members of a household engage in both intra-household negotiations with their spouses or partners, and external negotiations with organizations. The two levels affect each other. For example, a key determinant of bargaining power in the household is earning power outside of the home. Thus, if gendered norms hold women back in their salary negotiations, they may also affect their status within the household.

But of course the reverse can also be true: gendered norms within the household can influence women's outside opportunities. For example, we know little about how to change the expectation that husbands should earn more than their wives. Research suggests that violations of this norm have consequences. Based on US Census data, we can see that marriage rates decline as women become more likely to earn more than men. Similar trends can be found in other countries. For example, in Latin American countries marriage rates have also decreased as the gender gap in education has been reversing, producing more women who are better educated than men. What is more, Marianne Bertrand of the University of Chicago and colleagues find that as the likelihood increases that a wife's potential income will eclipse her husband's, the wife is more likely to stay at home. And when she does keep working and makes more money, she compensates by also doing more at home. Clearly running against the economic logic of division of labor, these findings strongly suggest that we need more research to better understand how negotiations within the household work.[14]

Nava Ashraf is among the few to experimentally examine the impact of bargaining power on how couples spend their money, conducting field research in the Philippines. She varied how much information spouses had on each other's financial choices. Knowledge means power, of course, as the more one spouse knows about the other's use of money, the more she or he is able to interfere and question decisions. It turns out that the information was particularly empowering to those in control of household savings, mainly women. When unobserved, husbands kept money for themselves, but when required to share information, they were more likely to put it into their wife's account.[15]

As we are rarely able to observe intra-household negotiations directly, researchers have relied on outcomes to infer how efficient the negotiation has been. Consider the example of farmers in Burkina Faso. It is not uncommon in Africa for men and women to own their own land, even after marriage. Spouses also pool their money to buy tools and other useful assets, such as seeds and fertilizer, and together work on each other's plot, sharing the collective spoils of their labor. But, as in the Philippines, household members in Burkina Faso had different preferences about how the pooled income was used—and this kept them from maximizing the size of the pie before haggling over who gets which slice.

It turns out that many more resources were used on the men's plots, making them much more productive than the women's plots over time. The main reason was the additional fertilizer applied (controlling for all other relevant variables). The irony, of course, is that the benefit generated by adding fertilizer to a plot of land declines steeply the more that plot is used. Fertilizer can help a plot of over-farmed field, but not as much as it can help an under-tilled field. Thus, men's plots benefited under-proportionally to what women's plots would have yielded, for it would have been those plots where the fertilizer could have made a huge difference. The households would have been significantly better off if the fertilizer had been allocated more wisely. Put differently, money quite literally was left on the table just to increase men's relative bargaining power in the household.

The implications of such inefficiencies in intra-household negotiations are important. In her insightful survey of the relationship between economic development and women's empowerment, Esther Duflo of MIT concludes: "This means that we cannot rely on the family to correct imbalances in society." Households are affected by the very same gender norms, leading not only to inequities but to everyone being worse off. If women do not contribute their knowledge in meetings and do not have access to the resources they need, we all are worse off for it.[16]

In an ambitious project, Ashraf and McGinn are studying whether teaching girls how to negotiate might be able to address some of this. Specifically, they examine the impact of teaching Zambian girls how to negotiate with their parents, guardians, and other adults about their future. The stakes are high. The girls they are teaching frequently must negotiate for the right to remain in school, marry later, or say no to "sugar daddies" offering to pay for school tuition and supplies in return for sex. Their randomized controlled trial is still ongoing. It aims to measure the impact of negotiation training on education and health outcomes in the lives of about 3,000 girls in eighth grade in Lusaka public schools. While early results are promising, they also show that these young women are up against a host of formal and informal constraints and quite aptly respond to them.[17]

However skilled you might be, overcoming biased environments on your own—in the workplace and at home, in Zambia or the United States—is hard and risky. In the spring of 2014, the failed attempt of an academic at negotiating a tenure-track job offer made the news in the United States. After she had made a few demands, the college withdrew the offer. A *New Yorker* article commenting on the case was aptly entitled "Lean Out: The Dangers for Women Who Negotiate."[18]

In order for everyone to be able to "lean in," we need to make it safer. And we can—by changing the constraints people face. Behavioral design focuses on changing these constraints. Clearly, this is a tall order in a complex environment such as the one the Zambian eighth-grade girls face. But we have had significant successes in the past. For example, women's willingness to invest in their education has been shown to be a response to changing constraints. When the Pill became available, more women started to pursue professional degrees and work more often outside the home. The introduction of infant formula had a similar effect on married women of child-bearing age. And better household technologies, from dishwashers to microwaves, have helped all women participate more.[19]

These technological innovations were neither low-hanging fruit nor behavioral interventions. But they move beyond "self-help" approaches, as Anne-Marie Slaughter refers to women's attempts at moving toward gender equality themselves in her illuminating book *Unfinished Business*, and illustrate the power of changing people's opportunity sets. Given an opportunity, many and perhaps most people will take it. Sometimes a nudge rather than a shove is all it takes. For example, while conditional cash transfer programs, typically paid out to households that commit to sending their children to school, have been successful in increasing children's school attendance, they are expensive and complicated to administer. Recent evidence from Morocco shows that similar and even bigger effects can be achieved with a much smaller investment. What the researchers referred to as a "labeled cash transfer" was given to fathers not on the condition that their children attend school, but merely as part of an education support program. The sum was modest and could not be considered a meaningful incentive on its own. However, by explicitly tying the gift to the goal of education, the government was able to send a signal about the importance of education, make this salient to parents, and influence behavior.[20]

Redesigning the context in which women and men negotiate works in the same way. The labeled cash transfer equivalents to helping women negotiate more effectively are transparency, relational accounts, and negotiating on behalf of someone else. While the latter two are helpful strategies that women should adopt, transparency is the design feature that countries and organizations should implement immediately. When given the opportunity to negotiate in a less ambiguous environment, women (and men) will take it.

The Obama administration has picked up on this evidence. On April 8, 2014, President Obama signed Executive Order 13665, which prohibits federal contractors from retaliating against workers for discussing their salaries with one another. The order states that when employees are prohibited from discussing their compensation with fellow workers, pay discrimination by sex and race is more likely to persist. Prohibiting employees from discussing their pay limits the information available to applicants and future employees, which creates an opaque process that inhibits salary negotiation. This order allows employees to talk about their compensation without fear of being fired, which may promote transparent hiring practices by employers and more equal pay for employees. Valerie Jarrett, then senior advisor to the president, commented on the executive order, saying: "With this new transparency, we can have an honest conversation. So many times women have no idea that they're being discriminated against. They have no idea what their counterparts are making."[21]

Increasing transparency is low-hanging fruit. It is an easy and practical de-biasing design. Failing to do it is not just ethically dubious, it is very much like leaving the most fertile plot you own undertilled.

Designing Gender Equality—Create Equal Opportunities for Negotiation

- Invite people to speak up or initiate negotiations.
- Increase transparency about what is negotiable.
- Have people negotiate on behalf of others.

4

Getting Help Only Takes You So Far

In German, they are called "Frauenförderungsprogramme," support programs for women. They have gained in popularity in Europe's largest economy. According to a law passed in March 2015, Germany's largest 100 DAX companies have to fill 30 percent of their supervisory board seats with women starting in 2016. Another 3,500 companies had to submit plans on how they intended to increase the share of women in senior positions in September 2015. But are these support programs, including leadership training, mentoring, and networks, effective?

With biases being so deeply ingrained in our unconscious minds, trying to de-bias people via diversity training has proven to be challenging. Asking women to do it themselves has been difficult and often risky, for women leaning in can experience backlash. If women cannot quite do it on their own, can they be much more successful with help?

To start with, not enough women have been getting help. According to the 1995 US Glass Ceiling Commission, lack of management training has been a key barrier to women's advancement in corporate America for decades. Indeed, research suggests that firms tended to statistically discriminate against women by offering them less access to development programs than their male colleagues. By now, many professional schools, including Harvard Kennedy and Business Schools, Stanford Business School, London Business School, INSEAD, and IMD, to name but a few, offer executive education programs focused on women's leadership. The programs vary in scope. Some use a generic leadership curriculum. Others aim to teach women the skills necessary to succeed in a "man's world." Yet others focus on the organizational context that makes it harder for women than for men to develop as leaders. Many combine these and different features.

That we have begun to level the playing field in terms of access to development opportunities is good news. But, of course, it tells us little about the impact of such access. I am not aware of any rigorous evaluation of leadership development programs for women. Recently, some critical voices were raised. A 2014 study reporting evidence based on interviews with personnel managers in Germany, Austria, and Switzerland went as far as to suggest that these programs might even be counterproductive: "Women are stuck in development and coaching programs while the men get the jobs." In the same year, a McKinsey report, "Why Leadership-Development Programs Fail" was equally skeptical and offered some suggestions for improvement: tailor programs to focus on the core competencies relevant for the business, couple them with on-the-job projects, and uncover "below the surface thoughts, feelings, assumptions, and beliefs" that slow or prevent behavioral change. The report concludes by lamenting the absence of rigorous evaluations of existing programs and a call to action, a point echoed by a 2015 *Harvard Business Review* article entitled "Evaluate Your Leadership Development Program."[1]

Shockingly, despite the $14 billion that, according to Mc-Kinsey, US companies spend on leadership development annually, the impact of leadership training, let alone leadership training specifically targeted at women, is largely unknown. A study that does allow us to make causal inferences about the relevance of leadership training is based on a hybrid program that combined leadership training with mentoring. It stems from an initiative sponsored by the National Science Foundation and the American Economic Association, and was inspired by Frank Dobbin and colleagues' findings that mentoring programs were associated with an increase in diversity in management in the over 800 companies they examined. Indeed, they reported that mentoring programs went hand in hand with the successful increase in diversity among all seven traditionally discriminated-against groups, namely, white women as well as African American, Hispanic, and Asian American men and women. While there is more research to be done, coupling leadership training with mentoring offers great promise.[2]

In 2004, the Committee on the Status of Women in the Economics Profession decided to offer a special workshop to female assistant professors. The program would turn into a much-loved and highly valued experience. Former doctoral students of mine who have had the good fortune of participating describe it as "wonderful" and "absolutely invaluable." In an exit survey, most participants gave the workshop the highest possible mark. But we do not only have to trust my students' word or even just judge from their exit comments whether and how the participants benefited from the program. The founders, four leading professors of economics, Francine Blau, Rachel Croson, Janet Currie, and Donna Ginther, designed the program so that it would allow us to draw conclusions based on hard evidence. They designed a randomized controlled trial examining its impact.

Like most other professions, the field of economics suffers from a "leaky pipeline." Many more women get PhDs in economics than there are tenured female economics professors. As in any profession, the causes of this are many, but one particularly striking feature in academic economics departments is the gender gap in promotion rates. Depending on the specific study, time frame and controls included, researchers have found a promotion gap of between 14 and 21 percentage points. Even granting for systemic gender inequality, this finding is notable. Women are less likely to be promoted to tenure in economics than in political science, statistics, the life sciences, physics, and engineering. To the discipline's credit, the committee decided not only to start a mentoring program to assist female junior faculty in overcoming the tenure hurdle, but to do so in a way that allowed them to judge its efficacy.

Since its inception in 2004, the program has been repeated every two years. After the first three iterations, the creators of the program took stock. Of the applicants to the 2004, 2006, and 2008 workshops, a bit more than half had been randomly assigned to receive the training. The others were relegated to a control group that did not receive the additional support. All applicants were aware of this possibility and accepted it as necessary to producing valid evidence.

The program brought participants together in a workshop that lasted two days. They were matched with senior faculty mentors in small groups based on research interests. The sessions included feedback on individuals' work as well as briefings on specific skills needed to succeed in academia, such as research and publishing, teaching, grant-writing, professional networking and exposure, the tenure process, and work-life balance. While some of the skills were directly related to the work of an academic, such as research and teaching, other skills the program focused on, such as professional exposure and networking, are nearly universal. Performance across professions is not based just on an individual's results, but includes how individuals and results are "sold." In their interim review, the four economists that designed the study compared the performance of those who received mentoring and those who did not. The evidence made clear that the program had worked: the young academics who had participated in the program had more publications and more success with their grant applications than the unlucky applicants not part of the treatment group.[3]

A meta-analysis on mentoring at work (not specifically focused on gender) based on forty-three studies also finds positive consequences measurable in compensation, promotion, and career satisfaction. However, the effect sizes were modest. Evidence from other domains comes to similar conclusions. A meta-analysis on mentoring of youth covering more than seventy studies, for example, found that overall mentoring was related to young people's developmental outcomes, but again, effect sizes were rather small and long-term benefits unclear.[4]

Catalyst, a leading NGO researching and advocating for the expansion of women's opportunities in business, as well as Sylvia Ann Hewlett of the Center for Talent Innovation and a number of other leaders in the field, have argued that sponsorship might be even more effective than mentorship. In 2008 and 2010 surveys of more than 4,000 employees, all 1996 to 2007 graduates of top MBA programs from around the world, Catalyst found that women were slightly more likely than men to have mentors. But they had different sorts of mentors than did men—less senior, with less organizational clout. In addition, the female employees' mentors tended to coach and advise them while the men's mentors took on a more active role and became advocates for their protégés, actively helping them advance their careers. They went beyond mentoring and into active sponsorship.

Sponsors make sure their protégés get visibility and are considered for promising opportunities. They negotiate on their behalf for interesting job assignments, promotions, and pay increases. Sponsors either vicariously or directly benefit from their protégés' successes. Some firms even hold sponsors accountable for how well their protégés do and reflect this in their pay. Why mentors of women did not become sponsors isn't clear. It is possible that demographics played the deciding role. The pool of available mentors for men and women was predominantly made up of men. Implicit biases may also have played a role, with female mentees being less aggressive in seeking the most from mentors, and male mentors unconsciously penalizing more assertive women. But what was clear was that by 2010, the men in the sample had received 15 percent more promotions than their female colleagues.[5]

Building on Catalyst's survey evidence, Katie Baldiga Coffman, together with her mother, Nancy Baldiga, constructed a lab experiment to take a closer look at some specific aspects of mentoring and sponsoring. Specifically, they were interested in two questions: How does the well-established gender difference in self-confidence affect sponsoring? Does sponsoring work better for men than for women because men are more self-confident to start with? And do instrumental approaches, such as rewarding sponsors, work for women as well as they do for men?

The team designed their study to examine these two aspects of sponsorship. Building on the work suggesting that women are generally less willing to compete than men, at least in the United States and many European countries, the two authors chose competitiveness as their outcome variable. Would being chosen by someone who cares boost women's self-confidence and make them more willing to compete? Presumably, by choosing a specific protégé, sponsors send a signal to that person that they believe in his or her talent. This signal might be particularly credible, however, when the protégé knows that the sponsor has a direct interest in his or her success. In the lab, the latter can be easily accomplished by tying the sponsor's compensation to how well the protégé is doing.

In both the Catalyst study and the Baldiga and Baldiga Coffman study, it turns out that being chosen by a sponsor works better for men than for women. The signal of being chosen increases most men's willingness to compete and their earnings, but it does nothing for most women—with one interesting exception: sponsoring helps the most talented women. Exactly why only talented women benefit isn't entirely clear. Maybe a certain level of self-confidence is required to profit from a sponsor's attention? With men generally being more self-confident than women, a topic we will discuss in detail later, they might find it easier to benefit from a sponsor's endorsement than women—with an exception for those women at the top who have enough data available to confirm that they "deserve" to be chosen.[6]

Firms with sponsorship programs generally report that they work. While hardly hard evidence, it is worth noting that the firms' findings do not run counter to the lab's. They cite that more of the protégés were promoted to more senior roles than a comparable group without sponsors, and turnover rates for protégés decreased. Obviously, the firms' evidence is not based on a random sample. They may have done a good job selecting the most talented protégés as well as offering them the right kind of sponsorship. And evidence from firms tells us little about potential gender differences in a program's effectiveness.

As someone who has assisted such programs, I have been struck by one particular comment that the female protégées typically make: to a degree far greater than the men, the women appreciate not only the knowledge gained and the support received from the leaders of their firm, but also the connections that they have been able to make with peers. Indeed, much has been written about the importance of networks. For example, it has been argued that same-sex networks are particularly important for women due to the scarcity of senior female role models. We tend to relate to and learn from similar others. When looking for sponsors or mentors, we typically try to find someone with the same demographic characteristics. But, of course, the demographic mix in an organization complicates and can even thwart such efforts.

In joint research with Farzad Saidi, I show that this puts women at an informational disadvantage. Our argument and experimental evidence is based on a simple statistical insight: the smaller the sample you have available, the noisier the information you receive. Consider the new hire trying to figure out what is deemed appropriate clothing for a client meeting. If you can only learn from the behavior of, say, two comparable others, and one of them wears a business suit and the other one is dressed casually, it is hard to know what the appropriate way of dressing is. If, on the other hand, there are fifty comparable others at your disposal, you will be able to make more precise inferences about the dress code. We show that such an informational disadvantage can affect performance, leaving members of smaller identity groups, such as women, worse off than members of larger identity groups, such as white men. But the logic does not only apply to gender. For example, religion-based, country-of-origin, or same-language networks have been shown to facilitate business relationships, job seeking, and even participation in welfare and social programs.[7]

In a network analytic study of men's and women's networks in an advertising firm, Herminia Ibarra of INSEAD shows that *organizational demography,* the relative fractions of particular demographic groups represented in an organization, not only influences the quantity but also the quality of relationships people have. Men tend to have both male mentors as well as male friends; women also have female friends. However, possibly by necessity due to the dearth of senior women or by choice in order not to use their same-sex friendships for strategic purposes, women tend to gain access to career and advancement opportunities through networks with men.

Building on these insights, Ibarra has developed a Network Assessment Exercise that allows people to better understand the networks they are part of and whether they help them identify career opportunities and advance professionally. The exercise is often used in leadership development programs where participants can assess how their networks compare to the breadth and depth of other people's networks. There is good news and bad news.

The bad news is that women are less likely to make strategic use of their friendships, viewing this as perhaps endangering or inimical to friendships. They also suffer from less free time than men: building relationships that one can benefit from often occurs during after-work activities that women, carrying a heavier domestic workload, participate in less often.

The research, however, has a silver lining: quality trumps quantity. Having a few sponsors who know and believe in a person may well be more important than relating to many others who take only a vague interest in your life. And while Dobbin and colleagues' work cannot establish a causal pathway between networks and diversity, they find a positive relationship between networks and the share of women in management.[8]

But much is yet unknown. A great deal of research still needs to be done to unpack what kinds of networks work for whom, why sponsoring and mentoring work for some but not for others, and how leadership development training can be improved to maximize its impact. We know even less about training targeting men. In 2015, the Australian Workplace Gender Equality Agency started to focus on helping men navigate work and life. It produced a documentary following the lives of five men in senior management roles who felt that, as one partner in a law firm said, "Flexibility in the workplace is equally important for both genders; we all have families and interests outside work." Another, a self-confessed workaholic and senior manager at Telstra, the country's leading provider of mobile devices, phones, and broadband internet, described the situation as follows: "A lot of my own work habits, I've spent about 15 years building up. They're a bit like smoking."

Conceptualizing work hours as an addiction offers an intriguing opening for behavioral interventions. It may also serve as an illustration for why training programs should tell us not just what to do, but also help us follow through. Consider smoking and the *present bias* that often thwarts people wishing to quit. Their System 2 plans to quit smoking but their System 1 wants to smoke—now. Their desire to quit is sincere, but quitting can wait until tomorrow, or even better next month. Smoking is part of a larger family of issues afflicted by present bias. Such present-biased preferences can help us understand why it is hard to quit smoking, eat healthily, or work out regularly. We want to have that chocolate now or sleep in today and defer eating an apple or going to the gym to another day. Humans are procrastinators, reliving the same experience again and again, as of course "tomorrow" never comes and that chocolate will taste exactly as sweet a month from now.[9]

The good news is that most of us can take inspiration from Ulysses. We understand that temptation exists and try to protect ourselves from it. Ulysses asked his crew to bind him to the mast of his ship so that he could listen to the Sirens' song but could not submit to the temptation to follow the Sirens into peril. (His crew had to put wax in their ears.) Some of us follow the crew's example and do not have chocolate in the house. Others have more intricate mechanisms and buy prepackaged rations to make sure that their unthinking, System 1 self eats only a set amount determined beforehand by their System 2 self. George Loewenstein refers to this reflective time as the "cold" state—but it changes to "hot" when we find ourselves in front of the dessert buffet at the next dinner party. When out with friends, it is difficult to exert enough self-control to say no to that additional drink, even though we had planned to have only one that night.

And the same is true for work, particularly for those of us who love our work. While System 2 promised our spouse in the morning to be home on time for dinner, System 1 tempts us at the close of the work day into quickly finishing that one brief. In that moment, you are up against the instant gratification of completing something specific versus the uncertainty of spending time with your family.

If you are a teacher or trainer who wants to help people better balance work and nonwork activities, or if you are a workaholic, you may want to consider introducing self-commitment devices. Maybe it is the time when you have to pick up your child from the daycare center or meet your friend in the gym. Generally, choosing in advance and making an active decision have been demonstrated to increase the likelihood that people follow through on their "should" choice. For example, when new employees were required to make a compulsory choice about enrollment in a pension plan instead of opting in at their leisure, this increased enrollment rates by almost 30 percent. But smart precommitment also includes buying smaller plates and glasses to reduce calorie intake. A word of caution, though: precommitment can be expensive. Paying for that yearlong gym membership may prod you to lift more weights or attend more spin classes but at a higher price. Ulrike Malmendier and Stefano Della Vigna have shown that gym-goers that choose long-term contracts end up with a per-visit cost that is 70 percent higher than what they would have paid if they had paid for each visit separately.

Alternatively, you can visit the website Stickk.com. The behavioral economist Dean Karlan and his colleagues wanted to create a mechanism that would help people stick to their plans. Stickk.com was their brainchild. The next time you plan to lose those twenty pounds, log on to their website and write a contract with your future self. Declare your goal and what you will do if you do not meet it—perhaps donate a certain amount to a charity.

Make sure you have a monitor controlling how well you do and make the price high in case your future self fails to perform. There's no use in committing to paying $10 in case you have not lost the twenty pounds within six months. Rather, $10,000 will give you pause and spur you to go to the gym. In order to provide a credible incentive, the amount must hurt. Karlan and a colleague were successful in losing thirty pounds over nine months, using a similar mechanism. If one of them did not meet the target, they had agreed to pay the other $10,000. They also instituted follow-through incentives and kept checking on each other for years. And there was at least one instance where one of them in fact had to pay the fine (which he did).[10]

Follow-through should also be an integral part of our leadership development programs. Some of the most interesting work on how this can be done is not from the corporate world. Rather, a number of nongovernmental organizations are experimenting with different types of leadership development programs. For example, several NGOs working on microfinance, having realized that microfinance was not able to live up to its great promise of lifting people out of poverty by itself, have started to couple it with business training.[11]

While obviously not the same pair of shoes as the executive education programs offered by universities and the leadership development trainings run by consultancies in the United States and Europe, the NGOs' evaluation still offers us a glimpse at the effects such programs can have. My colleague Rohini Pande of the Kennedy School and collaborators evaluated a two-day business training program offered to about 600 women micro-entrepreneurs between the ages of eighteen and fifty in Ahmedabad, India, by SEWA (Self-Employed Women's Association) Bank. The program focused on business skills, financial literacy, and leadership. The training worked for some but not for all. It increased borrowing and business income for upper-class Hindus but not for lower-class Hindus or Muslims. Such mixed results are not unusual for financial literacy training. A collaboration among more than one hundred researchers, the World Bank, the OECD, and the Russian Federation offers an excellent overview of the field evidence. It concludes that a broader definition of financial literacy is required, one that includes both training that raises awareness and provides knowledge and skills, as well as behavioral interventions making it easier for people to follow through on the knowledge gained. The report thus shifts from talking about "financial literacy training" to focusing on "financial capacity building."[12]

One of the most compelling findings is to keep it simple. A group of researchers compared the effectiveness of a traditional financial education program aimed at business owners in the Dominican Republic with a program that focused on delivering simple rules of thumb. Simplicity outperformed complexity by far—echoing the themes of two recent, important books: *Simpler* by Cass Sunstein, and *Scarcity* by Sendhil Mullainathan and Eldar Shafir. People, and particularly poor people who are worried about day-to-day survival, have limited attention and cognitive capacity available to learn about and implement new concepts.[13]

Supporting some of the lessons offered by McKinsey, another field experiment in India further found that microfinance clients benefited most from targeted training that did not just focus on general financial education but offered individualized financial counseling, including helping people set personal financial goals.

Goal setting matters. Much research suggests that establishing a goal increases performance. But not all goals are created equally, and there appears to be some art, in addition to science, in setting goals right. Specific, challenging goals tend to help us focus our attention and make us persistent, but they are particularly likely to work their magic if there are not too many goals and we are personally committed to them. Our values need to be aligned. And certain goals are by definition hard to reach and it might take months or years to do so. For commitments to survive in the interim and allow individuals and organizations to make progress, behavioral insights suggest that having clear goals achievable by making small steps might be more important than articulating the difficult, sweeping goal.[14]

Note, however, that goal setting can come with side effects. In a review of the evidence, Lisa Ordóñez and collaborators identify the neglect of non–goal-relevant activities, a potential increase in unethical behavior in pursuit of meeting the goal, and a reduction of intrinsic motivation as some of the core concerns. For example, consider the well-known study of *inattentional blindness* by Dan Simons and Chris Chabris showing that when people are given a clear goal, namely to count the number of passes in a video of a ball game, they fail to see a man wearing a black gorilla suit walking across the screen (he also stops in the middle of the screen and pounds his chest!). Thus, when using goals to motivate behavior, we need to do so with great care and eyes wide open for potential side effects.[15]

But goal setting can help bridge the intention-action gap. Microfinance clients intend to invest their loans wisely, but using the money to meet immediate needs today is tempting. Similarly, the participants in your training programs today might well mean to follow through on their virtuous intentions and implement what they have learned when they are back in their offices—but then, life takes over and great intentions remain exactly that, great intentions. To be able to meet our goals, we need to make plans on how to get there—much like the German companies that were asked to submit their plans on how to increase gender diversity in 2015. When persons or organizations are asked to make a plan for when, where, and how they will reach a certain goal, the plan can serve as a commitment device: a psychological contract that they write with themselves. Randomized controlled trials have shown that plan making can increase the likelihood that people follow through on their intention to vote, to exercise, and to get their flu shot. Plan making also helps people meet deadlines— quite relevant for someone working on a book.[16]

Feedback from others also matters, and that is where networks can come in handy again. A field experiment was set up in Uganda to evaluate how to best teach female cotton farmers proper growing techniques. A standard training program offered to both men and women did substantially worse than a program targeting women and establishing social ties among them. In the treatment group consisting of women only, each participant was randomly paired with a partner she did not know beforehand. The partners not only learned together during the program, but they also kept checking on each other throughout the season. This "buddy" system turned out to increase the productivity of most farmers by about 60 percent as compared to a 40 percent increase for those who had participated in the traditional training program only. Similar strong evidence on the importance of networks comes from randomized controlled trials on microfinance in India. When first-time borrowers met more often and forged stronger social ties, they were more likely to cooperate with each other later on, suggesting that group lending might work particularly well because it links people to each other in a new social network.

Social networks provide peer monitoring. Emily Breza of Columbia University and Arun Chandrasekhar of Stanford University show that helping households open an account and devise savings goals, coupled with regular visits to check on progress, has positive but only relatively modest effects on people's saving balances, increasing them by about 10 percent in India. When a peer monitor from a person's network is added, however, total savings increase by 34 percent. Interestingly, monitors are particularly effective when they are not chosen by the savers themselves but instead are randomly assigned. People need powerful monitors with a central position in their network. Peripheral network members do not have the social capital to request such a person on their own.[17]

All the available evidence points to the importance of training programs that go beyond educating people to building their capacity as well. Learning how to do something is different, and less desirable, than being supported in how you are achieving something. These lessons should be incorporated in training programs globally, whether in Uganda or in the United States, and whether your goal is gender equality or higher agricultural yields. In an executive program for the World Economic Forum's Young Global Leaders that I chair at the Kennedy School, for example, we assign participants to small leadership development groups at the beginning of the program. They then meet every morning before class to work through a leadership curriculum developed by my colleague, Bill George, of Harvard Business School. At the end of the almost two-week-long program, they share insights these small groups gained with the larger class. More importantly, they are encouraged to continue meeting, most often virtually, and to form a support group, which has proven invaluable for many. These highly accomplished men and women, all already in or seeking to join organizations of influence, whether in government or business, end up benefiting from the same framework for feedback as do Indian microfinance clients and Ugandan farmers.

To build leadership capacity, leadership training programs targeting women need to move beyond helping them navigate the existing playing field to more sustained interventions that can eventually redesign the field. Mentoring, sponsorship, and networking initiatives are a first step in that direction. They provide some of the knowledge and skills taught in leadership programs. In addition, they can have enduring effects by taking root in organizations and serving as commitment devices that help people follow through on what they have learned and on the goals they and the organization have set. But more systemic interventions are required to de-bias the system. And that is what we have to push for: redesign the environments in which we work, learn, and live.

Designing Gender Equality—Build Capacity

- Stop showering women (and men) with generic leadership development training.
- Build leadership capacity by supporting people with the resources required for success, including mentors or sponsors and networks.
- Use behavioral design to help people follow through, with actions such as plan making, goal setting, and feedback.

Part Two

HOW TO DESIGN
TALENT MANAGEMENT

5

Applying Data to People Decisions

"What does not get measured does not count," a saying goes. Even more important, though, is the truism "What does not get measured cannot be fixed." Any organization that hopes to learn and improve needs to base its decisions on evidence. This is particularly true when confronting problems that are the result of systematic unconscious bias. It also explains why a focused, data-driven effort to solve gender inequality can yield a double reward. By bringing its consequences to light, gender inequality can help organizations both do the right thing and invest resources in those policies, organizational practices, and structures that yield the highest returns. Before you can do any of that, however, you need to know what is broken. And to measure that, we are armed with not only new knowledge about how the mind works, but new tools to assess consequences. When it comes to improving our people decisions, few new tools promise to revolutionize human resource management as thoroughly as *people analytics*. It also holds out the promise of informing new designs to address gender inequality.[1]

The US workforce consists of more than 150 million people. More than 220 million are in the labor force in the European Union. In India, corresponding estimates suggest a labor force of more than 480 million and in China of almost 800 million. Globally, more than 3 billion people work or seek work. For the last thirty to forty years, we have been collecting a lot of information about these people: what they do, where they work, where they went to school, what their demographic characteristics are, how they perform and, maybe, even how much money they make. But only now are we starting to use this data to improve our people decisions.[2]

In its simplest form, people analytics collects large amounts of data and uses complex applications to measure relationships between variables and detect patterns and trends. For example, was your company right in assuming that graduates from the best colleges make the best analysts or salespeople or programmers? Maybe a degree from Harvard is highly correlated with job performance, or maybe not. Perhaps where an employee received her secondary education matters for some jobs, but not for others. You won't know unless you measure.

Data analytics has already been applied to combat crime, help prevent and manage natural disasters, improve health care, and make economies more productive. It has even been credited with helping people get elected. President Obama's campaigns were the first to make systematic use of big data, rather than the usual "gurulike intuition," to better understand how to mobilize support. This is far from just an American phenomenon. One reporter summed up the 2014 Indian elections this way: "It's no exaggeration to say that Big Data analytics, the process of capturing, managing and analysing massive amounts of data to generate useful information, was in part responsible in helping the Bharatiya Janata Party (BJP) and its allies secure the biggest election victory in more than three decades."[3]

Today many large companies use data analytics to better predict market trends, manage risk, measure customer needs, create improved customer experiences, optimize supply chains, and monitor compliance. Only a few, however, have started to apply data analytics to improve their people practices. One of them is Google.

Calling its Human Resources department "People Operations," Google has been at the forefront of this trend. The data told Google, for example, that an apparent gender gap—women were twice as likely to quit as the average Google employee—was in fact a "parent gap." Young mothers, it turned out, were twice as likely to quit. So Laszlo Bock, the head of the department, introduced a new maternity and paternity leave plan. Instead of the industry standard of twelve weeks, new mothers could take five months off and new parents seven weeks. The impact was immediate: new mothers at Google are now no more likely to leave than the average employee.[4]

Turnover is a big concern for many companies. It is expensive to find, recruit, train, and retain talent. Relying on big data, Google figured out how to best predict people's likelihood of leaving. They now use five diagnostic questions most predictive of employees' quitting. If the aggregate answers to these questions come back below 70 percent positive, Google knows it has to take action, otherwise the analytics make clear that people are very likely to leave the following year. The responses to the five questions allow Google to identify the issues costing them employees and target its interventions accordingly—without relating them to any specific individual.

Google's HR department has been compared to an employee science lab. Data are tracked and experiments are run constantly to optimize Google's procedures. For example, a few years ago, Google ran an analysis to determine the optimal number of job interviews. Todd Carlisle, director of staffing, collected all interview scores a candidate had received from the various people he or she had met. Repeating this for many candidates, he found that the optimal number of evaluators was four—well below the typical number of interviewers Google had been using. But the evidence was irrefutable: four independent assessments were enough for the candidate's average score to converge to a final score. Consequently, Google significantly cut back its interview times.

Google's People Operations has examined questions ranging from how to maximize employee happiness—higher salary, a bonus, or more time off?—to how to help employees save for retirement. Often collaborating with academics, Google makes many of its research findings public. Consequently, we know that the predictability that comes with salary increases makes "Googlers" happier than the possibility of a windfall bonus. Remuneration isn't the only thing that makes people happy. Research by Elizabeth Dunn and Mike Norton, for example, shows that companies can make their employees happier by letting them decide which charity receives corporate philanthropy. And if you want to motivate people to save more, you should remind them often and set goals, along with making participation in company retirement programs the default. Capturing the ambition behind all of these efforts, Prasad Setty, who leads the "people analytics" group within People Operations at Google, said: "We make thousands of people decisions every day—who we should hire, how much we should pay them, who we should promote, who we should let go of. What we try to do is bring the same level of rigor to people decisions that we do to engineering decisions. Our mission is to have all people decisions be informed by data."[5]

Organizations should follow in Google's footsteps. But this is easier said than done. A high-level partner in one company I worked with told me that his organization could never use the word "experiment." Doing so, he said, would suggest managers didn't know what they were doing. That, I told him, was exactly the point! People think they know what they are doing—based on a mixture of intuition, best practice, tradition, and industry norms. But only evidence can tell. Randomized controlled trials are the gold standard of evidence in medicine, the sciences, and increasingly in economics, sociology, and psychology (which has been employing the experimental technique in the laboratory for a long time). We all are thankful that the drugs we take to combat a migraine or lower our blood pressure have been tested in clinical trials, with treatment and control groups. Not only can organizations avail themselves of the same techniques, allowing them to fine-tune what works and design processes that lead to better people decisions, it is increasingly damning when they don't bother.

The power of data was jarringly brought to my attention by the students at Harvard Kennedy School. One day, I came to my academic dean's office to find a group of them camped out in front of my door. They needed to see me urgently, they said. So we met. They were concerned about the lack of women faculty. This was not a new concern, but given how much of my recent research had focused on how to equalize the playing field I found myself in an odd position. Even as I explained the progress we had made, I felt defensive. By statistical necessity, I explained, change was slow: we only hired about five new faculty members a year on average. I remember running impromptu calculations during the meeting, figuring out how long it would take to reach gender parity if we hired only women. A long time.

So I dug deeper. Much to my surprise, I realized that it was not primarily the number of female faculty or some abstract concept of gender equality among our faculty that concerned these students. Rather, it was the lack of role models for female students. They did not care that much about faculty statistics, but they wanted to see more women leaders—in the classroom, in seminars, at conferences, on panels, behind the podium, teaching, speaking, researching, tutoring, and advising. It turns out we had never paid attention to the gender breakdown of the people visiting the Kennedy School. On any given day, there are a multitude of talks and discussions taking place across campus, typically with a lead speaker or lead panelists. These experts—political, civil society, business, and academic leaders from around the world— were invited by different individuals, research centers, programs, institutes, and study groups. Some of those invited to campus visit for their presentations only and others stay at the school as visiting fellows for a year or longer. Many of them interact with our students, and all of them help complete the picture that represents Harvard. And we had never before collected their demographics.

So we did. We asked the sponsoring institutions and entities to include in their annual reports to the deans a gender breakdown of their guests. And our findings resembled those of most organizations that collect such data for the first time: the numbers were not pretty. However, they initiated a healthy discussion and some self-reflection starting in the first year we measured. And, of course, they have since allowed us to track change over time, design strategies based on the evidence—many of which are discussed in this book—and compare notes on what worked.

The potential of data analytics to help close gender gaps is enormous. After collecting and analyzing large amounts of data in the late nineties, the sociologist Janice Fanning Madden of the Wharton School found that female stockbrokers in two of the largest US stockbrokerage firms earned about 60 percent of what their male colleagues made. The stockbrokers received commissions from the sales of securities to their clients. Thus, the theory went, the female brokers made less money because they sold less. Without looking any deeper into these results, the easy assumption became this: women weren't as good as their male counterparts. But it turns out the women did not perform worse. How was it possible that they were paid less? The data told the tale.

The female brokers were treated differently. They were given inferior accounts and sales opportunities. Madden refers to this as *performance support bias.* Neither she nor the firms would have been able to deduce this if she had not had access to the stockbrokers' personnel histories, the firm's trading and asset records, as well as information on each broker's management of accounts. With this information she was able to carefully analyze the data to tease apart the various competing hypotheses, which included the theory that female brokers were less productive than men, with reasons cited being innate gender differences, earlier career discrimination, and consumer reluctance to work with female stockbrokers. None of these factors turned out to matter. Women were given worse-performing accounts to start with. In fact, when women were given more valuable accounts, the gender gap in performance disappeared.

We would not know if we had not measured, and the two brokerage firms would not have been able to fix what was both an inequitable and an inefficient allocation system of accounts. In this instance we know only because class action sex discrimination lawsuits filed against the two firms forced them to make their data available to Madden, who served as an expert witness on the case. It isn't just that what does not get measured doesn't count; it's worse. Set aside the substantial financial and reputational costs of a lawsuit. Because the best brokers weren't being identified and encouraged to be as productive as they could be, the firms served clients suboptimally and were less successful than they could have been.[6]

Here's the good news. Once you collect and study the data, you can measure progress. In 1999, MIT acknowledged that it had unintentionally discriminated against women. Charles M. Vest, then president of MIT, wrote in a preface to a report issued that year: "I have always believed that contemporary gender discrimination within universities is part reality and part perception. True, but I now understand that reality is by far the greater part of the balance."

Led by Nancy Hopkins, a professor of biology, an examination of data had revealed gender differences in salary, space, resources, awards, and responses to outside offers. Women faculty were being treated significantly worse than their as-accomplished male colleagues. Nancy and her colleagues' work incited a debate about gender inequality in academia across the United States, with some critics questioning the quality of the data and the subsequent analyses. MIT stood by its report and, indeed, its use of data. Then dean of the School of Science, Robert Birgeneau, said bluntly: "It was data-driven, and that's a very MIT thing."[7]

That data had real consequences. A follow-up study, published in 2011, showed that the number of women faculty in science and engineering had almost doubled, and several women held senior leadership positions. Inequities in resource allocation and salaries had been rectified. Learning from data, it turns out, is a very MIT thing, too. MIT is hardly alone. The Swiss government, for example, has developed an online tool called Logib, enabling companies to measure how well they are doing in terms of gender pay equity. More elaborate evaluation tools are now offered by a number of private providers and NGOs. I serve on the scientific council of one such provider. A few years ago, Nicole Schwab, one of the two cofounders and a former student of mine, came to see me to discuss a new idea, the Gender Equality Project. The discussion turned into advisory work in which we helped develop an evaluation and certification tool that allows companies to measure progress toward closing gender gaps in their organizations by assessing both outcome variables related to pay, recruitment and promotion, as well as input variables such as training, mentoring, and company policies and practices.

What started as a "project" has matured into EDGE, a private company and foundation led by the other cofounder, Aniela Unguresan. Companies that have met a global standard for workplace gender equality are EDGE certified. In March 2015, Jim Yong Kim, the president of the World Bank, announced that his organization would seek EDGE certification, joining already certified companies such as Banco Compartamos Mexico, CEPD N.V. Poland, Deloitte Switzerland, and L'Oreal USA, among others. In celebration of International Women's Day, Kim acknowledged that the World Bank could only be credible in its efforts to close gender gaps around the world if it walked the talk within its own organization. The EDGE-collected data allows the World Bank to uncover patterns in its management of human resources, better understand the dynamics of gender at work within its walls, and identify hot spots ripe for intervention.[8]

These are hindsight insights, using data to discover how current practices are influencing decisions and productivity. Predictive analytics, however, can also fundamentally change how we evaluate candidates in hiring, promotion, and performance appraisals, substantially decreasing the role that intuition has traditionally played.

Don't misunderstand me. Subjective performance appraisals are here to stay. Very few organizations can do away with them. Yet a multitude of studies have shown that the discretion they afford supervisors in evaluating their subordinates opens the door to all kinds of biases. As discussed earlier, pro-male bias for male-typed jobs and pro-female bias for female-typed jobs is prevalent, as is a pro-male bias for positions of leadership and authority. What is even more surprising, even when there are no gender differences in performance appraisals, identical ratings were found to be more likely to translate into promotions for men than for women. The sociologist Emilio Castilla of MIT found this *performance-reward bias* among employees of a large service organization. After having been given the same performance evaluation score as white male employees, women and other traditionally disadvantaged groups received lower pay increases. The finding was particularly striking as Castilla uncovered the bias just when the organization declared itself committed to creating a culture of meritocracy by explicitly linking rewards to performance.

To further explore what he later called the "paradox of meritocracy," Castilla and collaborators ran a number of follow-up experiments to examine whether emphasizing meritocracy could backfire, leading to an increase in biased performance rewards. Reminiscent of the *licensing effect* discussed earlier, the answer, sadly, was yes. Merit-based reward practices led to greater male favoritism as compared to a non-meritocratic work environment. Why is not entirely clear. Research has shown that when people are primed to feel objective—being offered the opportunity to disagree with sexist statements, for example—they afterward prove more likely to prefer male over female job candidates. Primed by a company's declared sense of meritocracy, evaluators may have felt licensed to act on their biased intuitions. Alternatively, as evidenced by the findings of another study, managers might treat men more favorably to avoid tough conversations. Just as women were not expected to negotiate and reviewed unfavorably when they did so, managers expected women to be more accepting of deviations from their performance ratings.[9]

The performance-reward bias is a substantial challenge for organizations interested in paying for performance. Compensation and promotion committees often add information not reflected in an evaluation score but still deemed relevant for compensation or promotion decisions. One of the most common additional considerations is a person's judged potential. Having worked with companies on their performance evaluations and compensation systems, I have found a widespread *gender potential bias,* in particular in male-dominated industries and work groups. And, like all biases, it is difficult to debunk.

Biased judgments are costly—for the employee as well as for the employer. And they affect women across industries, including in female-dominated sectors. According to a 2015 study published in the *Journal of the American Medical Association*, male registered nurses in the United States, who made up 7 percent of those in the profession, had higher salaries than the other 93 percent of nurses, who happened to be female. The wage gap applied across settings, specialties (with one exception, orthopedics), and positions and did not significantly change over twenty-five years (from 1988 to 2013).[10]

The gender pay gap is prevalent around the world, although the size of the gap varies by country, sector, and specific methodology used to assess it. The US Department of Labor reported a gender pay gap of 21 percent in 2014, where the gap represents the difference in men's and women's median earnings. The pay gap in 2014 was largest in Louisiana, where women were paid 65 percent of what men were paid, and smallest in the District of Columbia with an earnings ratio of 90 percent. In the European Union overall, the gender pay gap was 16.4 percent in 2013, and the gap represents the difference between average gross hourly earnings of male employees and of female employees. The country in the EU with the biggest gender pay gap, 29.9 percent, is Estonia, and the country with the smallest gender pay gap is Slovenia, with 3.2 percent. In terms of the OECD countries, overall, the gender pay gap was 15.5 percent in 2014, representing the difference between men's and women's median earnings. The OECD country with the biggest gender wage gap was Korea, with 36.6 percent, and the country with the smallest gender wage gap was New Zealand, with 5.6 percent.[11]

Not all of the gap is due to discrimination. My own discipline, economics, typically only deems someone to be discriminated against if people with the same qualifications and productivity in the same occupation are treated and compensated differently. This narrow definition does not capture earlier discrimination in access to education or skills. But even then, there remains a sizable "unexplained residual" that cannot be explained by any other characteristic than gender. The gender earnings gap also hides the fact that neither all women nor all men are treated equally. Race, ethnicity, geography, and sexual orientation, among other characteristics, all matter. For example, gay men have been shown to earn less and lesbian women to earn more than heterosexual men and women, respectively. In addition, both motherhood penalties and fatherhood premiums are well documented.[12]

Gender bias also hurts employers. Employees who feel discriminated against are less motivated to work and more likely to quit. Favoritism also sets the wrong incentives—indeed, it depresses effort among the discriminated *and* among the favored. The former know that there is no point and the latter know that there is no need. Favoritism sets arbitrary incentives and leads to the wrong people being promoted or assigned to jobs they are unqualified for. In addition, subordinates might try to influence their superiors to obtain better ratings and waste productive time lobbying for the desired outcomes. This is particularly true the more important incentive pay is. Salaried employees have little room to maneuver, but if money is on the line and, for example, the bonus makes for a sizable fraction of a person's compensation, the supervisor has real power to affect subordinates' welfare. These effects can be long lasting. A meta-analysis concludes that performance appraisals can turn into self-fulfilling prophecies. The effects appear to be particularly pronounced for men in the military and for people for whom low expectations were held from the beginning.[13]

Most managers like their discretion. I know that remains true for me. But, while I believe that I have some information about my team's performance that would likely not be captured by a formal evaluation system, I am keenly aware that it is almost impossible for me to be objective. There are just too many biases for me, or anyone, to monitor and fight them all. Thus, the real challenge organizations face is how to design evaluation and compensation procedures that balance the costs of supervisor bias with the benefits of an informed supervisor's discretion.

One small but surprising idea is to experiment with a behavioral intervention proven to increase ethicality in other domains. Lisa Shu and colleagues show that people behave more ethically when they sign a form before filling it out (instead of afterward, as is customary). Making morality salient before people are tempted to understate income, misrepresent expenses, or play favorites focuses the mind on honesty in a different way than signing after reporting, when it is tempting to come up with ex-post justifications. Perhaps we can decrease favoritism in performance appraisals, nudging supervisors toward honesty by having them sign first? An experiment to be run.[14]

Another solution is to hold supervisors accountable. Few firms track the impact of performance evaluations on job assignments, promotions, and the employee's subsequent performance. Supervisors should know that their assessments matter, not just to the employee but also to the firm. Favoritism is unjust and costly, and should be made costly for the supervisor as well. If supervisors are responsible for the promotions in their department, part of their compensation should depend on the department's performance, providing them immediate incentives to promote the most talented rather than the most favored employee. If promoted or recommended people are assigned elsewhere, more creative mechanisms need to be put in place. Analytics can help track and compare such employees with large numbers of others, controlling for many other variables that might also affect performance.

One study, for example, examined data of more than 8,000 employees in a financial-sector firm, finding a larger gender gap in bonuses and variable pay than in base salary or merit raises after controlling for performance. The former were distributed without formal rules, the latter were subject to formal rules. Generally, formulaic approaches measuring individual performance to determine compensation work better for women. Ideally, firms measure their performance relative to the performance of appropriate comparators to make sure they do not reward or punish for swings in the market or other idiosyncrasies specific to a firm or a team. Google explicitly uses such comparisons to help its supervisors calibrate their performance ratings and guard against bias. After having assessed their team members, managers meet to compare assessments across groups.[15]

Some firms employ rankings and curves to force supervisors to calibrate and be discerning among their subordinates. One ranking I have come across when working with a company was based on a three-point scale and had managers assign the best rating to 20 percent of their employees and the worst rating to 10 percent, with the remaining 70 percent being clustered in the middle. But there is nothing magic about this particular scale. In fact, the evidence on rating and ranking systems in performance management is not conclusive, and their impact on male and female employees is understudied.[16]

One of the few exceptions is the economist Iwan Barankay, who, working with a large office furniture company, set out to measure the impact of different evaluation systems on men and women. The company's salespeople were paid based on their absolute performance, measured by the value of their sales. The salespeople, about half women and half men, recorded their sales and learned about their commission rates and earnings on a private webpage. In the treatment group, salespeople were informed of their rank, based on the sales they had made to date, compared to their colleagues. It was kept private, with their ranking appearing next to their name on their personalized webpage. Also, their ranking did not affect their pay. Still, it influenced salespeople's performance—at least of some of them. Showing employees their rank decreased men's performance but did not affect women. Saleswomen, it turned out, cared less about their rank and, in contrast to their male colleagues, were not demoralized by knowing that they had received a lower rank than expected.

Independent of its gender effects, the evidence on the impact of sharing performance information remains unclear, however. Covering more than 13,000 subjects across some 130 studies in psychology, an early meta-analysis revealed mixed results. In about two-thirds of the studies, feedback increased performance, and in the other third, it decreased it. Many details seem to matter, which is why it is important for companies to collect their own data and begin collecting as soon as possible.[17]

For all its promise, and as much as I urge companies and organizations to embrace it, people analytics is not a first-best solution. Data collection has the potential to invade our privacy. It also opens the door to categorical judgments based on demographic characteristics. In addition, there are methodological concerns. It is tempting to make causal inferences based on correlations, which is wrong. But now that department stores can accurately predict a customer's pregnancy based on her shopping behavior (and inform her family with marketing materials before she is ready to share the news), it is safe to say that the influence of big data, for good or ill, is not going away.[18]

For most jobs, subjective performance appraisals will remain relevant—and this is where even a second-best approach can make things better. We now know a tremendous amount about the influence of unconscious biases on our intuitive judgments. At first blush, female stockbrokers seemed to underperform male stockbrokers, but in fact the unconscious biases of superiors were responsible for their assignment to weaker accounts—and clients, brokers, and firms suffered. People analytics can help us check the intuitive associations we make.

In many ways, people analytics is reminiscent of an earlier discussion that took place mainly among psychologists more than half a century ago. In his 1954 book, *Clinical vs. Statistical Prediction: A Theoretical Analysis and a Review of the Evidence,* Paul Meehl concluded that simple statistical algorithms tend to beat the predictions of experts. Many more experiments pitting humans against machines followed, providing strong support for the early findings. Simple models, often using just a handful of variables and linear specifications, were shown to outperform professionals' judgments in business, ranging from estimating the likelihood of success of new businesses to the career satisfaction of employees; in public policy, predicting recidivism among criminals; and in medicine, diagnosing diseases and survival probabilities, among others.[19]

Over the course of twenty years, Philip Tetlock invited almost 300 experts—economists, political scientists, and policy- and other decisionmakers—to make thousands of predictions that he compared with actual outcomes. Topics ranged from economic performance to interstate violence to nuclear proliferation. Soberingly, the experts did rather poorly, not much better than "dart-throwing chimps," Tetlock writes in his book *Expert Political Judgment*. They slightly outperformed Berkeley undergraduates, and did significantly worse than an algorithm extrapolating from the past and predicting more of the same for the future. The cumulative evidence is starting to have an impact. *Moneyball*, the 2004 best seller by Michael Lewis, demonstrated that even in sports it was better for scouts to entrust a machine with deciding which players to acquire. Developed by a Harvard graduate, the algorithm led the Oakland A's to 103 wins for the season, one of the best records in baseball. In the meantime, almost all major leagues have replaced human intuition with formulas, and other sports have followed suit.[20]

But despite the preponderance of the evidence, then and now, people remain skeptical of algorithmic judgment. A review of the evidence suggests that the instances when human judgment outperforms algorithms are extremely rare and typically involve situations where people have important information that the machine does not. But even then, challenges remain, for people cannot distinguish between beneficial adjustments due to information asymmetries and harmful adjustments due to overconfidence.

A group of researchers from the Wharton School documents how widespread is what they refer to as *algorithm aversion*. Across firms and forecasting domains (including banking, manufacturing, and beauty), professionals either did not use algorithms at all or placed too little weight on them. Strangely, people became even more averse to algorithmic forecasts after they saw them outperform human forecasters. Across five studies where participants either observed forecasts made by an algorithm, a human, both, or neither, those having seen the algorithm perform became less confident in it and less likely to prefer even a more accurate algorithm over the inferior human. We do not forgive an algorithm when it makes errors, even when it makes significantly fewer errors than humans do.

Digging deeper, the researchers learned that people think that while algorithms might well outperform human judgment on average, the algorithms are perceived as being unable to learn from their mistakes or respond to unusual events. Such agility of thought and ability to update based on past experiences is ascribed to humans—despite much evidence showing that when humans, drawing on their own observations, "correct" algorithms, they often make the algorithms less accurate. But could these adjustment costs be outweighed by the benefits people derive from being involved? Maybe giving people some control over algorithms might decrease their aversion, make them more willing to use them, and consequently improve forecasts.

It turns out we can design our way out of algorithm aversion. To test this, the researchers asked participants to predict students' performance on a number of tests based on some background information, for example, highest degree earned, number of friends not going to college, favorite school subjects, or whether or not they had taken any advanced placement tests. Study participants were paid for the accuracy of their predictions. Allowing people to "correct" an algorithm's forecasts decreased their aversion and made them more likely to use it. Interestingly enough, people do not appear to require a whole lot of leeway. Rather, the tiniest increase in their ability to make adjustments makes them more satisfied with the process and helps them remain confident in the algorithm even after it errs. Thankfully, a small degree of freedom is enough to substantially reduce their skepticism and let the algorithm do its work and—as the data would have forecast—outperform the human mind.[21]

The message of this chapter is straightforward: we should make more use of data and data analysis. We should use big data to understand whether there are gender gaps in pay or promotion in our organizations, diagnose why, and inform interventions designed to close the gaps. And we should employ experiments to evaluate whether or not our interventions work. Big data can also be used to better predict which employees and students will be most likely to succeed in our organizations and schools—and under which conditions. Algorithms will help. We can overcome our aversion to them by giving people the opportunity to intervene and adjust, ideally not too much lest we decrease the accuracy of the algorithms, but enough for people to be willing to use them.

Designing Gender Equality—Apply Data to People Decisions

- Collect, track, and analyze data to understand patterns and trends and make forecasts.
- Measure to detect what is broken and refine interventions. Experiment to learn what works.
- Give people some leeway to adjust algorithmic judgments.

6

Orchestrating Smarter Evaluation Procedures

Singapore's Ministry of Manpower (MOM) was owed money. Failing to comply with the law, employers of foreign domestic workers were not paying MOM their levies (temporary taxes). The ministry could have gone about trying to get its money in a number of ways. It decided to design a simple, inexpensive intervention that relied on the power of pink. In a field experiment, it sent half of the defaulting employers the usual reminder letter on white paper. The other half received pink letters, which included other design improvements. It worked. A far greater percentage of employers receiving the pink letter paid up.

There is nothing magical about the color pink. In Singapore, however, it is a powerful internal referent. Chew Ee Tien of the Behavioural Insights and Design Unit at MOM explains: "Mobile and utilities companies often print their late letter notices on pink paper. As such, the colour reinforces the message that payment is late."[1]

When designing solutions, the smallest details matter. The MOM design was influenced by one of the core insights of behavioral science: judgments are comparative. Whereas white paper recalls typical, undifferentiated mail, pink paper recalls a comparison to other late payment reminders. White stationery piles up in a way that pink stationery does not.

It is almost impossible for us to evaluate anything in absolute terms. Whether or not you like a particular cup of coffee has something to do with the type of coffee you typically drink. Whether or not you find yourself shivering or dying from heat in a conference room has something to do with the kinds of temperatures you are used to. Europeans visiting the United States tend to freeze in our conference rooms and restaurants. And Americans squirm and shed layers in the steamy boardrooms of Europe. Similarly, when we evaluate people, we instinctively compare them with others.

Consider the following problem: Linda is thirty-one years old, single, outspoken, and very bright. She majored in philosophy. As a student, she was deeply concerned with issues of discrimination and social justice, and also participated in antinuclear demonstrations.

Now, based on the above description, rank the following statements about Linda, from most to least likely:

a. Linda is an insurance salesperson.
b. Linda is a bank teller.
c. Linda is a bank teller and is active in the feminist movement.

If you are like most people, you think that Linda is most likely "a bank teller and is active in the feminist movement." Linda, the feminist bank teller, fits best with how she was described, even though we may have some lingering doubts about her career as a banker.

This is one of the most widely used tests that help people experience the representativeness heuristic we encountered earlier when thinking about who the typical Florida resident is (remember: not the elderly). It shows how our intuitions can lead us astray. Recall that you were asked to rank, from most to least likely, statements about Linda. It cannot be that the category "bank teller and active in the feminist movement" is more likely than a category, "bank teller," that subsumes it. A feminist bank teller automatically is also a bank teller—but not every bank teller, of course, is a feminist bank teller.

While logic dictates that there must be more bank tellers than feminist bank tellers, when contemplating Linda that point is not intuitive. Linda looks more like a feminist than a bank teller and thus, when we add a representative piece about her—feminist— to an unrepresentative piece—banker—she becomes more alive. Linda's description as a feminist bank teller is psychologically more appealing, albeit less probable, than her being just a bank teller. When economists Sendhil Mullainathan of Harvard University and Marianne Bertrand of the University of Chicago sent companies (fictitious) resumes, Lakisha Washington and Jamal Jones received fewer callbacks than the otherwise identical Emily Walsh and Greg Baker. Names that sounded white got 50 percent more callbacks than the African-American sounding names; indeed, Lakisha and Jamal needed eight more years of relevant work experience to gain equivalent attention. Across four occupational categories—sales, administrative support, clerical services, and customer services—Lakisha and Jamal were consistently perceived as the black salespersons or black assistants, while Emily and Greg were just salespersons or assistants. Just as Linda was a feminist first, for a clear majority of employers, when hearing Lakisha's and

Jamal's names, the internal referent is a black person, first and foremost.[2]

Together with Max Bazerman and Alexandra van Geen, I set out to find an intervention that would debunk the internal referent. In retrospect, the idea seems quite simple. We introduced an explicit comparator. Put differently, we wanted to confront evaluators with two applications at the same time. This would help them, we hoped, to explicitly compare job applicants rather than to implicitly judge them based on the internal referent.

This is how the experiment worked. Study participants had to hire a candidate for either a stereotypically male task, a math problem; or a stereotypically female task, a word assignment. They were paid based on their chosen candidate's performance. In the control condition, evaluators were informed of one single candidate's past performance and his or her sex (plus a number of filler characteristics that were identical for all candidates; for example, that they all came from the greater Boston area). In the treatment condition, in addition to the sole candidate introduced in the control condition, we added information on one additional candidate. Control condition evaluators had to decide whether to go with the candidate presented to them or be assigned a candidate at random, pulled from the pool of candidates. In the treatment condition, evaluators had to decide whether to go with one of the two candidates presented to them or draw from the pool. They were informed of how well the candidates in the pool had done on average, thus they knew what to expect by going back to the pool.

The experiment was designed to mimic real hiring and promotion decisions. According to one study, about half of real-world evaluators look at one candidate at a time. The other half pools a number of applicants and screens various candidates simultaneously. Another survey, this one of senior executives in large US companies, suggests that about 30 percent of promotion decisions involve one candidate only.

In our experiments, when evaluators looked at candidate profiles individually, men were more likely to be hired for the math task and women for the verbal task, including those who had performed below par. Our intervention, where evaluators were exposed to more than one candidate, was able to overcome these stereotypical assessments. Comparative evaluation focused evaluators' attention on individual performance instead of group stereotypes. When candidates were evaluated comparatively, not only did the gender gap vanish completely, but basically all evaluators now chose the top performer.[3]

This makes comparative evaluation not just more fair, but also profit maximizing. The right thing turned out to be the smart thing, too. Without hesitation, I recommend comparative evaluation procedures to all organizations I work with. It is an immediately available design that promotes gender equality and an improved bottom line. At the Kennedy School, whenever possible, we bundle our junior faculty searches. This allows us to not only evaluate the candidates comparatively, but evaluate searches comparatively, making performance criteria explicit and allowing us to calibrate our judgments across searches. By doing so, we also benefit from another behavioral insight, namely that variety is more likely to emerge when people make multiple decisions simultaneously rather than sequentially. In one experiment, researchers had volunteers choose three snacks—apples, cookies, and bagels—to be consumed on three different days—Monday, Tuesday, and Wednesday. The treatment group chose the snacks simultaneously. For example, on Monday morning they had to decide what snack they would eat that afternoon and each afternoon for the next two days. The people in the control group chose sequentially: they chose one snack each day. About two-thirds of the people who made choices simultaneously selected three different snacks, but only 9 percent of the people who made sequential choices selected three different snacks.

Such variety-seeking with simultaneous choice has been documented repeatedly. For example, people have also been found to buy a greater variety of yogurt when buying more yogurt at the same time. In many instances, diversification is a good thing. Most investment advisors will urge you to diversify your portfolio. Most nutritionists will recommend a varied diet. There are also obvious risks: the person who buys twelve flavors of yogurt may discover they dislike eight of them. Depending on your goals, package deals may or may not be optimal.[4]

We should be worried, however, when employers keep selecting employees of the same kind, namely employees who look like them. Or as Carlos, a Hispanic attorney, told the sociologist Lauren Rivera when she asked what evaluators looked for in a job candidate: "You . . . use yourself to measure [fit] because that's all you have to go on." Analyzing hiring in investment banks, law firms, and management consulting firms, Rivera found that *cultural fit,* the degree to which a candidate's backgrounds, hobbies, and self-presentation were similar to a company's existing employee base, was decisive in candidate evaluations across all three sectors. More than half of the evaluators interviewed described fit as the most important consideration when interviewing job candidates, more important than, for example, analytical thinking or communication skills. The preference for fit was most pronounced in law firms and least in consulting firms.

In some cases, unconscious bias translates into a deliberate strategy. Denise, a white attorney, reported: "I really do think it's about finding . . . something in common with your interviewee." To top it off, a banker named Arielle described one of her best interviews ever: "She and I both ran the New York marathon . . . we talked about that and hit it off . . . we started talking about how we both love stalking celebrities in New York . . . we had this instant connection . . . I loved her."[5]

Whether due to the chemistry that might develop between an evaluator and a job candidate or unintentional associations made during a job interview, we cannot help but be influenced by irrelevant details—a shared joy of celebrity stalking, the color of an application letter, or a person's appearance. Maybe an applicant's jacket is your favorite shade of blue. While this fact is unlikely to be relevant for the job he or she is applying for, after having seen a color you like, you will be more favorably disposed toward that applicant. This correlation, the halo effect introduced in Chapter 2, has been demonstrated again and again and belongs to the category of confirmation biases where first impressions affect how we assess subsequent information.

I find *confirmation bias* one of the most challenging obstacles to smart decision making. When people search for and assess information, they tend to favor evidence that confirms their existing beliefs. But it keeps them from assessing new information objectively. Indeed, it impedes their ability to learn. The consequences can be life threatening. Consider the following simulation conducted in Toronto: Medical doctors were given information on sixty-four patients having a heart attack. The doctors had to imagine being in the emergency room and having to make a ten-second decision based on a six-point history for each patient. They had two (fictional) drugs available. It was clear that they had to learn by doing, updating their beliefs about which drug worked best for which patient based on the feedback they received. After administering one of the two drugs, they were informed of whether it had been a success or not.

About a quarter of the doctors were able to work out the appropriate treatment for the patients: one of the drugs worked better for those with diabetes, the other for those without. What differentiated the minority of learners from the majority was visible in their brains: based on fMRI scans, the frontal lobes of the learners' brains were particularly active whenever a treatment failed. They seemed to "learn from their mistakes." In contrast, the laggards' frontal lobes showed heightened activity when the treatment worked. The researchers conclude that a process of disconfirmation, ruling out alternative hypotheses, is required to learn. If you fall into the majority and seek out confirming evidence, you are more likely to be fooled by wishful thinking and random luck.[6]

Learn from your mistakes! Don't celebrate successes (at least, not when you need to learn). Unfortunately, we know that simple admonishments do not work, at least not very well and in many cases not at all. Our desire for internal coherence makes us more likely to continue on the path we are on, our existing biases influencing, perhaps even dictating our choices. Consider the *attractiveness halo effect*. Given that in many situations we see people first and speak with them second, this halo effect has been studied in detail. A wealth of research suggests that attractive individuals are not only assumed to be more honest and responsible, they are also perceived as more intelligent. The *beauty premium* yields real returns in the labor market. Controlling for everything else, more attractive people earn more than less attractive ones.

Let's unpack this phenomenon a bit more. To better understand what people see in attractive counterparts, the economists James Andreoni and Ragan Petrie designed an experiment to measure people's willingness to cooperate with others. They found that people were more likely to assume (incorrectly) their counterparts would contribute to the public good when they were more attractive. It turns out attractive individuals are no more and no less cooperative than less attractive ones. When all participants learned about everyone's level of contribution, Andreoni and Petrie discovered that the beauty premium turned into a penalty. Given people's higher expectations of attractive individuals, their "only average" level of cooperation generated disappointment and an unwillingness to cooperate with them.

Above-average expectations of physically attractive people have been reported in many different contexts. In other research, attractive study participants were expected to be better at solving mazes, leading them to be offered higher wages. The above-average expectations were supported by the fact that attractive people were more self-confident and socially skilled. But it all proved unwarranted: beautiful people, it turns out, do not solve more mazes.

Adopting what worked for orchestras, namely having applicants audition behind a curtain, is not going to work in any number of situations, but at a minimum, countries, including much of Europe and Israel, that still encourage applicants to include headshots with their resumes are well advised to stop. To explore whether employers paid attention to these photographs, researchers sent more than 5,000 CVs in pairs to about 2,600 advertised job openings in Israel. Resumes with no picture attached were paired with resumes to which a photo of either an attractive man or woman, or an average-looking man or woman was attached. It turns out that employers were significantly more likely to call back attractive men than either average-looking men or men submitting resumes with no picture. Now pause: based on all you have read and your own intuition, how do you think employers responded to female resumes?

Somewhat surprisingly, attractive women did not reap a beauty premium. Employers demonstrated a clear preference for female CVs with no picture attached. One of the world's foremost experts on the economic consequences of the beauty bias, the economist Daniel Hamermesh of the University of Texas at Austin, tells us that we should not have been quite so surprised. In the Western countries studied to date, looks seem to matter more for men's labor market outcomes. In the United States, for example, better-looking men earn up to 5 percent more and worse-looking men up to 13 percent less than average-looking men, controlling for their education and experience. The effect is smaller for American women, though their earning potential is also improved or hurt by their looks.

Discrimination based on appearance is widespread, although the specific gender dynamics vary across countries. In the United Kingdom, the appearance penalty is also larger for men than for women, but the beauty premium does not differ across the sexes. In contrast, in China, women are more strongly affected. Below-average-looking women earn 31 percent less and above-average-looking women 10 percent more than average-looking women. Below-average-looking men earn 25 percent less and their above-average-looking counterparts 3 percent more. Height is also a factor. Taller people earn more and are more likely to get hired and be promoted up the career ladder.

Favoring the good looking strikes many of us as the epitome of shallowness, but attractiveness arguably influences the course of global events. William McKinley, the twenty-fifth president of the United States, assassinated in 1901, was the last president to be shorter than the average American man. And it is not just in the United States that attractive candidates are more likely to be elected. Knowing nothing about the candidates other than their looks, research participants (often foreigners) were able to accurately predict election outcomes in Finland, France, Germany, Sweden, Switzerland, and the United Kingdom based only on candidate photographs.

Clearly, looks help predict election outcomes—but do they also predict performance on the job? Although the debate is ongoing, the evidence presented in Hamermesh's fascinating book *Beauty Pays* does not suggest that beauty is a credible marker for underlying characteristics such as intelligence. When beauty pays, it appears to be mostly based on stereotypes. There may well be cases where customers prefer interacting with better-looking salespeople, translating into real economic returns for the company—but not because the attractive salespeople are more savvy. Rather, customers discriminate against worse-looking employees.[7]

If you want to hire talent and find the best match of skills for the task at hand, then jumping to conclusions based on first impressions (and, worse, a photograph appended to a resume) is not a smart strategy. Fortunately, we can design our way out of this thicket of biases. Simply acknowledging that you will be influenced by first impressions is a step in the right direction. Companies I am working with, learning from orchestras who hold blind auditions, now experiment with "electronic curtains." This entails not only the obvious—removing headshots from resumes—but removing all other demographic information, including names, from electronic job applications before reviewers see them.

Note the word "experiment" in the paragraph above. Even with something seemingly as straightforward as blind evaluations, much remains to be learned. In 2009, the French government launched an interesting experiment that would affect all firms that made use of the services of the public employment agency, Pôle Emploi (which until 2005 had the legal monopoly on matching job seekers with firms). Pôle Emploi invited firms to voluntarily participate in a blind recruitment process where the applicant's name, address, nationality, and picture would be removed. Depending on a given firm's preferences, Pôle Emploi employees thus either took the identifiers off applications or not in its standard pre-screening process before sharing the resumes with the employers.

Three economists, Luc Behaghel, Bruno Crépon, and Thomas Le Barbanchon, analyzed the impact of blind evaluations on the likelihood that members of traditionally disadvantaged groups—immigrants, children of immigrants, or residents of deprived neighborhoods—would be invited to an interview and eventually hired. Based on a sample of 600 firms, they found a surprising result: anonymization reduced the chance that a member of a disadvantaged group received an interview and eventually was hired. It turns out that a selection effect contributed to this unexpected and unintended outcome: the 62 percent of all of the invited firms voluntarily choosing to participate in the program were those that previously had hired many people of disadvantaged backgrounds, or as the authors state: "Anonymization then prevented selected firms from treating minority candidates more favorably during the experiment." Experimenting and evaluating what works, therefore, remains as important as ever. While other studies have found that blind evaluations indeed leveled the playing field, selection effects can lead to unintended consequences.[8]

But you can do more than anonymize applications. You could belong to the first generation of managers to overcome what a 2008 article on employee selection referred to as "the greatest failure of I-O [industrial and organizational] psychology": the inability to get employers to rely on "decision aids," including tests, structured interviews, and a combination of mechanical predictors "that substantially reduce error in the prediction of employee performance." When surveying human resource managers, time and again unstructured interviews receive the highest ratings for perceived effectiveness—higher than, for example, aptitude tests, personality tests, or general mental ability tests. However, when compared to such tests, unstructured interviews fare worse. The resistance to analytical approaches seems to be driven by the two factors discussed in the previous chapter: people's overconfidence in their own expertise and experience, and the dislike of probabilistic forecasts. And for precisely those reasons we are reluctant to believe, and act on, the evidence.

But know this: the data showing that unstructured interviews do not work is overwhelming. A few years ago, a rather unique opportunity to measure the value an interview adds to performance predictions presented itself in Texas. Realizing that Texas did not have enough physicians, the state legislature required the University of Texas Medical School at Houston to increase the class size of entering students from 150 to 200 after the admissions committee had already chosen its preferred 150 students from a pool of 2,200 applicants. Thus, in mid-May, the committee had to go back to the pool and select an additional 50 students from the previously rejected ones. As most students apply to several medical schools simultaneously, by that time all the top-ranked candidates had already been spoken for. This meant that by May the pool of still-available students was made up of candidates that had been previously ranked between 700 and 800 by the committee. To put this in the committee's perspective, back when it chose its original 150, the lowest-ranked student accepted came in at 350. Now they were getting ready to add another 50 students, none starting higher than 700. Of the 50 students finally selected, only 7 had received another offer from a medical school.

What at the time felt like an unfortunate government-dictated requirement causing much concern about the quality of these additional, low-ranked students turned into a very interesting field study allowing a group of researchers from the University of Texas to examine whether the initial ranking mattered for the students' performance in medical school and one year of postgraduate training. All 200 students, both the original 150 and the 50 late-admittees, were selected based on the following criteria: academic performance (GPA and MCAT), pre-professional adviser assessment, work experience, extracurricular activities—and an interview. Each of the 200 selected students had been interviewed by a member of the admissions committee and one other faculty member. The researchers report that "no attempt was made to standardize the interviews or to weigh the objective and subjective variables considered by the interviewers. Each interviewer submitted to the Admissions Committee a written assessment of the applicant."[9]

The shocking news, not so much for the informed readers of this book but for the evaluators, was that there was no difference in performance in medical school or afterward between the initially accepted and the initially rejected students. Indeed, the highest-ranked top 50 students did not outperform the initially rejected students ranked between 700 and 800.

How was this possible? Digging deeper, the researchers found that academic and demographic variables accounted for only about one-quarter of the difference in rankings between the initially accepted and the initially rejected students. For example, the average GPA of the initially accepted students was 3.48 and of the initially rejected students, 3.40, a tiny, hardly meaningful difference. Instead, about three-quarters of the difference was basically explained by whatever had happened in the interview. While the grades of the two groups were almost identical, the committee ratings substantially differed. Initial admissions were heavily influenced by the rating of the interviewers. The researchers concluded: "In summary, it appears that careful initial screening of medical school applications by a knowledgeable person who assesses the academic and demographic variables, the work experience and extracurricular activities, and the evaluations of pre-professional advisers establishes a good likelihood for successful performance in medical school. The traditional interview process does not appear to enhance the predictive value of such initial screening. Should initial screening be followed by a lottery among the viable applicants?"[10]

A review analyzing eighty-five years of research in personnel psychology and nineteen different selection methods concludes that unstructured interviews should not be your evaluation tool of choice. In contrast, structured interviews do much better, particularly when paired with a formal assessment of intelligence or general cognitive ability (there are a number of commercially available tests). General mental ability has long been shown to be the most valid predictor of work performance when evaluating job candidates without previous experience in the job. But, even among candidates with previous experience, when high levels of skill are required, it ranks among the top predictors.

A large meta-analysis conducted for the US Department of Labor, covering 32,000 employees in more than 500 distinct jobs, for example, reports that the validity of general mental ability in predicting job performance was high for most employment opportunities in the US economy, namely jobs of mid-level complexity, which account for 62 percent of all available jobs. General mental ability did better for the most complex jobs and worse for the least complex jobs that did not require any particular skills. To calibrate, reference checks and years of job experience did substantially worse than general mental ability. The overall predictive power of mental ability was maximized when this measure was combined either with a work sample test (very directly measuring the skill required to perform the job), integrity tests, or—and this is good news for all attached to interviews—with a structured interview.

In the extreme case, unstructured interviews make things worse. One of the leading researchers who explored their consequences, Robyn Dawes of Carnegie Mellon University, and colleagues show in a series of experiments that it is almost impossible for evaluators to ignore nondiagnostic information—even though it is well known that such information reduces an evaluator's reliance on more valuable information. To make matters worse, evaluators were very good at "sensemaking" after the fact. In one study, people even saw patterns in random sequences.[11]

Investing in structured interviews pays. What's more, it is easy and cheap. Here is advice I urge everyone to embrace: plan ahead, use a checklist to structure interviews and stick to it, and evaluate candidates in real time. If candidates are to be interviewed by several colleagues, do not compare notes until the very end. Finally, measure and experiment.

Before the first job interview, determine what you are looking for in a candidate. Draw up your list of questions beforehand. Any structured interview format will diminish subjectivity in evaluations, as the research by Barbara Reskin and Debra McBrier shows, but what feels more like an art can turn into science if you learn to rely on people analytics telling you which questions typically yield high correlations with the attributes you care about. Those insights come from deliberate experimentation. Create a scoring system on a scale from 1 to 10 (though feel free to adapt the scale to your needs) for each interview question, and think about how much weight you want to assign each question. Maybe you want to treat them all equally, or maybe some of your questions have been proven to better capture what you are trying to measure. If so, assign more weight to them.[12]

Be vigilant about the halo effect. Score each of the attributes you measure before moving on to the next one and ask all candidates the same questions in the same order. This is difficult, for invariably the interviews will follow different paths, and what seemed a logical follow-up question for the first candidate may seem awkward with the next. Don't give in. It is okay to say that you will revisit a topic later on, but greater benefits come from sticking with the structured interview. In *The Checklist Manifesto,* Atul Gawande reminds us that adherence to protocol is not rigidity, but rather frees up mental capacity to deal with the hard issues. What Gawande finds works in medicine, finance, and all high-stakes decision making works as well when interviewing.[13]

It is very important to assign scores right away. Our memory plays too many tricks on us. According to the Innocence Project, three-quarters of wrongful convictions later exonerated through DNA testing resulted from unintentional lapses in eyewitness memory. Like all of us, eyewitnesses are influenced by the many biases and heuristics affecting how we assess information. And so are job interviewers.[14]

Consider that we are more likely to remember vivid examples than boring numbers. What is more worrisome is that we tend to take the ease with which an event comes to mind as an indication for its likelihood. When asked to guess the more likely cause of death in the United States, murder or suicide, most people guess murder. Wrong. Suicide is more prevalent. This is a classic example of the *availability heuristic*, so named by Daniel Kahneman and Amos Tversky. Murders tend to receive more media attention than suicides; consequently, murder is the more available answer.

Evaluators misremembering is a real danger in interview-based quality assessments. According to the *peak-end rule* and *recency bias*, people make judgments based on the most intense and the most recent experiences rather than the total sum of the experiences or some average thereof. In addition, they may have been affected by framing during the interview process. It turns out that even just introducing random numbers, whether 100 or 1,000, will affect your best guess of, say, how many bridges there are in Venice. There are somewhere between 400 and 450. However, when I asked half of my students whether there were more or fewer than 100 bridges, and the other half whether there were more or fewer than 1,000 bridges, the first group, adjusting up from 100, guessed a substantially lower number than the second group, which adjusted down from 1,000. The *anchoring effect*, another heuristic coined by Kahneman and Tversky, has even been shown to affect how much people are willing to pay for certain goods.[15]

To guard against evaluation biases, frames, and anchors, evaluate candidates comparatively. Once you have interviewed all candidates, compare their responses horizontally across candidates, question by question. This is a procedure many academics employ when grading exams. We have already learned to identify exams by student ID numbers rather than by names, but then I do not evaluate a student's exam by reading his or her answers to all questions. Rather, I grade all students' answers to Question 1, then their answers to Question 2, and so on. Ideally, I hide my assessment of Question 1 from myself to make sure I evaluate the next question uninfluenced by first impressions. You will likely experience some discomfort—I know I have—as you discover that a student can give superb answers to the first two questions but deeply disappoint in the answer to your third and fourth questions. But acknowledging this internal inconsistency is worthwhile.

Likewise, avoid the consistency commonly known as "groupthink." The idea that groups might perform worse than individuals because they tend toward uniformity and censorship was first introduced by Irving Janis. Since then, much research has been conducted on the phenomenon, and collectively it paints a somewhat more complex picture, recently discussed in the 2015 book *Wiser* by Cass Sunstein and Reid Hastie. Most important for our purposes, groups have been found to be even more prone to rely on the representativeness heuristic and show more pronounced overconfidence in their judgments than individuals do.[16]

If you currently use panel interviews, where a group of interviewers meets with a job candidate all at the same time, stop. Instead, the ideal is independent, uncorrelated assessments, uninfluenced by what the other interviewer thinks. We all have been in meetings where it was obvious that the group did not reach the best outcome but rather followed the loudest voice in the room. By now we know too much about unconscious biases to accept such outcomes without complaint or concern. To benefit from various sources of expertise, we should try to keep interviewers as independent of each other as possible. To state the obvious, if you have four interviewers, four data points from four individual interviews trump one data point from one collective interview.

Slightly higher-altitude fruit: you might want to invite the evaluators to submit their assessments before a meeting to discuss an applicant. This would allow an organization to aggregate answers—those one-to-ten weighted scores to questions asked in the exact same order—perhaps even automatically. Assessments with candidates above a certain threshold—both in terms of average scores as well as in terms of minimal number of evaluations with a certain score—would advance for consideration, whether this entails hiring or promotion. Go one step further and have a computer program evaluate these suggestions for shared biases.

Armed with individual evaluations, the outcome of the aggregation process, and the bias analysis, then have the evaluators meet and discuss controversial cases. For particularly important appointments or promotions, you might want to consider a slightly more elaborate design: employ the previous process, but have it conclude with two meetings. In the first meeting, the committee members are randomly assigned to smaller subcommittees to discuss the candidates, and at the second meeting, the full committee discusses the recommendations of the subcommittees. It is likely impossible to avoid groupthink in the final stage of the process, but this approach will allow for more than one groupthink to evolve in the subcommittees before the full committee meets.

Generally, research suggests that groups will reach better decisions if they adopt more structured processes, including having subgroups or an assigned devil's advocate.[17]

This starts to sound like complicated, hard work. It is. But technology can help. A few tools are now on the market, assisting employers in evaluating talent more objectively. The Behavioural Insights Team in the United Kingdom has developed Applied, a tool building on much of the evidence discussed in this chapter. Applications are blinded and assigned to different evaluators, work sample tests that assess applicants on real tasks required for the job emphasized, and independent assessments centrally aggregated. Similarly, GapJumpers and Unitive have also created recruitment platforms that anonymize the gender and race of the applicant. Unitive also exposes hiring managers to one piece of information at a time—separating where applicants went to school, for example, from their previous employers—to make sure an evaluator's rating is not unduly influenced by false inferences.[18]

If you still think that this is too labor-intensive and time-consuming, consider the high cost of bad appointments, and our inability to deal with them well. Most of us are enthralled by the current state of affairs and experience change as a loss. This means bad appointments are mistakes that are not easily fixed. In a survey of corporate directors about their company's talent management practices, Boris Groysberg and Deborah Bell found that fewer than 10 percent of directors thought that their companies did a good job dealing with such mistakes. The harder work is arguably letting go a poor hire.[19]

Don't let that happen to you. Pay more attention to whom you select. But don't just take my word that adopting these design features for recruitment and promotion are a benefit. Measure and

Interview Checklist ✓

Prepare

1. Determine number of interviewers and their demographics (use your own data!).
2. Determine questions (use your own data!).

During

3. Interview separately (no group interviews).
4. Ask questions in the same order and stick to it.
5. Be aware of framing effects: anchoring, representativeness, availability, halo...
6. Score answers to each question and score immediately afterwards.

& After

7. Compare answers to questions across candidates. One question at a time.
8. Use pre-assigned weights for each question to calculate total score.
9. Submit your scores to the lead evaluator.
10. Meet as a group to discuss controversial cases. Consider sub-groups for important hires.

A checklist for comparative, structured interviews

experiment. And let me help you by offering a checklist for your next interviews.

Designing Gender Equality—Create Smarter Evaluation Procedures

- Evaluate comparatively and hire or promote in batches.
- Remove demographic information from job applications.
- Use predictive tests and structured interviews to evaluate candidates. Do not use unstructured interviews.

7

Attracting the Right People

If you manufacture diet sodas, you face a challenge: men, or a bit less than half of the potential worldwide market, do not seem to like drinking your products. At least, they drink them much less often than women do. Your challenge boils down to answering why this is so. Maybe men start off less concerned about how many calories their sodas contain. Maybe they just drink fewer sodas. Or, maybe, there is just something about diet soda that turns them off. Confronting this same challenge, several companies concluded that the latter was likely the case and further suspected that there was something about the label "diet" that did not agree with men. Put differently, they suspected that "diet" just didn't align with male gender identity.

They started to experiment with different messages. For example, Coca-Cola introduced "Coke Zero"; PepsiCo, "Pepsi Max"; and the Dr Pepper Snapple Group came out with "Dr Pepper Ten," a ten-calorie soda whose slogan announced that "It's Not for Women." When Coke Zero was introduced to the United Kingdom, it was referred to as "bloke Coke," and the head of

Coke's integrated marketing communications in North America went as far as to comment at the time of the launch: "We're positioning Coke Zero as a defender and celebrator of guy enjoyment."[1]

Not all marketing plays as overtly on gender stereotypes, but gendered messages are more prevalent than you might think. For example, Gillette expanded the appeal of its brand, traditionally associated with personal care products for men, to include women by designing women's razors in pastel colors and naming them "Venus Divine," "Daisy," or simply "Gillette for Women." Gillette's dark-colored razors for men instead carried names like "Mach3 Turbo" or "M3 Power Nitro." And while yoga is most often marketed to women, I recently learned that "Broga" is specifically for men.[2]

What messages do you send in your job advertisements, newsletters, web pages, blogs, and other communications? Are your messages framed to appeal equally to all, or are they more likely to speak to some but not to others? Clearly, for any organization, attracting the right people, whether employees or clients or customers, is paramount—and it starts with smart advertising. One takeaway: the right language matters.

Linguists have long pointed out that language is gendered. In English, pronouns can present a problem. You need to hire a new marketer and you hope he is skilled. Or should it be she? Using "he or she" in such sentences has only recently become accepted. In other languages, even nouns can be gendered. In German, for example, a male professor is a "Professor" and a female professor, a "Professorin." But often, professors are only referred to with the male noun. In fact, there is a lovely German word for this, "mitgemeint," which is hard to translate but means that women are also included when a male noun is used. But, of course, this is not what the evidence tells us.

It is well known that women are less likely to apply for jobs that are male-labeled, and men are less likely to apply for jobs that are female-labeled. For decades in the United States, it was common to place advertisements in sex-segregated newspaper columns—jobs for women and jobs for men—until civil rights legislation made the practice unconstitutional in 1964. Jobs used to be advertised to attract male candidates for male-dominated professions, such as linemen being sought by a power company, or to attract female candidates for jobs traditionally occupied by women, such as stewardesses being sought by airlines. By the early 1970s, the practice had completely vanished—and it had real consequences. When ads do not make reference to the desired sex of the ideal candidate, research shows that both men and women are substantially more likely to seek nontraditional jobs. Placing ads in integrated columns organized alphabetically rather than segregated by sex proved to be a particularly powerful solution—much more effective than disclaimers saying that "job seekers should assume that the advertiser will consider applicants of either sex in compliance with the laws against discrimination." Once a job was assigned to a sex-identified column, disclaimers helped very little.[3]

Job ads targeting a particular sex are still common in some parts of the world. For example, an examination of more than 1 million job ads aimed at highly educated urban job seekers posted during 2008 and 2009 on Zhaopin.com, one of the leading online job boards in China, revealed that about one-third of the more than 70,000 advertising firms used job descriptions identifying the sex of the ideal employee in one or more of their ads. The gender-specific ads, which favored women and men in about equal measure, were quite explicit as to what they were looking for. When they targeted women, the ads encouraged young, tall, and attractive applicants; when they targeted men, they encouraged older applicants.

The gender targeting followed an interesting pattern, however. Firms seemed most explicit about the preferred sex of their ideal candidates when the size of the labor pool meant that they could afford to do so. They relied on more objective measures of performance in tighter labor markets and for higher-skilled positions. One of the most robust findings of the study was a negative "skill-targeting relationship": as a job required more skills, whether measured by educational background, experience, or even the pay offered, fewer ads made reference to a particular sex. The analysis may remind you of our earlier discussion of Gary Becker's argument that a "taste for discrimination" should disappear as competitive pressures on firms increase. Left behind and most vulnerable to such discrimination are those who do not possess skills differentiating them from others and who live where the supply of labor is abundant.[4]

Even in countries where job descriptions no longer make explicit references to the sex of the ideal candidate, more subtle cues remain. A group of researchers set out to measure how gendered the wording in job advertisements remained in the twenty-first century and whether the use of words associated with stereotypical gender roles, such as competence for men and warmth for women, has an impact on how applicants perceive these jobs. The team content-coded job advertisements on Canada's leading job search websites, Monster.ca and Workopolis.com. They focused on male-dominated and female-dominated occupations. These included plumbers, electricians, mechanics, engineers, security guards, and computer programmers, where men occupied between 99 percent and 74 percent of the jobs, and administrative assistants, early childhood educators, registered nurses, bookkeepers, and human resources professionals, where women occupied between 97 percent and 71 percent of the jobs.

To measure whether advertisers had selected masculine wording for male-dominated occupations and feminine wording for female-dominated occupations, they relied on published lists of agentic and communal words, such as individualistic, competitive, ambitious, assertive, and leader in opposition to committed, supportive, compassionate, interpersonal, and understanding. Each ad then received a score based on the fraction of male- or female-gendered words it contained. Unsurprisingly, the ads were heavily gendered. Indeed, the fraction of gender-stereotypic words was even correlated with the proportion of men and women in a given profession. This means that more male-stereotypic words were used for plumbers than for computer programmers and more female-stereotypic words were used for administrative assistants than human resources professionals.

Such wording matters. In follow-up experiments examining the impact of masculine wording, the authors found that people inferred from the ads how male- or female-dominated the profession was. The more women inferred a profession to be male-dominated, the less they found these jobs appealing. Tellingly, it was not a matter of perceived competence to succeed at the job. Gendered wording told the applicants something about whether or not they "belonged," but did not affect whether or not they thought they had the skills to do the job.[5]

People self-select into jobs based on their preferences and their beliefs about whether or not they belong. Job descriptions provide information and behavioral cues about both. And if you are not careful, both speak immediately to gender identity fit. Economists refer to such behavior as *sorting*. People sort into neighborhoods, schools, jobs, clubs, and social groups. Some of them charge high "membership" rates and offer specific privileges to attract those who value these privileges enough and have the capacity to pay for them, thereby deterring others. Among members, linguistic cues are like price tags. They signal to some that they belong and are welcome but deter others who, consciously or unconsciously, realize that they would have to pay too high a price to fit in.

Sorting is not a bad thing—in fact, in many circumstances we might want to encourage people to self-select. They have much more information about themselves than any outside observer or evaluator ever will. But we should be aware of what the basis of their sorting is. This is the moment for design. You need to scrutinize your messages for the signals they send to the world. Maybe elementary schools want to add still more women to their roughly 80 to 90 percent female faculty by specifying in their ads that "they look for a committed teacher with exceptional pedagogical and interpersonal skills to work in a supportive, collaborative work environment." But I doubt it. Most schools want to benefit from 100 percent of the talent pool and not deter skilled male applicants simply because the gendered adjectives in their advertisements signal to men that they do not belong. And schools are also keenly aware that boys need same-sex role models. This is an easy fix. Schools, and any other organization for that matter, can use inclusive language in their ads. With a few simple word-choice changes—"they look for an excellent teacher with exceptional pedagogical skills"—you have expanded the potential talent pool.

In many ways, by de-biasing job advertisements, we are helping the market do its job. It should bring those who offer services together with those who demand them. And it should do so efficiently, aiming for the best possible matches. Elaborate matchmaking algorithms now help schools find the right students and hospitals identify the right residents, and vice versa. For example, in 2003, New York City adopted a new method for matching students with high schools. The system is based on a "deferred acceptance algorithm" designed by a team of academics, including my former colleague and 2012 Nobel Laureate in Economics, Alvin Roth. The algorithm matches the best available school with the best available students, based both on the student's school rankings and the school's student rankings. The rankings are based on the signals the students and the schools send about what they have to offer and what they are looking for. Of course, the algorithm can be designed to be blind to demographic characteristics. In his illuminating 2015 book *Who Gets What—and Why: The New Economics of Matchmaking and Market Design,* Roth provides many more examples of successful matchmaking, including between people in need of an organ and those willing to donate. The beauty of an algorithm for finding a compatible organ donor is that it strives to include all medically relevant information—and nothing more. We should apply the same high standards when matching employees with employers.[6]

While many of us charged with hiring might not engage in a formal matchmaking process, we can improve our search procedures. In addition, we should be wary of the language used not only in our own communications but also in the ones we receive. Letters of recommendation, for example, are another place where gender-biased language often creeps in. According to one study, letters written for female medical faculty tended to be shorter, more likely to raise doubt (faint praise; hedges; negative, unexplained comments) and refer to her teaching instead of her research, reinforcing stereotypes portraying women as teachers and men as researchers. For an example of gendered language, consider this: "On a personal level Sarah is, in my opinion, the quintessence of the contemporary lady physician who very ably combines dedication, intelligence, idealism, compassion, and responsibility without compromise." Doubt raisers included language such as this: "It appears that her health and personal life are stable," or "While not the best student I have had," or "As an independent worker she requires only a minimum amount of supervision," or "She worked hard on projects that she accepted."[7] Eliminating gendered language in letters of recommendation and job ads is low-hanging fruit. But we do not always know a priori what wording works best to attract the right kinds of employees. Sometimes, it pays to test the impact of your messages, even as you are sending them.

Testing is exactly what the Government of Zambia did when it was looking to fill the newly created position of community health worker, or CHW. It collaborated with researchers to better understand how it could attract the right people through messages in job advertisements. In a field experiment, the researchers learned that while the job required people who wanted to do good and care for others, putting such information in the job advertisement attracted the wrong kinds of people. "Want to serve your community? Become a CHW!" attracted less qualified applicants than ads that made the extrinsic benefits of the job salient: "Become a CHW to gain skills and boost your career!" Such career incentives led more qualified people to apply who were then more effective at delivering health services. Interestingly, they also proved no more likely to leave the job for better opportunities than the health workers who had responded to the service-oriented advertisement. It turned out that both groups wanted to do good, but higher-ability workers also wanted to have a career. Neither the government nor the researchers would have known this without actually testing the impact of various messages.[8]

Sometimes, even the gender effects of our messages cannot be known ahead of time without running an experiment. Consider gender differences in attitudes to risk and competition. If they exist (we will discuss this in more detail in Chapter 8), we might expect men and women to respond differently to ads depending on how competitive a workplace they describe. That is what Jeffrey A. Flory, Andreas Leibbrandt, and John List sought to find out. They ran an advertisement in sixteen cities across the United States for a "News Assistant," in which the primary responsibility was described as creating news digests by summarizing stories and writing short reports. The researchers examined whether women were indeed more attracted to less competitive compensation schemes. Job seekers encountered ads that randomly described the position's compensation as being fixed, partially dependent on job performance, or substantially dependent on job performance. Across all sixteen cities, almost 7,000 people applied—but far fewer women applied when the position's compensation was advertised as extremely competitive. While neither women nor men embraced competitive environments, women disliked them decidedly more than men.[9]

This problem seems general, even global. Laboratory experiments conducted in various countries all present similar evidence. Women tend to opt out of competitive and variable pay schemes, typically due to their more pronounced aversion to risk, lower self-confidence, and dislike of competition. There seems to be at least one design that affects this gendered self-selection. Interestingly, the gender gap in competitive environments reverses when people compete in teams. This appears to be a pull-push phenomenon, with teams attracting women even as they push certain men away. Working in groups appears to boost women's self-confidence, while men grow concerned about their team members' abilities. In particular, high-performing men shy away from competitive pay schemes when pay depends on team performance.[10]

As is often the case with gender inequality, women may well have highly practical reasons for avoiding competitive compensation schemes, just as men have reasons for embracing them. An analysis of German labor data suggests an additional reason for why women self-select into piece-rate schemes: compensation tied more closely to objectively measured performance leaves less room for discrimination. In the sample of blue-collar workers analyzed, piece-rate schemes indeed worked better for women, with a smaller unexplained gender wage gap in the piece-rate regime than in the time-wage regime. History lends support to this observation. Claudia Goldin took the long view, studying where women have historically worked in the United States. She discovered that women tended to work in occupations that rely heavily on objective performance measures.[11]

Goldin also showed that women self-select into occupations that allow for more flexibility. In her 2014 presidential address to the American Economic Association, she identified the premium that women place on flexible work conditions as a key factor affecting gender segregation in the labor market. It also helps explain gender differences in pay and promotion in occupations that make flexibility available to employees only at a high cost. These include the corporate, finance, and legal sectors, which disproportionately reward people who work long hours continuously, without taking time out for family care. In contrast, in science, technology, and health care, demands on people's time have started to change. Goldin points out pharmacists as an interesting case in point. Pharmacology, where earnings have a more linear relationship with hours worked than is true in business or law, is the third-highest-paying occupation for women and the eighth-highest for men. The more hours pharmacists work, the more money they make, irrespective of whether they work part time or full time, or take time out to care for their family. Correspondingly, the occupation has one of the lowest gender pay gaps among high-paying jobs and over-proportionally attracts women.[12]

Sectors trying to attract more women use this knowledge in their job descriptions. And some go further and try to change the very dynamics that led to Goldin's conclusions. In an interview with the *Financial Times,* Niall FitzGerald, then co-chair of Unilever, explained how this could work: when one of his colleagues said, "We must identify very clearly those jobs which can be operated in a flexible manner," his response was, "You're going in absolutely the wrong direction. We will say: 'In principle, every job can be operated in a flexible manner unless it can demonstrably be shown to be otherwise.'"

There is a reason for the due process requirement in criminal law that stipulates a defendant is presumed to be innocent until proven guilty. Defaults are powerful, and requiring the government to prove the guilt of a defendant and not the other way around safeguards justice. As a default, "flexibility unless proven not to work" would dramatically change the structure of work. If flexible work arrangements were the default until proven objectively untenable, or until employees decided that they wanted to opt out, many more people would embrace working flexibly. Much research by behavioral economists underscores that moving from "opt-in" to "opt-out" defaults can have huge impacts. The now-iconic example is how participation in employer-sponsored 401(k) plans increases dramatically when companies automatically enroll their employees compared to when employees have to take the initiative. A well-established bias explains why: people tend to cling to the status quo, aptly named *status-quo bias* by William Samuels and Richard Zeckhauser in 1988. In particular, when people face complicated decisions, such as planning for retirement, they tend to avoid making one and procrastinate. In addition to defaulting people into a particular savings plan or flexible work arrangement from which they can opt out if they wish, simplifying the process and requiring people to make an active choice can also help them save more.[13]

The Australian company Telstra, mentioned earlier, is showing how this might work. It made flexibility the norm. "Flexibility applies to every kind of role at Telstra," it now states on its website. Conversations I had with Telstra employees while I was in Australia in 2015 suggest that "All Roles Flex" in fact has become the default work arrangement. Before implementing the change across the board, Telstra ran a three-month pilot program in its customer sales and service business unit, which it described as "a new and disruptive position around mainstreaming flexibility that would amplify productivity benefits, lift engagement, establish a clear market position, and also enable a new way of working." During the pilot phase, it monitored who applied for posted job openings and for what reason. As expected, the share of women in the applicant pool increased, and about one-third of the candidates reported that they had applied because of Telstra's stance on flexibility. While not a randomized controlled trial, the Telstra experience provides some hints at how flexibility might affect who companies are able to attract.[14]

Of course, if flexible work arrangements were no longer a woman's issue, there would no longer be the gender-specific career penalties that Goldin writes about. With increased demand for flexibility, we can (and you should) anticipate that competitive labor markets will adjust to employees' preferences and stop discriminating against people seeking flexibility.

When seeking to hire, in addition to worrying about the content of your message, you also need to consider the context in which your job advertisement is read. Framing does not end with the language you choose or the defaults you set but includes, as marketing experts would tell us, all aspects of design, including the placement of the ad and the proximity of other ads. Recall the lesson learned in Chapter 6: our minds want to evaluate everything comparatively. Today, technology even allows job seekers to take what other applicants are doing into account.

Benefiting from the large amounts of data collected by the professional social networking website LinkedIn, Laura Gee of Tufts University was able to measure how job seekers respond to information on what other applicants are doing. She analyzed the job search behavior of almost two million job seekers from more than 200 countries viewing 100,000 job postings in March 2012. About two-thirds of the job seekers were male, thirty-six years old on average, and almost half came from the United States. Most everyone had a bachelor's or a post-bachelor's degree.

Job seekers looked at a wide variety of jobs and responded to postings from about 21,000 companies, with the two most prevalent sectors being high tech and finance. Gee was interested in better understanding one particular aspect of the job search, namely how job seekers responded to information on what other applicants were doing. In line with the above findings, it could be that knowing others are also applying for a given job encourages women to shy away, disliking the competition that comes with popular jobs. Alternatively, perhaps knowing what others are doing provides additional information on the potential attractiveness of the job. The more applicants are averse to ambiguity, the more they might appreciate this additional piece of information, making them more likely to apply.

To investigate, Gee ran a field experiment where job seekers were randomly assigned to one of two conditions: they either saw the number of others who had started an application when they viewed the online posting or they did not. Interestingly, the additional information hardly matters for men, but it increases the likelihood that women apply by 10 percent. On any given day, this means employers seeking 100 percent talent could receive thousands of additional applications from women, including in industries where the fraction of women is still small, such as high tech and finance. Being more averse to ambiguity and less confident, women were reassured that a job was worth applying for when they knew that others found that job appealing. Being less averse to ambiguity and more confident, men found the additional information of little importance. Whereas women generally have been found to shy away from competitive environments, knowing about the desirability of a job seemed to outweigh whatever concerns they have about stiffer competition.[15]

Attracting the right kinds of people to apply for a job is hard. Along with the various biases employers can anticipate and adjust for, there are associations and contextual factors—whose ad is next to yours, for one example—that are beyond your control. But as I have noted, and any human resources manager can attest, handling bad hires is difficult and sometimes costly. Zappos, the online shoe store, used an innovative design to make sure it ended up with the right kinds of employees. After a few weeks on the job, when new hires spend much of their time in training, the company offered their new employees an opportunity to quit—accompanied by a "golden handshake" consisting of one month of salary in addition to whatever they had already earned. Why would Zappos do such a thing? Because it allowed employees to "sort." Those who liked the company and their job stayed, valuing the opportunity to be a Zappos employee more highly than the cash bonus offered to them for quitting. Others left without imposing additional costs, either to the company or themselves.[16]

Attracting the right people instead of managing the wrong ones is one of the most important tasks any organization confronts. This is the mantra Google lives by—or, as Laszlo Bock writes: "Only hire people who are better than you." In an interview on the company's hiring and corporate culture, Eric Schmidt, the executive chairman, explained that in addition to judging the technical qualifications of potential hires, a key focus at Google was to determine whether they were passionate and committed to innovation. Surely, allowing all Google engineers to spend 20 percent of their time developing their own ideas serves as a sorting device. It attracts creative, independent minds who invent Google News, Orkut, or a social networking site. The time is not written in stone nor necessarily utilized, but it matters as an idea: "No one gets a

'20 percent time' packet at orientation, or is pushed into distracting themselves with a side project. Twenty percent time has always operated on a somewhat ad hoc basis, providing an outlet for the company's brightest, most restless, and most persistent employees—for people determined to see an idea through to completion, come hell or high water."[17]

Not many of those "seeing an idea through to completion, come hell or high water" are women. In the spring of 2015, a gender discrimination trial brought by a former junior partner at a venture capital firm in Silicon Valley drew renewed attention to the low fraction of women in technology. While in the end a jury found against the plaintiff, the low numbers were undeniable: fewer than 20 percent in most tech companies and even fewer in Silicon Valley's venture capital firms. Some argue that the "tech bros" mentality of Silicon Valley keeps women out and even discourages female students from focusing on computer science. Perhaps. Surely, the male-dominated environment does not help tech firms attract women. As we know, deviating from behavior that is expected of a social category, either by others or by oneself, can be costly. A woman who acts against the norms by definition doesn't "belong"; not surprisingly, the fear of not belonging is influential.[18]

Indeed, research by Boris Groysberg, Ashish Nanda, and Nitin Nohria (now dean of Harvard Business School) suggests establishing *belonging* turns out to be a major concern of female job seekers. They report that women consider more factors than men when screening jobs; in particular, cultural fit, values, and managerial style. There is a surprising silver lining to this research, however: it carries hidden benefits for women and their employers. In follow-up work, Groysberg identifies this scrutiny as one of the key variables explaining why women transition more successfully to new companies than men. Women know better what they are getting themselves into.

The researchers analyzed the performance of more than a thousand "star" analysts working for almost eighty different investment banks over a nine-year period. Analysts were labeled "stars" if they were ranked as one of the best in the industry by *Institutional Investor* magazine. The team was interested in better understanding whether the analysts' skills were portable when they switched companies. It turns out most analysts lost their stardom when they changed employers unless they moved to a better firm or brought their whole team along—with the exception of female analysts. Not only had the women studied a potential new employer more carefully before joining, they had also built their expertise differently than their male colleagues. The top-performing female analysts had "built their franchises on portable, external relationships with clients and the companies they covered, rather than on relationships within their firms." Or as one female star analyst put it: "For a woman in any business, it's easier to focus outward, where you can define and deliver the services required to succeed, than to navigate the internal affiliations and power structure within a male-dominant firm."[19]

People choose organizations based on their preferences and their beliefs about whether or not they could thrive in a given organization. Messages shape those beliefs. Consider the messages sent when Lieutenant General David Morrison stated in a video posted on the Australian army's official YouTube channel that he was committed to inclusion. "If that does not suit you, then get out," Morrison flatly declared. "There is no place for you amongst this band of brothers and sisters." Acting in response to a 2013 investigation into sexual abuse, Morrison sent a strong message. In 2014, Morrison joined the Australian delegation to the Global Summit to End Sexual Violence in Conflict in London. Speaking again with admirable bluntness, he said that armies that assign more value to men than to women and tolerate sexual violence "do nothing to distinguish the soldier from the brute."[20]

Will these messages attract and retain soldiers valuing equality and inclusion? Time will tell. And while actions have followed his words, we all know that talk can be cheap. When and how messages affect behavior is a large field of inquiry in itself, but experimental evidence is rare. One example, however, is encouraging.

Robert Jensen and Emily Oster took advantage of the fact that cable television became available at different times in different parts of India, allowing them to trace whether attitudes and behaviors went along with exposure to the new information cable programming provided. They found that the introduction of cable television was associated with improvements in women's status in rural areas, including female school enrollment, decreases in fertility, as well as reported increases in autonomy and decreases in the acceptability of beating women and son preference. The information conveyed via cable television, often through somewhat surprising means, such as soap operas, exposed rural viewers to gender attitudes and ways of life, including within the household, more prevalent in urban areas. And it changed behavior.[21]

Sorting mechanisms are powerful and often overlooked. Those charged with attracting the largest, most talented pool of applicants should make sure they scrutinize the messages, overt and biased, conveyed in their advertisements, websites, or other communications. The wording used, the incentive schemes employed, the work hours required, or even the number of others applying may unintentionally attract some but not others. And while talk definitely can be cheap, sometimes people do listen. They care about what people they look up to have to say, including the heroes and heroines of soap operas, who may even become role models—a topic we will turn to in Chapter 10.

Designing Gender Equality—Attract the Right People

- Purge gendered language from job advertisements and other company communications.
- Pay for performance, not for face time.
- Make the application process transparent.

Part Three

HOW TO DESIGN
SCHOOL AND WORK

8

Adjusting Risk

Guess what? Women do not like to guess. And it matters. Consider the widely taken Scholastic Aptitude Test (SAT), used for generations to help determine college admissions. Female test-takers are more likely than male test-takers to skip questions rather than to offer a guess. In one of the most consequential design innovations promoting gender equality in recent history, the people behind the SAT took risk out of the multiple-choice questions.

Introduced in the United States in 1926 to create a meritocratic screening device, the SAT is used to select students for college based on ability (or "innate intelligence," as it was originally purported) rather than their demographic characteristics, where they come from, or how much money their families have. It is administered by the not-for-profit College Board and considered to be one of the most important tests American students ever have to take. Despite its honorable aspirations, as early as 1938 students started to take preparatory classes with Stanley Kaplan to improve their scores. This turned into a multi-billion-dollar industry with preparatory courses now being offered by many other companies and private tutors. The expensive classes and tutors focus on knowledge, skills, and, often most important, test-taking strategies—a far cry from the test's original intention of encouraging meritocracy instead of reinforcing existing privilege.[1]

These and other concerns led the newly appointed president of the College Board, David Coleman, to initiate a fundamental overhaul of the SAT in 2012. Among the revised SAT's new features is a design that equalizes the playing field between risk takers and risk avoiders. Starting in 2016, the SAT no longer penalizes test-takers for incorrect answers in multiple-choice questions. In the past, test takers received one point for each correct answer, but lost a quarter of a point for each incorrect answer. Test-takers could also skip questions, which had no impact on their raw scores. The redesigned SAT does away with the quarter-point penalty for incorrect answers.[2]

What were Coleman and colleagues thinking? Surely, the College Board did not just want to encourage wild guessing. Or did it? Under the old regime, the smart strategy was for a test taker to guess whenever he or she could exclude at least one possible answer. Here's why. Each multiple-choice question had five possible answers. If a test-taker could eliminate one, then randomly guessing meant a one-in-four chance of picking the right answer. If people adopted this strategy on, say, forty questions, on average they would get ten right and thirty wrong. For each correct answer, they would gain one point; for each wrong answer, they would lose one-quarter of a point. Thus, they would end up with ten points for ten lucky answers and lose seven and a half points for thirty unlucky answers for an expected gain of two and a half points. (If you were unable to eliminate an answer for each question and blindly guessed, the result would be a wash, on average gaining eight points and losing eight points.) Thus, a person's SAT score was determined by a combination of knowledge, some understanding of probability theory, a willingness to take a risk—and pure luck. Guessing did not hurt—the worst possible outcome from pure guessing was an expected value of zero. And if a test-taker knew something and could exclude some alternatives, guessing definitely helped.

With the penalty abolished, guessing becomes even more attractive. Using our example from above, with the quarter-point penalty gone, a pure guessing strategy now yields an expected value of 8. Guessing on the SAT has always been advisable, but with the new scoring system it has become all the more so. The College Board has taken the risk out of guessing. As a consequence, those more averse to risk, including women, should benefit.

Indeed, a number of studies suggest that women are more likely than men to skip multiple-choice questions. An analysis of the Fall 2001 mathematics SAT scores shows that women's tendency to skip more questions can explain up to 40 percent of the gender gap in SAT scores. Similar effects have been found for multiple-choice tests in South Africa, microeconomics tests in the United States, and Hadassah aptitude tests in Israel. In the United States, 20 to 40 percent of the well-established gender gap in political knowledge has been documented as resulting from men providing substantive but uninformed answers to surveys rather than marking "I don't know."[3]

Katie Baldiga Coffman took these results to heart. She developed experiments to measure not only any gender gap in willingness to guess on SAT-like tests, but also whether the gap was due to men being more willing to assume risk. And even more importantly, she tested whether decreasing the risk involved in guessing, that is, doing away with the penalty for wrong answers, would help close the gap.

It turns out that even among equally able test-takers, men were more willing to guess and women more likely to skip questions. Coffman's experiment was the first study designed to measure what people would have known if they had been forced to answer. She learned that it was not gender differences in knowledge that led to differences in test scores. Rather, women's reluctance to guess lowered their test scores significantly. About half of the gender gap in willingness to guess was due to differences in willingness to take risks—enough for the design innovation to work. Indeed, her findings are quite dramatic: when no penalty was assigned for a wrong answer, all test-takers answered all questions.[4]

Literally hundreds of studies, with a very small number of exceptions, support the notion that women are more averse to risk than men. In a large representative sample of more than 22,000 in Germany, Thomas Dohmen and colleagues found that women assessed themselves lower on a risk scale as well as made more risk-averse choices in a lottery for real money. Controlling for lots of other possible determinants of risk taking, the authors also report that shorter respondents, older people, and children of less-educated parents were all more risk averse.

In addition to collecting data on people's general willingness to take risks, the authors also focused on five specific domains: sports and leisure, health, career, driving, and finances. Women were less willing to assume risk in each. However, the gender gap was most pronounced in financial matters and in driving, and it was least pronounced in matters of career. Still, the differences were large enough to help understand some career choices. For example, individuals who are less willing to take risks have been shown to choose occupations with more stable and predictable, albeit lower, average earnings.[5]

Along with being less likely to guess, women are also less likely to speak up or offer opinions. They also need more assurances before being willing to run for public office. While there are many barriers to women's political participation and leadership, gender differences in willingness to take risks may contribute. Armed with the fact that serving in a state legislature is predictive of who runs for a US congressional seat (often more than half of sitting congressmen and congresswomen have served in state legislatures), Sarah Fulton, a political scientist at Texas A&M University, examined how many men and women currently serving as state-level legislators were considering a move up to Congress. Put more precisely: how high did the odds of winning have to be for male and female state legislators to consider running? For women, those odds had to be at least 20 percent. Men, on the other hand, were willing to jump into a race if the chance of winning was larger than zero. Female politicians do not gamble on long odds. They compete when the probability of success is decent. When they do run, however, their chances of winning are identical to men's.[6]

The Women and Public Policy Program offers an extracurricular training program, *From Harvard Square to the Oval Office: A Political Campaign Practicum,* for students who want to consider running for public office. The program provides students from around the world hands-on training in public speaking, fundraising, data-driven voter targeting, and Get Out the Vote strategies, as well as navigating political parties and campaign media. It also provides students the chance to grow their professional and personal networks, in part by exposing them to political role models at all levels of government, such as former US secretary of state Hillary Rodham Clinton, Minority Leader of the US House of Representatives Nancy Pelosi, former congresswoman Anne Northup, and former governor Christine Todd Whitman.

In one particularly noteworthy session, Jennifer Lawless, a political scientist at the American University in Washington, DC, one of the leading experts on women in politics, shared US statistics on what she refers to as the "gender gap in political ambition." Even though many things have changed over time, this gap has not. Women remain less ambitious to run for office than their male counterparts. The reasons are numerous, but include—based on people's self assessments—risk aversion, lower self-confidence, and less competitiveness. Women also perceive the electoral environment as more hostile and biased than men do—and, based on Lawless's work, they are right. Finally, and this is something you and I can start correcting today, they are less likely to be asked to run. This points to one of the easiest design interventions this book will offer: urge a woman to run for public office today! (Later in this book I will introduce you to startling evidence from India that underscores how profoundly women in public office can change, and indeed improve things.)[7]

Becoming a politician is a complex business, and disentangling exactly which part of a person's decision is due to his or her risk preferences is a difficult science. This is why TV game shows can be useful. Consider that female contestants have been found to take fewer risks than men on shows such as *Who Wants to Be a Millionaire* or *Deal or No Deal*. Natalia Karelaia of INSEAD and collaborators, for example, analyzed women's and men's behavior in a Colombian game show, *El Jugador* (The Player). In this game, contestants had to answer general knowledge questions for up to five rounds. They started by competing against five other players.

After each round, each contestant has to decide whether to continue to the next round or quit. If no one voluntarily quits, the player with the lowest score is forced to leave. Players who quit voluntarily can keep the money they have accumulated. If they stay and end up with the lowest score after the next round, however, they lose all their earnings and are sent home.

Similar to most game shows, substantially more men than women audition for *El Jugador*. Because the organizers made an extra effort to recruit women, they ended up with an almost equal gender split among contestants. But women were substantially more likely to quit voluntarily than equally skilled men. Why? Can this be explained by general differences in men's and women's willingness to take risks, or is something happening during the contest that makes men even more willing to assume risk?[8]

In his 2012 book *The Hour Between Dog and Wolf,* John Coates examines the impact of success and failure on risk taking. Having once been the head of a derivatives trading desk, he had the network and wherewithal to collect saliva samples from traders to measure their biochemical responses in "moments of transformation," namely after wins and losses. It turns out winners show heightened levels of a particular hormone, testosterone, found to lead to an increased appetite for risk, while testosterone levels in losers were reduced. Coates argues that such chemical reactions exaggerate booms and busts: when things go well, male traders seek ever more risk; when things go badly, they become overly risk averse. Women, however, seem to be largely immune to this *winner's effect.* Alexandra van Geen of Erasmus University Rotterdam shows in her experiments that men who have just won a lottery are more willing to take on risk than men who just lost, while winning did not matter for women. Women, of course, start out with only a fraction of men's testosterone levels. New work by John Coates, involving another hormone, cortisol, suggests that reducing stress on the trading floor might go a long way toward more accurate risk taking. Having more women on Wall Street would by biological necessity increase the diversity of testosterone and cortisol levels—an intriguing reason for firms to hire more female traders?[9]

Recent evidence from an experimental asset market and a meta-analysis based on thirty-five different markets from earlier studies by Catherine Eckel and Sascha Füllbrunn suggest that the answer is "yes." Earlier studies using the same paradigm had found a consistent bubble pattern: in these asset markets, prices typically start below fundamental value, then increase way above it and crash before maturity. But they had never tried the paradigm with women only. A replication with exclusively male or exclusively female traders revealed substantially larger speculative bubbles in all-male than in all-female markets. In some cases, all-female markets even produced negative bubbles with prices below fundamental value. A follow-up experiment showed that mixed-gender markets fall somewhere in between. The meta-analysis supports these findings, showing the smaller the price bubbles, the larger the share of women in a given market. The authors conclude: "These results imply that financial markets might indeed operate differently if women operated them . . . Our data suggest that increasing the proportion of women traders might have a dampening effect on the likelihood and magnitude of bubbles."[10]

The pressures on the trading floor perhaps mask another, subtler effect of mixed groups. Who else is present when a particular task is undertaken may affect performance. Consider the finding that when put in groups of three and asked to complete a difficult math test, women did worse in the presence of men. Consider as well that this wasn't true when completing a difficult verbal test. Men, however, were not affected by the gender of the people present. Or consider a curious and worrisome pattern researchers detected when analyzing all 2005 SAT scores: taking the test in a smaller, less crowded venue increased your score. To the rationalist, this seems bizarre. Student test-takers are all aware that thousands and thousands of people take the test on the same day; the number of people who happened to be in the room with you during your test shouldn't matter. Yet it did, introducing another unintended bias—*test-taker density*—in SAT results.

Clearly, the design of the test matters, but so does the physical environment in which the test is taken. Seeing so many other students taking the SAT may have reminded test-takers of how competitive this business of getting into college is. The environment increased the perceived risk of not making it, and undermined people's self-confidence and effort.[11]

An entirely different question is whether the SAT, or any test for that matter, helps us predict students' future performance. The SAT is still widely used to determine college admissions in the United States on the belief that students' test scores do a good job of predicting college achievement. The evidence, however, is mixed. And even those studies that suggest a link exists between test results and college grades, completion rates, and even post-graduation income, also find that SAT scores under-predict women's college performance compared to men's.[12]

A series of studies examining how well various tests predicted student performance in the University of California system support these concerns. They suggest that the SAT is a relatively poor predictor of college performance. High school grades proved to be the best predictor of college grades and graduation rates, irrespective of the school the test-taker had attended. What is more, and in keeping with findings regarding the value of workplace performance evaluations, the UC report raises concerns about using a student's potential as criteria for admittance as it tends to unfairly disadvantage poor and minority applicants.[13]

To make matters worse, we need to add another concern. Knowing how well someone performed—a student, a subordinate, or a teammate—might affect how you treat them. In this way, test performance becomes a self-fulfilling prophecy. The top students or employees do not necessarily do better because they are in fact better performers, but because you give them more attention, offer them better opportunities, and create work conditions in which they can thrive.

A well-known study originally published in 1966, by the Harvard psychologist Robert Rosenthal, drives this point home. He joined forces with Lenore Jacobson, the principal of an elementary school in San Francisco, and administered a cognitive ability test in eighteen different classrooms, ranging from kindergarten through fifth grade. He then informed the kids' teachers of the test results. About 20 percent of the students showed the potential for "unusual intellectual gains." Indeed, the test proved to be right. A year later, the 20 percent of students identified as having unusual potential had gained an average of twelve IQ points, compared to an average of only eight points for the rest of the students. Two years later, the top students still outperformed their classmates. They got smarter more quickly than their peers.

What the teachers didn't know was that Rosenthal had chosen the initial "top" 20 percent at random. The difference "was in the mind of the teacher." Teachers who believed students to be gifted paid more attention to the children, set higher expectations, and supported the pupils in their learning and development. While several studies have confirmed the effect of self-fulfilling prophecies in the classroom, a review of the evidence suggests that the impact is likely more nuanced. The most worrisome news is that teacher expectations seem to be particularly relevant for groups who traditionally face discrimination. The better news, however, is that the effects of self-fulfilling prophecies are not as significant as feared and do not tend to accumulate over time.[14]

Still, we need to remain vigilant, as even very subtle cues can affect what people believe possible for themselves. *Stereotype threat* is one of the most widely studied topics in social psychology since its introduction by Claude Steele and colleagues in 1995. It argues that certain situational factors can lead people to confirm the negative stereotypes about the social group they belong to. For example, Steele showed that when women were told that a math test was particularly difficult for women, they performed worse than men. When the tests were presented as being equally difficult for both genders, the gender gap in performance disappeared. Neuroscience now offers clues as to why. When women are confronted with threatening environmental cues, neural activity increases in the ventral anterior cingulate cortex, the affective network involved in processing negative social information. As this activity increases, their math performance worsens.

Stereotype threat starts early. The psychologist Nalini Ambady and colleagues tested its impact on Asian American children's math performance in the Boston area. Before solving a few age-appropriate math problems, the youngest girls, five to seven years of age, were asked to color one of three pictures: a girl with a doll, priming their gender identity; Asian children eating from a bowl with chopsticks, priming their Asian identity; or a land-scape, which was the control condition. When reminded of their gender, the girls performed significantly worse than the control condition. When reminded of their ethnicity, they did better than the control condition. Related studies found similar effects for German and Italian girls. In literally hundreds of studies and many different endeavors, ranging from golfing to standard-ized test-taking to entrepreneurship, stereotype threat has been found to reduce the performance of the negatively stereotyped group members.[15]

What can be done? Consider offering a friendlier environment. Remember that women tend to do better on math tests when the proportion of men around them is small. Fifteen-year-old girls in single-sex schools in the United Kingdom, for example, are as willing to take risks as their male counterparts. Girls from mixed-sex schools, however, are substantially more averse to taking risks. While you might (rightly) worry that different types of children attend single-sex as opposed to mixed-sex schools, an experiment conducted in Switzerland, where high school students were ran-domly assigned to single-sex and mixed-sex classes, rules out self-selection effects. The Swiss girls did substantially better in mathematics in single-sex classes, were better able to judge their abilities, and were more self-confident.

Instituting same-sex schools would be difficult and expensive, and as we will see when we spend more time thinking about di-versity in Chapter 11, controversial. But there are incredibly simple fixes that can move the needle. Relocating the boxes where test-takers are asked to select their gender and ethnicity from the beginning to the end of a test is one of them. While the impact of such changes is a matter of debate, I take a pragmatic view:

moving the box from the beginning to the end of the test harms no one and may help some.[16]

In mixed-sex classrooms, make sure everyone is able to contribute. In my classroom, I have two important rules: I count to five before I call on anyone to make sure I do not always choose the people whose hands are up first. And I ask students to build on each other's comments to encourage listening—and a more productive classroom discussion. As I have not always been successful at promoting the latter, I have started to experiment with a little behavioral intervention. Early in the semester, I pick three students at random and ask the first one to summarize in one minute why he or she has decided to take the class. I give the person a little bit of time to think about what to say. Excellence is not the point of the exercise, the class later learns. Then, I ask a second person to do the same. Of course, that student has had more time to prepare and thus often does a little better. Finally, I invite the third person to stand up. But the rules have changed. I ask that student to summarize what the second person just shared with the class. Usually, that's impossible. The student has been so focused on preparing a story that he or she forgot to listen.

The exercise has several goals: First, I want to highlight that what most professors ask students to do, namely listen to what others have to say and build on their arguments to advance learning in class, is easier said than done. Awareness is a first step toward improving. Second, the exercise helps them experience firsthand the scientific evidence which indicates that most people are not good at multi-tasking. Listening to others and developing an argument at the same time is hard, let alone when these tasks are combined with the all-too-common student habit of surfing the internet or texting friends while in class. Finally, I use the opportunity to explain my five-second rule and a few other strategies to provide a welcoming environment for those who need a bit more time to combine thinking with listening. For those who would like to test their ideas first before speaking up publicly, having people meet in small groups first to discuss complex or controversial topics strikes me as a very elegant design feature to level the playing field and enable everyone to contribute.[17]

Indeed, a desire to create small group contexts was one of the reasons for Harvard Business School (HBS) to launch a new course called "Field" in which students have to work in teams. Analyzing class participation in the typical first-year MBA course with eighty or ninety students in the room revealed that women and other traditionally disadvantaged groups were less likely to contribute. Under the leadership of Dean Nitin Nohria, HBS has been working hard to create an environment where women—as well as men—can thrive. Small groups provide a learning space that differs from the large classroom, where students compete for the professor's time and attention and where their participation determines a large percentage of their grade. Working in teams, of course, also helps students develop important interpersonal skills.

A big part of the behaviorally inspired design changes at HBS was ensuring fair, gender-neutral performance evaluations. Understanding that we have to help faculty, students, and staff get it right by making it easier for them to do the right thing, HBS has scribes in classrooms to help faculty monitor who they call on. They have developed online tools for professors to instantly track class participation and grading by collecting data by gender and other relevant metrics. One such metric is whether English is a person's native tongue. Even proficient English speakers take longer to insert themselves in a discussion if English is not their first language. Any grade based on class participation should be designed to take this into account.

HBS has made tremendous progress, increasing both the fraction of women students as well as narrowing the gender grade gap, but this is a work in progress. As Robin Ely said in a 2013 *Atlantic Monthly* article, "There are no silver bullets for dealing with second-generation bias—not scribes in the classroom, not software that ensures all students have a chance to participate, whether male or female, on the left side of the room or the right—because no two or three things hold women back." Frances Frei summed it up nicely in a 2013 *New York Times* article: "We made progress on the first-level things, but what it's permitting us to do is see, holy cow, how deep-seated the rest of this is." Ely and Frei, both faculty members at HBS who have been instrumental in changes made there, are too modest. Precisely because we can now see how ingrained unconscious gender bias is, we can start to design and experiment our way out of the thicket of bias. They and their colleagues have started to redesign HBS much like David Coleman and colleagues have started to redesign the SAT—removing bias from risky environments to level the playing field and let talent speak for itself.[18]

Designing Gender Equality—Reduce Bias in Risky Environments

- Adjust risk when gender differences in willingness to gamble may bias outcomes.
- Remove clues triggering performance-inhibiting stereotypes.
- Create environments inclusive of different risk types.

9

Leveling the Playing Field

The word *bloke* is not only used to make Diet Coke appeal to men. I was introduced to it in a different context when our two boys attended school in Sydney, Australia, where I worked for a semester. Various Australian schools had launched a new program: Boys, Blokes, Books and Bytes (B4). Its goal is to motivate boys to read. In short, it is a design that addresses one facet of gender inequality. B4 offers events and activities reflecting male learning styles and involving male role models, a.k.a. blokes, in an effort to close a gender gap in literacy.

Across the globe, boys are increasingly falling behind in reading and writing, as measured in tests such as the National Assessment Program Literacy and Numeracy (NAPLAN) in Australia or the National Assessment of Educational Progress (NAEP) in the United States. Many researchers and policy makers wonder whether teaching styles, such as requiring students to sit still for long stretches of time, might inhibit male learning. The dearth of male teachers and male role models who read likely does not help either. After he and his son had participated in one B4 program, one father, Gary, reported: "I will recommend this course to other dads because for me it broke down the fear of doing the wrong thing when reading with my son."

The right thing to do likely entailed nothing more than a father reading to his son. I will spend more time discussing the role model effect in Chapter 10, but it ought to be stated here that there is increasing evidence that having a teacher of the same sex improves how not only boys but girls perform and how their teachers perceive them.[1]

A 2015 report by the OECD titled *The ABC of Gender Equality in Education: Aptitude, Behaviour, Confidence* found that in all sixty-four countries studied, girls outperformed boys in reading and writing. By age fifteen, the gender gap in literacy corresponds to an extra year of schooling. By comparison, the gender gap in mathematics is shrinking. By age fifteen, boys are ahead of girls by just three months. In science, girls and boys perform about equally.

The problem is well documented, and with varying degrees of concern many countries have come up with interventions to address it. What is interesting is that no country has been able to close the gender gap in mathematics and in literacy at the same time. In fact, it appears as if there was a trade-off between gender equality in literacy and gender equality in math. In Latin American countries, such as Chile, Colombia, Mexico, and Peru, the gender gap in reading is small, but the gender gap in mathematics is large. In contrast, in Nordic countries such as Iceland, Norway, and Sweden, girls do as well as boys in math while boys have not caught up with the girls in reading.[2]

How can we design environments in which both boys and girls thrive? What if we cannot have it all? If boys and girls differ in how they learn best, designing environments that truly level the playing field between men and women will prove difficult. Instead, it will favor one of the two sexes. Maybe this is what the apparent trade-off between gender equality in math and literacy across countries is telling us. In some cases, trade-offs are explicit and certain games are zero-sum. Given that budgets are limited, and even more so in poorer countries, every scholarship to improve access only for girls or only for boys is a scholarship that does not go to a member of the other sex. What is more, this is funding that is not being used for interventions that might benefit boys and girls equally.

While it is true that coming up with gender-neutral procedures is hard, it is not impossible. Recall again the blind auditions used by many orchestras. Creativity, data, and experimentation will help. And while some situations involve trade-offs, others clearly do not. Firms and schools want their workers and students to play their very best game. Thoughtful design architecture will help. That male and female students, workers, managers, politicians, and leaders do not necessarily thrive under the same conditions will require care and attention when choosing behavioral designs that may impact groups differentially.

To better understand potential trade-offs, researchers have started to tease apart three effects: the impacts on the targeted group, the untargeted group, and overall. For example, a randomized controlled trial evaluating the impact of merit-based scholarships for girls in Kenya found that they significantly improved the recipients' test scores. Interestingly, what could have been an intervention favoring one sex over the other turned out to have broader beneficial effects. The scholarships also had a positive impact on their female and male classmates who had not received any support. What is more, the treatment schools eligible for the scholarship program also saw a 5 percent increase in teacher attendance rates as compared to the control schools that did not have access to the program, benefiting boys and girls equally. Thus, a program aimed at a small subset of the population can benefit the entire population through spillover effects, in this case, through peer effects and motivational impacts on teachers.

This is good news—but of course, that is not always the case. More importantly, we cannot stop there. Another question a responsible designer has to ask is whether merit-based scholarships to girls were the most cost-effective way to achieve the positive impacts mentioned above. In this case, they were not. To better understand this much understudied question, a group of researchers at the Abdul Latif Jameel Poverty Action Lab at MIT recently set out to develop a framework for "comparative cost-effectiveness analysis" and used educational interventions as their first application. As you might expect, scholarships are an expensive way to improve school attendance and performance in developing countries. But it is not textbooks, subsidized meals, or free school uniforms that promise the most impact at the lowest cost. Instead, one of the most cost-effective ways to improve school attendance came as a big surprise. It was identified shortly before the turn of the century and since has become one of the most impressive success stories of evidence-based decision-making: deworming, an intervention aimed at improving children's health. In many cases, the binding constraint keeping both boys and girls out of school is their poor health.

Based on the evidence collected by two development economists, Michael Kremer and Ted Miguel, in randomized controlled trials in Kenya, school-based deworming programs have now been scaled up by Evidence Action, a nonprofit organization that implements cost-effective and evidence-based interventions, to almost 100 million children in Kenya and India through its Deworm the World Initiative. In their evaluation in Kenya, school-based deworming decreased serious worm infections by half and school absenteeism of boys and girls by one-quarter—at a cost of less than fifty cents per child per year.[3]

So the answer to my question is: yes, we can design environments where both girls and boys thrive. Learning from deworming and the redesigned SAT, we can equalize the playing field. Deworming is a cost-effective intervention that does not have sex-specific impacts, and taking out risk from the SAT turned a gender-biased instrument to measure ability and performance into a gender-neutral one. Sometimes particular cases resist gender-neutral redesign and will continue to impact men and women differently. Even in such cases not all is lost.

Consider overconfidence, one of the most potent and pervasive biases. Overconfidence "has been blamed for wars, stock market bubbles, strikes, unnecessary lawsuits, high rates of entrepreneurial bankruptcy, and the failure of corporate mergers and acquisitions," as Max Bazerman and Don Moore report in their review. While it appears in various shapes and forms, one simple illustration is the "better-than-average" effect. When I ask my students to indicate how well they drive or what they expect their final grade to be, 70 to 80 percent believe that they are better than average. Thirty percent expected their grades to be in the top 10 percent. Much research suggests the phenomenon "not only to be marked but nearly universal."[4]

But not quite. It turns out that men tend to be substantially more overconfident than women. They are not only willing to take more risks when the risk factors are known, as discussed in

Chapter 8, but they are also more optimistic when assessing risky situations. Men seem to be particularly overconfident in areas where they are expected to have expertise. For example, Brad Barber and Terry Odean looked at data from a large discount brokerage firm and found that male investors were so overconfident in their own ability that they traded 45 percent more than female investors and as a consequence made significantly less money than the women did.

The evidence suggests strongly that it is almost impossible for us to assess ourselves objectively, and de-biasing employees who think more highly of themselves than others is very challenging. A meta-analysis examining perceptions of leadership effectiveness across nearly 100 independent samples found that men perceived themselves as being significantly more effective than women did when, in fact, they were rated by others as significantly less effective.

Women tend to be overconfident to a lesser degree and in some instances even underconfident. For example, women tend to underestimate their ability in mathematics and overestimate how good they have to be to succeed in higher-level math courses. Generally, female students are more likely than male students to take grades as an indicator of their mastery of a given subject. They are more likely than their male counterparts to drop courses in which their grades are lower; in the United States this is sometimes referred to as the "fear of B- effect." The loss of self-esteem in introductory math and science courses has been identified as an important factor explaining why women drop out of science and engineering majors.[5]

We have discussed performance appraisals previously, but it is worth revisiting them here: gender differences in self-confidence are also a concern for performance appraisals. Many firms ask their employees to evaluate themselves and then to share these self-evaluations with their supervisors. Consider the following scenario: supervisors must rate subordinates on a scale from one to ten, with ten indicating perfect performance. On their own, the managers would give each of their two direct reports, a man and a woman, a score of seven. But the male employee is overoptimistic about his abilities and the female employee underconfident; the former evaluates himself as a nine and the latter gives herself a five. Keeping the average score across the two constant and thereby meeting firm requirements regarding curves, the supervisor is tempted to adjust his or her initial score, making the male employee less unhappy by only downgrading him to an eight and making the female employee happy by upgrading her to a six. This is another example of the *anchoring effect*: inadvertently, subordinates have thrown a reference point at their managers who then cannot help but take it into account when making their own assessments.

Fixing anchoring effects in performance appraisals is easy: simply do not share employees' self-evaluations with their managers before they make up their own minds. Or even better: do away with self-evaluations altogether. To date, I have not come across any evidence suggesting that having people rate themselves yields any benefits for themselves or the organization. Consider junking self-evaluations as a mitigation strategy. While you cannot keep women from evaluating themselves more harshly than their male colleagues evaluate themselves, you can contain the impact the gender difference in this bias has on people's lives.[6]

Sometimes, you can intervene even a little bit earlier. You can give people feedback on how well they are doing, maybe as compared to others, to help them update their biased beliefs and reassess their standing. This design has proven to be particularly effective in mitigating against the gender gap in willingness to compete. The original studies examining men's and women's willingness to compete with others were conducted in Israel by Uri Gneezy, Muriel Niederle, and Aldo Rustichini. The researchers had the participants of their studies join in a task for which they either were paid a fixed amount for every problem solved correctly (a piece rate), or participated in a tournament style, where earnings depended on relative performance. Men and women performed about equally in the piece-rate scheme, but in the tournament setting men worked harder and did better. What is more, when given the choice between being paid based on a piece rate or a tournament scheme, women "shy away" from competition while men "embrace" it, subsequent research with American study participants by Niederle and Lise Vesterlund showed.[7]

This leads to inefficiency: we have too many of the low-performing but overconfident men and too few of the high-performing but less confident women choosing to compete. Gender differences in risk aversion and overconfidence can explain some of this, but it also appears as if women just disliked competing more than men. And, again, it matters. In the Netherlands, willingness to compete has been shown to predict which high school tracks students choose. The more competitive Dutch students, who tend to be the male students, are more likely to choose mathematics and science, which are the more prestigious, higher return tracks. For MBA graduates at Booth School of Business at the University of Chicago, interpersonal differences in willingness to compete translate into significant differences in earnings, explain part of the gender gap in earnings, and have long-lasting effects:

competitive graduates are more likely to work in higher-paying industries nine years after graduation.[8]

The impact of gender on competitiveness has been studied extensively in the laboratory and the field. Results appear to be sensitive to the task involved, the composition of the team, and the context in which it is undertaken. One study, particularly interested in these contextual effects, pushed the envelope to find two societies with substantive differences in their gender relations. The researchers chose the Maasai in Tanzania, an extremely patriarchal society where "women are said to be less important than cattle," and the Khasi in Northeast India, a matrilineal society in which women are the heads of households. They invited the villagers to participate in a task where they had to try to throw a ball in a bucket ten times. The participants were asked whether they wanted to be paid a piece rate, receiving a fixed sum for every successful throw, or to compete with another, anonymous villager participating in the same task at a different location. If they chose the tournament, the winner would receive three times the fixed amount and the loser would receive nothing.

The Maasai behaved pretty much like Americans: half the men and only a quarter of the women decided to compete. In contrast, more than half of the Khasi women decided to compete while men were about 15 percentage points less likely to enter a competition. While the Maasai and Khasi differ in many ways in addition to their gender relations, the experiments provide support for a nurture-based account of competitiveness.

Other work suggests that the gender difference in competition is particularly pronounced for male-typed tasks, such as a math task, while it disappears in female-typed tasks, such as a verbal task. As in test-taking, who else is in the room matters. When it was only women in the room, women were more likely to compete and did better in competitions. Another interesting example involved seven- to ten-year-old Swedish children, male and female, among whom Anna Dreber of the Stockholm School of Economics and her colleagues found no gender differences in competitiveness at all. In their sample, it did not matter whether the kids tried to out-run or out-dance each other, activities associated with maleness and femaleness respectively.[9]

Sweden appears to have created an equal playing field where there are no gender differences in competition. More generally, Sweden and other Nordic countries consistently appear at the top of rankings measuring gender equality. But turning countries like the United States into Sweden is a tall order. While a topic of extensive debate, gender equality in the Nordic countries is likely the result of a complex interplay of a large number of factors. Fortunately, without attempting to turn countries into Sweden, there is lower-hanging fruit anyone can harvest.[10]

For example, we can help people make more accurate self-assessments. The larger goal, both societal and within organizations, is to encourage the right people to participate in competitions—not the overconfident ones but the most able ones. Good feedback on how well someone is doing compared to others can do this for your organization. In various experiments employing the designs introduced above where people participate in piece-rate or in tournament schemes, information about relative performance has been shown to move high-ability women to more competitive environments and low-ability men to less competitive forms of compensation, such as piece rates. It eliminated gender differences in choices.[11]

Feedback about relative performance can help those less confident about their abilities, more risk averse, and less inclined to compete know if their hesitation is warranted or not. In addition, it also provides a reality check for those too eager to compete but unlikely to win. A while back, Robert Frank and Philip Cook wrote a fascinating book, *The Winner-Take-All Society*, in which he suggested that too many people waste their lives running after the big prize. Achieving the successes of Serena Williams or Roger Federer in tennis indeed is rare and becoming a professional tennis player truly is risky business. Overconfidence in pursuit of the unattainable is costly for individuals and organizations; calibrating ambition to ability is a lifelong lesson. Designs can help.[12]

Not sharing biased self-evaluations with others to avoid contaminating their judgments, and offering feedback to the under- and overconfident to help them make more accurate assessments are attractive designs that help equalize the playing field among people with different degrees of self-confidence and competitiveness. But we enter rocky terrain here. There has been much rhetoric, much of it overblown and not well grounded in evidence, about the differences between men and women. Are women really "from Venus" and men "from Mars," as a 1992 best seller by John Gray, a relationship counselor, suggests, and do these differences indeed predict "The End of Men," as a much-discussed 2010 article by Hanna Rosin in the *Atlantic Monthly* and a later book argue?[13]

Whatever the mechanisms driving differences in values and attitudes between men and women, the variance across countries suggests that they cannot be attributed to nature—at least, not exclusively. To be sure, various hormones have been identified as being related to certain behaviors. In Chapter 8 we discussed the relationship between testosterone and risk taking. Additional evidence from Swedish university students suggests that prenatal exposure to testosterone influences a child's willingness to take risks. In addition, the menstrual cycle has been shown to affect women's willingness to assume risk. But I do not expect science to ever resolve this question and determine what fraction of the observed gender difference is due to nature and what is due to nurture.[14]

Consider another potential gender difference about which there is much speculation: do women care more about others than men do? Richard Zeckhauser and his collaborator, John Rizzo, set out to examine whether or not this was relevant for physicians. They analyzed data from a nationally representative sample of young physicians in the United States from the 1987 and 1991 Practice Patterns of Young Physicians Surveys. The data showed that female physicians tended to work fewer hours per week and spent more time with their patients than their male counterparts. They also opted for less costly and invasive treatments. For example, female obstetricians/gynecologists performed cesarean sections and hysterectomies significantly less often than their male colleagues. But how does this work? Do male and female physicians "want" to do this, or are there other forces at play?

It turns out that young male physicians set higher income goals for themselves (what they refer to as "adequate income" in the survey) than women did and then needed to live up to them. We do not know what causes this. It may be due to men caring more about money, as the question might have suggested, but it could also be a reflection of the expectation that men be the main breadwinner in a family. Or it could simply reflect male overconfidence as discussed earlier. No matter the underlying cause, physicians who want to close an earnings shortfall between their aspirations and reality have two options: they can work more hours, or they can try to make more money per hour worked (or, of course, some combination of the two). They can boost their hourly incomes by charging more, seeing more patients per hour, and prescribing more procedures, particularly choosing those that reimburse the prescribing doctor at a higher level. Or they can move their offices to an area that commands higher prices for medical services. Women, it was found, pursue none of these strategies. Of course, having set lower income goals for themselves, they have a smaller shortfall to close. In contrast, male physicians typically choose the second option: they raise their hourly incomes by pursuing an array of strategies aimed at boosting their earnings to better align with their goals. In this study, the gender gap in income goals and in responsiveness to those goals fully explains the substantial gender gap in earnings and in earnings growth over time.

Based at least on this study, female physicians do not intrinsically care more for their patients but rather can afford to do so given the goals they set for themselves. While patients likely care little about where the difference in their treatment quality comes from, for a behavioral designer the root causes are key. If the reason for the difference in care is doctors' aspirations, as the study suggests, we clearly have to attack the doctors' goal-setting process. If the root cause lies in how much doctors are concerned with others' well-being, changing values should be our objective— which is likely the harder problem to address through design. Thankfully, the evidence does not suggest that we have to try to attack values. In fact, the evidence on potential gender differences in regard for others is less clear than you might think.

Much of the laboratory evidence on "other-regarding" behavior stems from a simple experiment called the dictator game. Two people are involved. One of them is randomly chosen to receive a certain amount of money. The other person does not receive anything, and, indeed, is a passive participant. The first person is then asked how much, if anything, he or she wants to share with the second person. Women tend to share a bit more with their counterpart and keep a bit less for themselves than men do. But the differences are generally small and depend on context. For example, men have been found to be more responsive to the price of altruism than women. When the rules of the game stipulate that giving up $50 will translate into someone receiving $100, they are more willing to do so. In contrast, women willing to give up $50 hardly care about whether their donation translates into a benefit of $50 or $100 for others. (This means that charities in countries offering tax deductions to donors are marginally better off targeting men than women.)[15]

Even if the gender differences in how others are regarded are tiny and depend on context, they can turn into self-fulfilling prophecies, and belonging to a social category expected to be more other-regarding can turn into a liability. Consider the following clever experiment by Lise Vesterlund, Linda Babcock, Maria Recalde, and Laurie Weingart. Motivated by their own experiences as female faculty members, they wanted to explore whether women had a harder time saying "no" when asked for a favor. They were worried that women might spend more time on what they refer to as "non-promotable tasks" such as serving on administrative committees, organizing an event, or mentoring and evaluating others, and thus have a harder time climbing up the career ladder. Their experiment was designed to capture the incentives people confront when asked to undertake a task that they would benefit from, but which they would prefer to leave to somebody else. Most university faculty members prefer someone else to organize their department's speaker series and most partners in law firms would rather have someone else mentor their firm's summer associates. But in both cases, faculty and partners benefit from great talks and wonderful future colleagues.

In the experiment, people were assigned to groups and their earnings depended on finding one group member willing to volunteer. They were all better off if one person volunteered, but volunteering was costly for the person doing it. When in same-sex groups, women and men were equally willing to volunteer. But when grouped with members of the opposite sex, the pattern suddenly changed. Women volunteered more and men less. Everyone, including the women, assumed women would volunteer more than men. Accordingly, men adjusted their behavior, expecting to benefit from the women, and women lived up to their expectations.

This is a common pattern at universities. Researchers at one large university confirmed that there, too, female faculty were more likely to say "yes" to a request to serve on an administrative committee than their male counterparts. Committee work is an important service to the university, but it rarely benefits the individuals participating. It is troubling that this pattern appears to be generalizable. In an excellent review of why there are so few women working in STEM fields, Stephen Ceci of Cornell and colleagues discuss various studies finding that male faculty spend less time on service activities and teaching but more on research, the most promotable task in academia. To what degree these differences inhibit women's careers is an open question. To answer it, we would need a detailed analysis of gender differences in time allocation by field. For example, do female academics in fields where women have traditionally been under-represented, such as engineering, economics, or mathematics, have less time to do research than women in psychology, and the social and life sciences? We do not know. For now, Ceci and colleagues conclude that mostly, "current barriers to women's full participation in mathematically intense academic science fields are rooted in pre-college factors."[16]

If you are concerned about gender-based imbalances in your organization, you can easily follow in Harvard Kennedy School's footsteps. We try to measure (and compensate) as many contributions relevant to the institution as possible. We employ a point system to measure faculty's workload. A full-time faculty member's workload is 100 points, with a margin of error of 10 percent plus or minus. If faculty members contribute substantially more, the school compensates them more. If a faculty member falls significantly short of workload expectations, explanations and sometimes adjustments in compensation or time status are in order. Points are allocated for teaching and administrative tasks, and faculty have substantial flexibility in how they meet their obligations. Some might choose to teach more than the minimal requirement, others might give more of their time and effort to service or organizational leadership opportunities.

The point system has lots of advantages, providing incentives for people to deliver the public goods everyone benefits from. The flexibility allows them to trade off activities they are less good at for tasks they are better at, making everyone better off. As a design, this is almost a pure win-win. True, not everything is quantifiable, which is why every few years we have a discussion about whether our workload system rewards effort adequately and does not crowd out intrinsic motivation. But I do not mind, and I believe most of my colleagues prefer our system to the less flexible, more opaque, and seemingly less equitable systems followed at other academic institutions. At the very least, the Kennedy School's points bring inequities out into the open and make service activities a part of any conversation about faculty contributions.

The larger issue is, of course, this. Through the measurement of all contributions, we can correct for differential impacts of gender bias ex-post. Ideally, we would level the playing field ex-ante or intervene to mitigate impacts before they fully hit. But if we can't, ex-post compensation for career-relevant imbalances resulting from the expectations placed on one's gender can be a helpful design feature.

Designing Gender Equality—Level the Playing Field

- Prevent gender bias from having an impact: use gender-neutral designs.
- Mitigate the impact of gender bias on yourself and others; do not share biased self-assessments with supervisors; give feedback to help people correct their biases.
- Compensate for differential impact due to gender bias.

Part Four

HOW TO DESIGN DIVERSITY

10

Creating Role Models

Like most office lobbies, when you enter Harvard Kennedy School you will see portraits on the wall. They hang in our public spaces, classrooms, conference centers, and office suites. Inspired by research findings, we recently added a few new ones. Made possible through the leadership of my colleague, Jenny Mansbridge, and the Women and Public Policy Program, they now include Ida B. Wells, the US civil rights activist and suffragist; Abigail Adams, the second First Lady of the United States; Edith Stokey, economist and "founding mother" of the Kennedy School, and Ellen Johnson Sirleaf, President of Liberia, winner of the Nobel Peace Prize, and a graduate of the school.

This is a work in progress. Harvard still has more to do. The student newspaper, the *Crimson,* reported in March 2012: "Of the more than 60 figures portrayed in the art of Annenberg Hall, three are women—two of them are tending to children, while the third welcomes her warrior husband home to a life of domestic tranquility."

New portraits of women leaders at Harvard Kennedy School: Ellen Johnson Sirleaf, President of Liberia

Does it matter? Yes. Students' attitudes can be affected by subtle and simple changes. Sapna Cheryan of the University of Washington has demonstrated that just by changing decorations in a computer science classroom, losing the Star Wars and Star Trek images for gender-neutral art and nature pictures, female students' associations between women and careers in computer science were strengthened. Even one's choice of screen saver can have a consequence. One study subtly exposed people either to a picture of Hillary Clinton, Angela Merkel, Bill Clinton, or no picture before they had to give a public speech. Women who had seen a picture of a female leader gave longer speeches that were rated higher both by external observers as well as by the women themselves than those who had seen a picture of Bill Clinton or no picture. Role models did not affect men. They did equally as well, whether exposed to Bill or to Hillary Clinton or to no picture. Another study showed that pictures are not even necessary—just asking people to imagine what a "strong woman" looks like can undermine stereotypes.[1]

Most organizations confronted with such simple design choices act unthinkingly. When entering a board room, you typically meet the previous—typically all male—company leaders. Correcting this sort of gender inequality through design is the very definition of low-hanging fruit, or at about the height one hangs a picture. One multinational I advise often gathered in one room when reaching important promotion decisions. Its walls were decorated with the portraits of previous CEOs. All were men, of course, and, as I pointed out, this was hardly conducive to triggering counterstereotypical associations between gender and leadership. Indeed, only ten years ago, all portraits at the Kennedy School had been of men.

The ability of role models, in portraits and more importantly in the flesh, to influence gender inequality is both encouraging and muddy. We have already encountered in Chapter 9 research pointing out the positive consequences of having same-sex instructors and students, whether to encourage boys to read or girls to excel at math. But the promise of role models promoting the moral imperative of gender equality may be far greater. In 1993, the Indian government amended its constitution with the following provision: Going forward, village councils needed to reserve one-third of their seats for women. Additionally, one-third of council leaders, the pradhans, had to be women. Described as "landmark legislation" that would "forever change the face of rural Indian politics" and as "one of the best innovations in grassroots democracy in the world," more than 1.5 million women were to be elected representing 800 million people in the world's oldest and largest democracy.[2]

In a speech late in 2011, then US secretary of state Hillary Rodham Clinton built on India's amazing innovation to launch the Women in Public Service Project, a collaboration between the US State Department and five all-female colleges—Barnard, Bryn Mawr, Mount Holyoke, Smith, and Wellesley—aimed at empowering women from around the world to serve in the public sector. The tangible accomplishments of India's experiment inspired the project's aims. When introducing the project, Secretary Clinton described just some of the Indian legislation's impact: "Over a very short period of time, studies showed that women in these positions [India's village council leaders] started investing more in public services, from clean water to police responsiveness, than their male counterparts had. And there were other benefits. With more women installed as council leaders, more women spoke up in council meetings than ever before. And in a nation where the under-reporting of crimes against women is widespread, more women came forward to file complaints about abuse, because they were more confident that the police would take action."

We know this and more because India's path-breaking legislation was implemented in a way that allowed a number of social scientists, including Esther Duflo of MIT and Rohini Pande of the Kennedy School, to rigorously evaluate its impact. Not only did the law mandate that one-third of village leaders in a district have to be women, it also required that these villages be picked randomly out of a hat in each election cycle. This turned the intervention into a "natural experiment" where some random sample of villages received the "treatment," in other words, a female leader, while others did not. Thus, the researchers could analyze villages that were comparable other than for the sex of the village chief and measure what difference the new enforced gender difference really made.

I often describe this research as constituting the "gold standard" of how to measure the impact of quotas. The evidence gained from India's intervention is based on a true experiment, allowing us to make causal inferences about the impact of quotas. In no other country in the world have quotas been introduced randomly. Usually, we have to rely on "before-and-after" comparisons or correlational analyses. While helpful, this data is much less reliable than experimental evidence.

Through the Panchayati Raj Act, as the amendment is commonly called, India was able to increase the share of women in local government from 5 percent in 1993 to 40 percent by 2005, well exceeding the mandated quota of 33 percent. And despite early rhetoric suggesting that the female council members were either ill qualified or the relatives of powerful men just serving as their proxies, the women village leaders did all the good things Secretary Clinton mentioned in her speech: they provided more key public goods such as drinking water, roads, and education, increased the reporting of crimes (including of rapes), and accepted fewer bribes than their male counterparts.

The women leaders also substantively changed the face of politics. They served as role models in various ways and with measurable consequences. With the advent of female village leaders, the likelihood that a woman spoke up in a village meeting increased by 25 percent. If a seat had been reserved for a woman in the previous election cycle, women were more likely to run in a subsequent open election, competing with men, a study for the state of Maharashtra showed. Seeing women leaders changed perceptions—making women more confident that they could run for public office and making men more accepting of women as leaders.

Villagers who had been exposed to at least two female chiefs in West Bengal overcame their initial bias against women as leaders and rated male and female leaders equally. This included male villagers who, when the quota was first introduced, declared that they did not like voting for women. But after being exposed to a minimum of two female leaders, they had become comfortable with voting for them.

Administration of the Implicit Association Test confirmed that female role models influence gender bias, up to a point. Male villagers who had never had a female as chief consistently rated them lower than male chiefs. But male villagers who had had female chiefs rated male chiefs as less effective. This finding is particularly remarkable given the evidence from a survey that sought to discover if ratings in effectiveness translated into differences in who people liked. Sadly, the answer was no. Male villagers exposed to female chiefs might rate them higher, sometimes even higher than male chiefs, but they still found male leaders more likable—suggesting that the competence-likability dilemma that American women in male-dominated fields face also applies to female leaders in India.

Evidence for the positive benefits of India's grand experiment, however, do not stop with perceptions of effectiveness. Perhaps most strikingly, female chief role models affected parents' career aspirations for their children. After having experienced a female chief twice, parents were more likely to want their daughters to study past secondary school, basically eliminating the gender gap in aspirations. The influence didn't end with the parents but extended to their daughters. Girls exposed to female village chiefs spent less time on household activities and wanted to marry later. The quota system had created role models for the girls and their parents, enabling both to imagine and see the value of a different future. A comment made by Abhijit Banerjee of MIT—the author, together with Esther Duflo, of the important book *Poor Economics*—gets at this shift in attitudes. Interviewed for the film *Gender Equality: The Smart Thing to Do*, which the Women and Public Policy Program produced in 2011, he reported hearing something unexpected and attributable directly to the Panchayati Raj Act. When he talked with parents in rural India, they spoke of a new aspiration for their daughters, "to be in politics because there's a lot of reservations for jobs for women in politics. That's an answer that I would not have expected, or didn't hear, ten years ago."[3]

Overall, the introduction of political gender quotas in India was a success. The act of seeing women lead increased women's self-confidence and their willingness to compete in male-dominated domains, and it changed men's and women's beliefs about what an effective leader looked like. This mattered for elections, making everyone more willing to vote for women. It also influenced parents and girls, allowing them to anticipate and strive for political office.

At the time India passed the amendment, nothing was certain. No one knew what would happen. Indeed, many feared that mandating exposure to women leaders through reservations would completely backfire. People, it was thought, would perceive gender quotas as unfair or as violating gender norms, or they might simply dislike the restrictions quotas impose on their free exercise of choice. While surely some Indian villages must have felt, even acted on some of these concerns, the mandate solved a "chicken and egg" problem: If people are biased against female leaders and never see a woman in a leadership position, they can never update their beliefs. With a third of village council seats reserved for women, Indian voters were given a chance to evaluate real female leaders carrying out their duties in office instead of basing their beliefs on stereotypical caricatures. And all Indian women were given role models to learn from and be inspired by.[4]

Norway is another case in point. In 2003, Norway legislated a 40 percent minimum representation of each sex on the corporate boards of public limited and state-owned companies. While it is still early days, Marianne Bertrand and collaborators tentatively conclude that the introduction of the board quotas may have triggered further corporate changes at the top, increasing the share of top managers who are women, but did not influence the total number of women employed in a given firm. A study for large corporations in the United States finds similar positive associations between an increase in the number of female directors and moves toward more top female executives. Overall, however, the research does not suggest that more women on corporate boards and in corporate suites produced gender de-biasing outside of the firm. Compared to India's experiment with village chiefs, the role-model effects of Norway's corporate quota seem to be limited to those with direct exposure. Stating perhaps the obvious, the Norwegian and US evidence underscore that a female director of a corporation is much less publicly visible than a female politician.[5]

Senior managers might well be important role models. Based on panel data from over 20,000 US firms across all states and industries from 1990 to 2003 provided by the Equal Employment Opportunity Commission, researchers have found that when the share of female top managers increased, subsequently, the share of women in mid-level management also rose. The effect was most pronounced for white women, but African American, Hispanic, and Asian women also benefited from same-sex, same-race superiors.[6]

Do not let the obvious point hidden in these analyses be missed. The evidence on role models points to some of the easiest solutions: role modeling can start with you. Learn from the people who have inspired you. Often, this starts at home with parents and grandparents, brothers and sisters, nieces and nephews, in-laws, and other relatives and friends. Or take a look at Melanne Verveer and Kim Azzarelli's inspiring book *Fast Forward,* where you will learn from more than seventy "trailblazing women." You will encounter former US secretaries of state Madeleine Albright, Hillary Rodham Clinton, and Condoleezza Rice; Managing Director of the IMF Christine Lagarde of France; founder of the Self-Employed Women's Association (SEWA) Ela Bhatt of India; the Nobel Peace

Prize Laureates Leymah Gbowee and President Ellen Johnson Sirleaf of Liberia, Tawakkol Karman of Yemen, and Malala Yousafzai of Pakistan; US talk show host Oprah Winfrey and Chinese talk show host Lan Yang, and change-makers Cherie Booth Blair, Tina Brown, Katie Couric, Geena Davis, Abigail Disney, America Ferrera, Melinda Gates, Senator Kirsten Gillibrand, Arianna Huffington, Katty Kay, Helena Morrissey, Maria Shriver, Justice Sonia Sotomayor, Meryl Streep, Aude de Thuin, and so many more.[7]

As a director on the board of a large multinational firm, I hope my presence has positive effects on the company's female employees. But I also appreciate that it matters how visible the director is. The more visible I am, the more likely the positive effects. So, whenever possible, I try to meet with women's groups or speak at gender-related events sponsored by the firm. The title of a paper on the topic, "Seeing Is Believing . . . ," resonates with me: people need to see counterstereotypical role models often for beliefs to change. In their paper, Nilanjana Dasgupta and Shaki Asgari show that exposure to female role models, encountered either through biographical information about famous female leaders or by seeing female professors in a classroom, decreased women's stereotypical beliefs about themselves. In both a women's college and a coeducational college, the greater the proportion of female faculty, the more female students were likely to associate women with leadership and with math.

While a number of studies have shown correlations between female students' achievements and the gender of the instructor, particularly in male-dominated fields, only recently have researchers been able to exploit a naturally occurring experiment to test causal links. The Air Force Academy randomly assigns students to courses, allowing us to measure what impact the faculty's gender had on the students. In introductory STEM courses, female students were more likely to choose a STEM major when they were assigned to a female professor instead of a male professor. The gender of the faculty had no effect, however, on male students' choices.

Examining a nationally representative sample of 25,000 middle school students in the United States, Thomas Dee of Swarthmore College finds that the gender match between students and teachers matters dramatically. Among thirteen-year-olds, almost a third of the gender gap in reading was eliminated if the English teacher was male. The gap was reduced because of a gender match for boys, improving boys' performance, and a gender mismatch for girls, hurting their performance in English. Similarly, half of the gender gap in performance in science and the complete, albeit much smaller, gender gap in math was eliminated if the teacher in those subjects was a woman. Given that most teachers are female, 83 percent at the time of this study, and often comprise about half of the workforce in math and sciences, Dee concludes that "the gender dynamics between teachers and students at this level amplify boys' large underperformance in reading while attenuating the more modest underperformance of girls in math and science."[8]

The dearth of role models can create self-fulfilling prophecies. Two studies in large law firms suggest the low number of female partners has a significant impact on women law associates' careers. Kathleen McGinn and Katy Milkman had access to five years of personnel data and employee interviews from a US-based law firm. They found that retention of junior-level female employees was highly correlated with the number of female supervisors. The fewer role models (who may also have served as mentors or sponsors) there were, the fewer female associates were promoted or stayed in the firm. What is more, Robin Ely's study of a law firm suggests that scarce role models render the few that are visible less useful: female associates assessing the lone two female law partners with wildly divergent habits confront a challenge that male associates assessing dozens of male law partners do not.

A scarcity of role models can in fact promote gender inequality, even as a firm or organization works to address it. Employees were more likely to have left the law firm by their fifth year if the fraction of same-sex or same-race peers was larger in their work group. Apparently, law associates believed that their chances for promotion diminished the more people "like them" there were at their same level. If ten female associates see only one female partner, they could well make the inference that their chances of advancement to partner are quite limited. Women and minorities may assume that they are in a fierce competition with members of their own demographic group for implicitly reserved seats.

Indeed, a very similar dynamic has been uncovered by a number of other studies. Based on an examination of job interviews in a large professional services firm, being interviewed by a woman hurt female applicants who the interviewer perceived as most likely to turn into competitors, namely the most competent women, and benefited the less able female applicants.

In Spain, academic promotions from assistant professor to associate professor and then to full professor are determined by randomly created evaluation committees, leading to random variation in the gender composition of the committees. It turns out that female associate professors evaluating assistant professors for promotion were more likely to be in favor of promoting male junior colleagues. But this effect was only evident when evaluator and candidate were at the same institution. It appears as if the evaluator again feared same-sex competition, perhaps assuming some implicit gender quota. In fact, if a male evaluator was replaced by a female evaluator of the same institution, this decreased the likelihood that a junior female candidate was promoted by 38 percent. It did not affect female candidates from other institutions. Nor did the researchers observe any of this behavior for promotions to full professor. When full professors evaluate associate professors to join their ranks, they need not fear same-sex competition. Full professor is the highest rank possible in academia, and at that point, evaluators, looking for friends and people like themselves, exhibited an in-group preference, favoring candidates of the same sex and academic network.

Both biases, in-group preferences and in-group discrimination, obviously are bad for an organization hoping to hire and promote the best talent. The evidence increasingly suggests that in-group discrimination is driven by a fear of same-sex competition, or the concern that there are only a fixed number of positions available for women, and a woman promoting another highly capable woman has only made the competition for one of those positions more fierce. In contrast, a dislike of in-group members appears to turn into a preference for them once people have climbed up the career ladder. To what degree this is caused by the scarcity of role models, and consequently the scarcity of perceived slots, is an open question. Maybe male nurses or teachers would also feel more threatened by same-sex competition? Unfortunately, no research on this question has been conducted yet.[9]

Role models are everywhere, of course, starting with parents. Mothers are often the first role models for young girls. Based on data from an eighteen-year panel study, researchers concluded that the egalitarianism of people's views is related to whether or not their mother worked outside of the home. Adolescents seem to be particularly influenced by their mom's employment status. Interestingly, women's willingness to work can also be traced back to the proportion of men with working mothers. Similar to the Indian evidence, exposure to working women, in this case their own mothers, seems to have made men more accepting of women's participation in the labor force.

Several researchers built their analyses on the efforts during World War II to recruit women to the labor force. Mobilizing men into the armed services during the war affected more than just the generation of women who were consequently pulled into the labor force. Its effects were longer lasting.

The circumstances arising during World War II were unprecedented. Labor demand alone would have pulled some women into the workforce. But as George Akerlof, a 2001 Nobel Laureate in Economics, and Rachel Kranton argue, role models supported by an extensive marketing campaign were necessary to help women picture how they could take on a "man's job" without losing their "femininity." Rosie the Riveter was born and has since become a cultural icon in the United States. Rosie's British equivalent is Ruby Loftus, whose picture now is part of the Imperial War Museum's art collection. Little if at all considered at the time was how these working women would influence, as role models, younger generations of men and women who watched them head off to work.[10]

Another fascinating and understudied issue is the influence daughters have on their parents. Justice Harry Blackmun, a Republican who served on the US Supreme Court from 1970 until 1994, is best known for writing the court's opinion on *Roe v. Wade*, the landmark decision decriminalizing abortion in 1973. He would become one of the most liberal justices in the court's history, writing in *Stanton v. Stanton*, which in 1975 ruled that a state could not specify different ages of adulthood for men and women: "A child, male or female, is still a child . . . No longer is the female destined solely for the home and the rearing of the family, and only the male for the marketplace and the world of ideas . . . If a specified age of minority is required for the boy in order to assure him parental support while he attains his education and training, so, too, is it for the girl."

Justice Blackmun was close to his family, including his daughter Sally. When his archives became public in the winter of 2004, Sally talked with *Women's eNews* about her father, and shared some of her own story. She was nineteen and a student at Skidmore College when she found out in 1966 that she was pregnant. "It was one of those things I was not at all proud of, that I was not at all pleased with myself about. It was a big disappointment to my parents . . . I did what so many young women of my era did. I quit college and married my 20-year-old college boyfriend. It was a decision that I might have made differently, had *Roe v. Wade* been around."

A few weeks after the wedding, Sally had a miscarriage. But it was too late to return to college. Instead, she joined her husband, then living in a different state. They got divorced six years later and Sally eventually completed college, became a corporate lawyer, remarried, and had two daughters. She describes how, nine years after her unexpected pregnancy, her dad sought his family's input in *Roe v. Wade*: "*Roe* was a case that Dad struggled with. It was a case that he asked his daughters' and wife's opinion about."

Might his daughter's experience have influenced him? Maybe. Using data from almost 1,000 gender-related cases of the US Courts of Appeals and the information as to the makeup of the families of 224 judges sitting on the court, Adam Glynn and my colleague Maya Sen found that judges with daughters are more likely to support women's causes than judges with sons only (controlling for the total number of children). It appears that Republican judges, much like Justice Blackmun, are more affected by the gender of their children than their Democratic peers: their opinions demonstrate a more marked shift in support of women's causes when they are the parents of girls.[11]

Glynn and Sen's work was inspired by Ebonya Washington of Yale University, who took a closer look at politics to examine whether decisions by male members of the US Congress were affected by the gender of their children. Indeed, holding the total number of children constant, each daughter significantly increases a congressman's likelihood of voting liberally, particularly in regard to issues involving reproductive rights. In addition to impacting legal and political decisions, daughters also play a role in business. Evidence from Denmark suggests that male CEOs who have daughters, and in particular firstborn daughters, are associated with a difference in female employees' wages. In this study, the more daughters a Danish CEO has, the better his employees are paid.[12]

Enlisting men as agents for change is the goal of a number of innovative initiatives, including the UN's HeForShe campaign, a "solidarity movement for gender equality that brings together one half of humanity in support of the other half of humanity, for the benefit of all," represented by the actor Emma Watson. Australia's

Male Champions of Change "use their individual and collective leadership to elevate gender equality as an issue of national and international social and economic importance." The organization was founded by Elizabeth Broderick, Australian sex discrimination commissioner from 2007 to 2015. Many other organizations, too numerous to list here, honor women as role models.[13]

"Seeing is believing," whether to inspire women in India to run for public office and men to vote for them, or to help male politicians walk in women's shoes in the United States. The evidence is overwhelming that role models influence behavior, whether daughters affecting fathers, female village council chiefs impacting male Indian voters, or female corporate board members influencing the gender makeup of top management. The stunning example of India's amendment reinforces the promise of quotas. Even as we unpack the concerns quotas still legitimately raise (to be discussed in the next chapter), we can acknowledge that they offer a potentially influential tool. And while increasing the number of female partners in law firms has proven and will continue to prove difficult, every woman in a position of prominence may choose to act as a role model. At a minimum, if you care about gender equality or are a woman weighing job offers or candidates to vote for, learning how many daughters a CEO or candidate has is not a bad idea.

This is why leaders across Australia received a present in 2014—"Daughter Water." Labeled water bottles were distributed with this explanation: "Women being paid fairly shouldn't hinge on a CEO having a daughter, and it doesn't need to. The Workplace Gender Equality Agency has all the tools employers and employees need to make sure gender bias plays no part in pay decisions."

Daughter Water, created by the Australian Workplace Gender Equality Agency in partnership with DDB

Designing Gender Equality—Create Role Models

- Diversify the portraits on the walls of your organizations.
- Increase the fraction of counterstereotypical people in positions of leadership, through quotas or other means. Seeing is believing.
- Know that fathers with daughters are more likely to care about gender equality.

11

Crafting Groups

Around the world, microfinance institutions provide credit to the poor. About three-quarters of their customers are female: why? For starters, being among the poorest of the poor, women's need of credit is acute. But creditors seek female customers for a more pragmatic reason: they are more likely than men to repay their loans. Micro-credit groups are not alone in marketing their services to women. Rotating Savings and Credit Associations, or ROSCAs, are groups in which members make regular contributions to a fund that is then distributed among the participants, overwhelmingly consisting of women. In Kenya, for example, public goods such as schools are often provided by women through *harambee,* the Swahili expression for "let's pull together."

When thinking about diversity, we must understand why, sometimes, people are drawn to homogeneity. Why do women-only groups appear to be particularly adept at loan repayment, cooperation, and contributions to public goods? Seeking answers, Fiona Greig traveled to a slum in Nairobi, Kenya, and ran a number of experiments. The female slum dwellers were indeed more likely to cooperate with other women than with men because they expected women to be more cooperative. It turned out that they were too pessimistic about their male counterparts, who the experiment showed would have been more cooperative if given the chance. But expectations became self-fulfilling prophecies: women were more likely to trust other women, and were rewarded in return for such cooperation.[1]

What works in a Nairobi slum also works on an American game show. *Friend or Foe,* a variant of the classic prisoner's dilemma studied extensively by game theorists and behavioral scientists, started airing in the United States in 2002. Two players have to simultaneously decide whether to play "Friend" or whether to play "Foe." If both of them play "Friend," they share a pot of money. If both play "Foe," they both get nothing. And if one plays "Friend" and the other plays "Foe," the "Foe" player gets the whole pot of money and the "Friend" player gets nothing. Thus, people are motivated to play "Foe" to maximize their earnings, but must fear that the other person will do the same, leaving both empty handed. But cooperation is risky, of course. If you choose "Friend" and your counterpart chooses "Foe," you will have been played for a sucker. The stakes varied between $200 and $16,400, and across 315 games, 630 contestants made over $700,000.

About half of the participants typically played "Friend." Specifically, they cooperated if they had reason to believe that their counterpart would cooperate as well. But how could they know? What clues did they look for? Contestants met briefly, and they had to answer trivia questions together, but otherwise they knew very little about each other. They could, however, watch earlier episodes and learn what typical cooperators looked like. What they would have learned is that they were more likely to be female.

Accordingly, pairs of women were most likely to expect each other to cooperate, and many fulfilled these expectations.[2]

What works like a charm in this version of a prisoner's dilemma is not necessarily helpful in other contexts. In their review of the experimental evidence on the role of gender and cooperativeness, Rachel Croson and Uri Gneezy stress that the results seem to depend on social cues about appropriate behavior that women in particular take from their environments. Such cues help them form expectations. But, of course, sometimes expectations clash. Consider the following. Imagine that you and I are negotiating over who gets what amount of a fixed sum of money. Because I am a woman, you might expect more from me—and because you are a woman, I might expect more from you. If those expectations go unmet, we could be at an impasse. This is the exact pattern found in an experiment where one of two players, the proposer, was given a pot of money and had to decide how much of it to offer to a second person, the responder. In the traditional version of this game, the ultimatum game, the responder then decides whether or not to accept the offer. If he or she accepts, the deal stays as proposed. If he or she rejects, neither of the two players gets anything. In this particular experiment, the responders had to write down the minimum amount they would accept before they saw what they were offered.

It turns out both male and female responders expected more from women. They set higher minimums when their proposer was a woman than when he was a man. But expectations clashed. Both male and female proposers offered less to women than to men. In fact, the clash was worst for female-female pairs: Female proposers expected kinder, more generous female responders, and on average expected them to accept a 43 percent share of the pie. In comparison, women offered men 51 percent of the pie. But the same was true for responders: female responders expected kinder, more generous female proposers and on average, demanded a 42 percent share of the pie. When paired with men, they demanded only 28 percent.

In this experiment, female-female dyads stood out, with female pairs clashing 23 percent of the time with the result that both participants ended up with nothing. By contrast, all other gender pairings hardly clashed at all. Men expected more from women—and they got more. Women expected less from men—and they got slightly less, but were content with it. Male-male pairs worked out because men expected the least from male proposers—and were treated better than expected. Homogeneity helps in some contexts but not in others—and some of these contexts are quite controversial. For example, consider the hotly debated question of sex-segregated education.[3]

In what is widely considered the most significant policy change since the prohibition of sex discrimination in educational institutions, Title IX, which passed in 1972, the George W. Bush administration in 2006 relaxed constraints on single-sex education in public schools. It ruled that districts could create single-sex classes and schools as long as the district offered coeducational schooling of equivalent quality and students and their parents could choose which form of education they wanted. Though heavily criticized by some civil rights and women's groups, who feared it would legitimize discrimination in schools, the ruling had sufficient backing from Republicans and Democrats and passed. Subsequently, the number of public schools catering to boys or girls exclusively rose substantially. According to some estimates, in 2015 there were more than 1,000 public single-sex schools in the United States, though compared to the country's nearly 100,000 public schools, they remain a small fraction.[4]

In addition, and by statistical necessity, if single-sex schools are provided primarily for one gender, in this case girls, they will increase the gender imbalance in other schools, leading to an overproportional share of boys. This matters. Caroline Hoxby of Stanford estimated the effect of the gender composition of the classroom on academic achievement in Texas. Both girls and boys did better when there were more female students in the classroom, including in math, where on average girls had lower test scores than boys. This is not just a spillover effect, with better students benefiting the less skilled students. This is a *girl effect*—a pattern that has also been found in Israeli and Spanish schools.

The effect varies somewhat by grade, subject, and location, but overall the studies estimating peer effects in classrooms suggest that while girls might well benefit from single-sex classrooms, they hurt boys. Both genders, but particularly boys, benefit from being surrounded by girls. Although explaining why requires further research, the Israeli study shows that a larger share of female students led to more satisfied students, less exhausted teachers, less classroom disruption and violence, as well as better relationships between teachers and students and between students.[5]

How groups are composed matters. Too much data has been collected for anyone to form them thoughtlessly. How you design work teams, classrooms, and corporate boards should at a minimum be accomplished with an awareness of potential gender dynamics. And gender is present always, whether the group consists of a single sex or all one sex but for a lone member, or a neat (and rare) equally split group.

Knowing about group dynamics, you can also create groups strategically to meet a particular objective. Consider the work on peer effects that supports the notion that exposure to the "out-group" can improve cross-group relations. A group of researchers looked at what happened when students with different racial backgrounds were randomly assigned to live together at the beginning of their college year. White students who were randomly assigned to live with African-American students were more likely to support affirmative action and endorse diversity on campus. They also reported that they were more comfortable interacting with people of color and were more likely to do so. (Due to the small sample size, the authors could not draw inferences on how racial diversity impacted people of color.) And the random assignment of roommates at Dartmouth College has been shown to influence substantially academic efforts and social behaviors. Group composition matters.

Looking beyond the dorm room, where incentives for getting along are great, experiments suggest that size also matters. Based on datasets about friendships and social interactions at the classroom and the school level, researchers conclude that adolescents in small schools have a more diverse set of friends. In bigger schools, students have a larger range of potential friends to choose from and opt to cluster by sex, race, age, and socioeconomic status, leading to segregation and cliques. In short, we like being surrounded by similar others. But if people do not have much choice, social category–based differences lose their relevance. And contact across groups matters. A meta-analysis of more than 500 studies and over 700 independent samples shows that contact typically reduces intergroup prejudice, supporting what in psychology is known as the *intergroup contact theory*.[6]

While we are not inclined to seek diversity unless we have to, there would be lots of advantages if we did. A large number of laboratory studies suggest that diversity can increase productivity. A particularly comprehensive study assigned about 700 people to groups of two to five and had them participate in a variety of tasks, including brainstorming, solving visual puzzles, making moral judgments, conducting negotiations, and playing a collective game of checkers against a computer that took up to five hours. The researchers, Anita Williams Woolley of Carnegie Mellon and collaborators, used a team's performance on these tasks to calculate its "collective intelligence" factor, which by assessing how well a group does on a set of tasks can help predict the group's future performance on different tasks.

It turns out that individual team members' average or maximum intelligence is a bad predictor of a group's collective intelligence. Instead, the higher a group scored on social sensitivity, the more opportunities to speak were equally distributed among members, and the larger the share of women in the group, the higher its social intelligence. Or, as Woolley and her colleagues put it, "collective intelligence of the group as a whole has predictive power above and beyond what can be explained by knowing the abilities of the individual group members." The importance of including women in a group so that it could reach its potential came as a surprise to the authors of the study. It appears as if it was partly due to female team members scoring higher on the social sensitivity measure than male team members, thus providing the necessary glue to connect all members' contributions and create a whole that exceeded the sum of its parts.

Such results are tantalizing, suggesting that further research might be able to turn collective intelligence into a diagnostic tool, allowing us to predict which teams will perform well and which will struggle. In addition, tools might be developed to help teams manage themselves—ensuring a more equitable share of speaking times, for example—producing the social sensitivity to allow a group to benefit from everyone's contributions.[7]

Groups can also rely on decision rules that make sure every opinion counts. Decision rules could stipulate that a team must reach a decision by consensus or backed only by a majority of the team. Comparing unanimity with majority rules, experimental research by Christopher Karpowitz, Tali Mendelberg, and Lee Shaker shows that unanimity leads not only to every vote counting but also to a broader sharing of "voice," with more people participating in the deliberations. Unanimity rules appear to be particularly important for groups in which women are in the minority. The researchers conclude by arguing that "deliberative design can avoid inequality by fitting institutional procedure to the social context of the situation."

In addition, and somewhat counterintuitively, groups might want to constrain themselves from speaking freely. The study "Creativity from Constraint" presents experimental evidence on how imposing a norm of political correctness (PC) that specifies how men and women should interact with each other enhances creativity in mixed-sex groups. The PC norm increased the exchange of ideas by clarifying the rules of engagement and providing assurance to those, predominantly women, for whom speaking up was associated with counterstereotypical behavior.[8]

Although randomly formed groups are easily created in the laboratory, when doing research in organizations, we typically have to work with existing teams. But while selection issues are real, organizational settings have other advantages. Typically, the time frame of an organization's team is longer and the stakes higher than one created in the laboratory. Some of the dynamics seen in the laboratory emerge in the field, too. In one study examining team performance and employee satisfaction in a global professional services firm, more gender-diverse offices generated more revenue. The same study also found that employees in more diverse teams were less comfortable and less willing to cooperate, though the latter effect was mitigated when employees believed that the firm endorsed diversity.[9]

In a similar finding, gender diversity in senior management teams has been found to be associated with better firm performance under some conditions but not under others. As always in correlational analyses, causality could go in either direction: high-performing firms might attract an over-proportional share of women, for example. To overcome this shortcoming, one study examined start-up firms where the sequence of events can be better controlled. Using a large Austrian database, the study's authors looked at whether there was a relationship between women being among a start-up's first highest-paid hires and the firm's survival. Controlling for a large number of additional variables, they found that firms with at least one woman among the first hires were more successful and stayed longer in the market than all-male start-ups. Similar positive impacts of gender diversity on firm performance—measured by sales, profits, and earnings per share—were found for randomly created student start-ups in the Netherlands.[10]

In short, diversity can lead to better performance—but not always. When might we reasonably expect its benefits? Suppose that you need to create a new team to work on a special project and have five positions to fill. You evaluate the applicants based on ten different characteristics and assign scores from one (worst) to ten (best) for each characteristic. It turns out that exactly five of the applicants have a total score of 91, with the best possible score on nine of the attributes that you are looking at and the worst possible score on one of them. These are your highest total scorers and you might consider yourself lucky to get all five on your team. Or should you? While the five are the highest total scorers, they may not provide you with the diversity you need. None of the five scored high on one of the attributes you care about, say creativity. Shouldn't you choose at least one or possibly even more than one candidate with a lower total score but high marks on creativity?

One study, aptly entitled "Too Many Cooks Spoil the Broth: How High-Status Individuals Decrease Group Effectiveness," looked at equity research analysts on Wall Street and found that groups enjoyed ever-smaller benefits from including more and more star performers. As the share of stars increased, the benefit each additional star brought the team declined and eventually even became negative.

When we build teams, we look for complements, not substitutes. The diversity of viewpoints may trump average excellence when we have to solve problems collectively. In his wonderful book *The Difference,* Scott Page helps us understand why a successful team does not necessarily consist only of star players. Both ability and diversity are required for collective intelligence to reach its potential. Of course, complements must overlap. To state the obvious, an excellent Mandarin speaker without any knowledge of English and a superb English speaker without any knowledge of Mandarin are complements but do not make the whole greater than the sum of its parts.[11]

For gender diversity to increase group performance you need team members whose different perspectives add value while keeping the cost of coordination as low as possible. Indeed, diversity theories in organizational behavior, psychology, sociology, and economics expect performance to improve the more diversity is based on different sets of competencies relevant to the task. The more relevant knowledge increases with each additional team member, the more positive the impact. In contrast, the more differences are based on categories not related to the task at hand or on deeply held values, the more diversity is expected to hurt team performance. Of course, variables can interact in many different ways and correcting for most of them is challenging. In certain fields, these differences can even prove insurmountable.[12]

Based on data from more than 2,000 management teams from several different organizations in the equity mutual fund industry in the United States from 1996 to 2003, differences indeed hurt team performance: homogenous teams significantly outperformed mixed-sex teams. Every team's job was to manage an equity fund, with expectations clearly defined and performance easily measurable based on fund returns. High fund performance was rewarded by compensation and promotion. Many teams worked together for several years, optimizing team performance and developing relationships.

With only about 10 percent of fund managers being female at the time of the study, homogeneity basically meant all-male teams. Only 2 percent of the teams consisted of women only. With such little variation, the researchers had to measure gender diversity with a dummy variable that took the value of one if the teams consisted of men and women, and zero if they were exclusively male or (much more rarely) exclusively female. Furthermore, if a team was diverse, in almost all cases female managers constituted a small minority of a team. In this heavily skewed micro- and macro-environment, the study showed that heterogeneity did not pay.[13]

Organizations pondering how to best create teams should focus on "critical mass." A seminal paper that my colleague Rosabeth Moss Kanter of Harvard Business School wrote in 1977 suggests that one of the key factors determining team performance is the relative share of people from different demographic categories represented, or a group's critical mass. Having studied American corporations in the 1970s, she observed that the "relative numbers of socially and culturally different people in a group" were "critical in shaping interaction dynamics in group life." In groups dominated by one social type, as in the mutual fund industry, members of the minority group are likely to be treated as tokens among their peers. Their minority status makes them visible and easily reduced to their demographic characteristics. Regarded as symbolic representatives of their social category, they may be unable to fully contribute their complementary expertise.

Many of you have likely experienced what it feels like to be the obvious outlier in a group, perhaps due to your sex, race, ethnicity, nationality, religion, or sexual or political orientation. The Hispanic accountant is very often considered the spokesperson for Hispanics rather than the expert in accounting and the Chinese professor of computer science teaching in the United States becomes the go-to person on all things Chinese. Tokenism of this sort is uncomfortable and can easily undermine the group member's credibility. Differences tend to be stressed, sometimes compelling the token member to adopt the majority's style and opinions. In addition, tokens may feel the need to overachieve to prove their worth. What often is referred to as the *queen bee syndrome,* describing the lonely woman at the top, can be the result. Rather than pave the way for those who follow them, token members look up to their majority peers, and assimilate and distance themselves from new entrants of their own social category. This seems particularly true for first-generation women in counterstereotypical roles.

In more balanced groups, stereotypes lose their importance and minority members are regarded as individuals rather than just token representatives. While the exact tipping point from scarcity to balance is hard to determine, it appears as if equal representation is not required to change experiences and team performance. Many argue that a critical mass of one-third in relative terms and at least three in absolute numbers is required to move groups from being haunted by the dynamics of social categorization to being able to seize the benefits of diversity.[14]

A decade after Rosabeth Moss Kanter's article, the political scientist Drude Dahlerup applied critical mass theory to politics. Politicians in committees or parliament appear to be affected by relative numbers in the same way employees are influenced by the sex composition of their work groups. In addition, in politics the business case for making sure that we seize the benefits of diversity might be even more critical. If male and female voters have different policy preferences, they may care about the sex of their representatives for substantive reasons. Female suffrage, for example, has been shown to lead to an increase in spending on health care in the United States, and reserved seats on local governing committees for various castes in India resulted in more support of these groups.[15]

Tokenism, critical mass, and queen bee syndrome present a challenge to many organizations that start off with skewed demographics. A boutique eighty-member consulting firm with only eight women will have a hard time putting into practice the insight that homogeneity and balanced heterogeneity both likely outperform skewed heterogeneity. When Katherine Phillips and Damon Phillips of Columbia University studied the performance of NHL hockey teams between 1988 and 1998, they discovered this pattern. Focusing on national heterogeneity in teams with twenty-eight different nationalities represented, the hockey teams won more games when their heterogeneity was either low or high. Relatively homogenous groups had few coordination issues and extremely heterogeneous ones had no choice but to deal with them. With many different nationalities represented on a team, fault lines started to blur. If almost every player comes from a different country, social categorization based on country of origin loses its importance. In contrast, if only a couple of nationalities are represented on a team, players are attracted to others like them, inviting inter-group differentiation and conflict.[16]

When I form teams in my classes, I take these considerations into account. My students often express surprise when they find themselves in same-sex teams. In the executive program for the World Economic Forum's Young Global Leaders at the Kennedy School, such assignments led to outright protest. People wanted to be in diverse teams. I had to explain to them that not everyone could be on a diverse team without turning some people into "token" group members. A rich classroom discussion broke out, in which I shared many of the insights of this chapter and distilled for them a cheat sheet of group formation:

- If a task involves coordination, say the provision of a public good like clean water or better health care, homogenous groups can be helpful. All-women teams, for example, outperformed mixed and all-male teams in *Friend or Foe* because they correctly believed that women would be more likely to cooperate than men, leading to a virtuous cycle.

- If a task involves individual problem-solving, say test-taking, be aware of peer effects. Diversity might produce spillovers (or, more formally, "externalities") affecting, for example, how students perform in a class. If one group is more likely to work hard or disrupt less, as has been found to be true of girls, having them over-represented can help others, in this case boys, perform better.

- If the task involves collective problem-solving, say the building of a house, you should go for heterogenous groups where the individual knowledge and perspectives of group members complement each other. A particularly useful skill to incorporate in groups is listening and bridge-building, both shown to be correlated with the fraction of women present. And to reduce the challenges associated with social category diversity, you need to make sure demographic minorities are represented by a critical mass of members. If you start out with a population of, say, 20 percent men and 80 percent women and then want to create work teams, do not allocate people proportionally. Instead, form a few balanced teams and assign the rest of the women to all-female groups.

Does perceived fairness matter? Students and participants in executive education programs always express concern with how their groups were formed. Was it done randomly, based on merit, or using some intricate algorithm? They care for many different reasons. An obvious one is that in some cases their grade depends on their team's performance. But they also look for subtle clues to help them better understand their place and purpose in the group. Finally, they also care about fairness. Much research suggests that people are more likely to accept an unfavorable outcome if they believe the process was fair. But what characterizes a fair process? Surprisingly, what many consider the epitome of fairness, a random process, is not typically what people like best. Bruno Frey of the University of Zurich and colleagues have studied this question in many different environments, and what they typically find is that bureaucratic or traditional procedures such as "first-come first-served" win the day. Much to my surprise, my students often prefer that I form the teams rather than that they create their own.[17]

One much-debated bureaucratic mechanism we mentioned in Chapter 10 for composing teams is quotas. Guaranteed political seats in Indian villages and corporate board quotas in Norwegian firms have created role models. At the same time, a laboratory study that Johanna Mollerstrom conducted in Boston found that people did not perceive quotas as fair. When team membership was decided by quotas as compared to a random process, it turned out that people were less willing to cooperate with one another. Similar evidence stems from an experiment conducted in Australia where study participants in the quota treatment went as far as to sabotage each other. In addition, quotas do not always achieve their purpose. For example, though Spain passed a law in 2007 mandating that at least 40 percent of each sex be represented in national parliamentary elections, actual numbers have fallen short. And the women who were included were not always helped. One study shows that parties positioned their female candidates disadvantageously. For example, in a Senate election women were placed by their party in only 20 percent of the winnable seats whereas 53 percent of the slots that were expected to be lost were assigned to women. Similar issues have been raised in France where an equal representation of men and women on candidate lists was mandated in 2000.[18]

Much has been written about the advantages and disadvantages of quotas. Predictions about their overall performance tend to depend on the theory of the world people have. If you think that there is a "pipeline" problem, that there are too few qualified women for a given job, or that such mandates undermine the functioning of a team, you will expect quotas to decrease performance. On the other hand, if you believe that stereotypes keep qualified women from being selected, you will be optimistic about the impact of quotas. Which theory wins the day often depends on context. For example, pipeline issues are real in some fields, as a survey of the research on women's underrepresentation in STEM fields suggests. Only about 20 percent of women graduate with a bachelor's degree or a doctorate from engineering schools in the United States. Arguably, there are just not enough female engineers in the pipeline to dictate a quota in some circumstances— for example, a 40 percent quota for federally financed projects.

However, inferring from this that quotas do not make sense more generally would be grossly misleading. In an elegant experiment that Muriel Niederle, Carmit Segal, and Lise Vesterlund conducted in the United States and which has now been replicated in other parts of the world, quotas were shown to induce more talented women to compete, those who should have competed all along but held back due to a lack of self-confidence and self-stereotyping. In their study, there were enough women in the pipeline; they just did not dare to put themselves forward.[19]

Concerns about adequate numbers of sufficiently skilled women and people of color in the pipeline are repeatedly raised in the context of affirmative action policies. There is reason to doubt the severity of such worries. In the United States, such policies have played an important role for federal contractors and, despite many people's fears that affirmative action would negatively impact firms' performance, a review of the evidence suggests no such effects. There were enough qualified job candidates who had been formerly discriminated against to fill the open slots, and the firms were able to find and hire them. Examining how, researchers surveyed firms in four large US cities: Atlanta, Boston, Detroit, and Los Angeles. The firms reported that they had broadened their searches, looking in places that they had not looked before, and looking for candidates that were not the usual suspects. The result was a more diverse candidate pool to choose from. And it worked: comparing federal contractors with nonfederal contractors, the proportion of women employed rose substantially faster in some periods when firms were affected by the policy. According to the most comprehensive study to date by Fidan Ana Kurtulus of the University of Massachusetts, Amherst, analyzing data over the course of three decades between 1973 and 2003, however, the primary beneficiaries of affirmative action were African American and Native American women and men.[20]

The pipeline concern is stubbornly persistent, however, and certainly having firms lower their standards to comply with a quota or affirmative action is in nobody's interest. Among other things, it can further bolster negative stereotypes about the discriminated-against group. Indeed, studies suggest that employees hired under gender- or race-based policies experience stigmatization, both by others as well as by themselves, but that such negative stereotyping can be attenuated if merit-based criteria played a dominant role in the hiring decision. A two-stage process, thus, seems imaginable where first merit is determined and then members of certain demographic groups are preferentially treated.[21]

More important, perhaps, is that the pendulum appears to be swinging in the direction of the second quota theory: they boost the participation of well-qualified but previously underrepresented individuals. Today, more than half the countries in the world have adopted political quotas. They range from party quotas—a certain representation of female candidates on party lists, whether voluntarily adopted or mandated by law—to reserved seats for a fraction of women who must be represented in elected office. Some of this reflects the realization that the self-perpetuating effects of discrimination can only be broken if opportunities for the traditionally discriminated-against are created. If people assume women are unsuited to leadership, women invest less in leadership training and seek out fewer leadership opportunities. And when they do seek to become leaders and confront the stereotype, they are less likely to be chosen. Quotas can short-circuit this cycle. Far from elevating the under-qualified, quotas prove in fact to broaden the pool of qualified candidates.

This is perhaps why quotas have started to spread in the business world. In 2003 Norwegian legislation mandated that 40 percent of each sex be represented on its corporate boards. This was followed by similar laws in Belgium, France, Germany, Iceland, Italy, the Netherlands, and Spain. Board quotas and related target-based schemes are currently under discussion in various other places, including Brazil, Canada, the Philippines, Scotland, South Africa, the United Arab Emirates, and the European Union. In Germany, Chancellor Angela Merkel surprised many with a change of heart when in 2014 she affirmed the plan to introduce board quotas of 30 percent for the largest German companies in the Bundestag: "We can't afford to do without the skills of women," she said.[22]

But was Chancellor Merkel right? Does the evidence suggest that a larger share of women on its corporate board is good for a company? The short answer is that based on the available data, it is almost impossible to prove either way. No study to date has been able to establish a causal relationship between corporate board diversity and company performance. Boards are not created randomly nor imposed on firms randomly. If there was a relationship between board diversity and firm performance, we would not know whether it was the board that affected the company or whether the company influenced the composition of the board.

Even though causality cannot be established with the available data, much research has gone into understanding whether there is a relationship between board diversity and company performance. Deborah Rhode and Amanda Packel of Stanford University provide an excellent review. The evidence is mixed. A number of studies report positive correlations between the fraction of female directors and company performance. Taking a global perspective, the Credit Suisse Research Institute, for example, found a substantial gender diversity premium in an analysis of more than 2,300 companies across the globe from 2005 to 2011—but only after the financial crisis in 2008. Maybe diversity is particularly relevant in turbulent times? Miriam Schwartz-Ziv's analysis of Israeli companies suggests that critical mass mattered and that companies with at least three female directors had higher ROEs (returns on equity) and net profit margins. Others have found no or negative correlations between gender diversity and performance.

Given the mixed evidence of individual studies, a meta-analysis combining the results of 140 studies is particularly helpful in this context. Across all studies, it finds a small positive relationship between female board representation and company profitability (accounting returns). Market performance, on the other hand, was only positively related to board diversity in countries with greater gender parity (as measured by the World Economic Forum's Global Gender Gap score) and negatively otherwise. Investors' evaluations of a firm's future performance may well be influenced by gender norms prevalent in a given country. In more gender-equal countries, they expected gender diversity on corporate boards to be a good thing; in less gender-equal countries, they saw it as a disadvantage.

To put these findings into perspective, recall that generally there is little empirical evidence that any of the board characteristics we typically worry about, including board size, number of independent directors, time and effort spent by directors, director indemnification, director duties, or whether or not the CEO serves as board chair are related to firm performance.[23]

In addition, the above studies do not distinguish how diversity was brought about. Understandably, as gender quotas on corporate boards have only been introduced very recently, we know very little about their impact on company performance. The little we do know is based on Norwegian companies. There the evidence suggests that the introduction of quotas had negative short-term impacts, both on profits and on company valuation. One study compares the profits of Norwegian companies after the introduction of quotas with how well other Scandinavian companies did in the same time frame. It finds that the introduction of quotas led to an increase in spending on labor, driven by employment levels, not compensation packages. Survey evidence supports the notion that female directors may indeed be more concerned with employees than their male counterparts. Could this have hurt the performance of companies affected by the quotas in Norway at a time when many other companies laid off people due to the financial crisis in 2008?

We will never quite know what the channels of influence were as the research does not allow us to recreate what happened in these companies. There are too many possible variables: perhaps the female directors were indeed decisive, or their presence influenced opinions of male directors, or management reacted negatively to the gender quotas or the increased diversity on their boards. It is also possible that all this had little to do with the specific composition of the boards and instead was the result of teams being newly formed. Teams, and in particular heterogenous teams, do become more effective over time. Richard Hackman, for example, reports that how long an airline crew has been flying together is a good predictor of aircraft "incidents:" 73 percent of incidents occur when a crew flies together for the first time.[24]

To be clear, quotas are not behavioral interventions, but they affect people through behavioral channels. Whether or not they should be introduced is a political decision, weighing their benefits and their costs. Their beauty is that they change numbers quickly, sparing the team the stereotyping and painful assimilation processes that go along with a more incremental approach, which can depress performance. Yet a two-stage process where candidates are first reviewed for merit, ideally in blind evaluations, seems advisable in order to address fairness considerations.

The composition of groups clearly matters. And while getting it right is not easy, some behavioral design principles can help us move in the right direction. The most important one is critical mass. When forming diverse teams, make sure every subgroup is represented by at least three people or makes up about a third of the total. When you next appraise the performance of your team members, take a moment to reflect on this. Women have been found to receive lower-quality performance evaluations than men in work groups where they compose less than 20 percent of the group. As their relative presence increased, so did the scores on their performance evaluations. Shortlists and the much-celebrated diverse slates are another place to look for potential improvements. Some executive search firms have pledged to always include a woman on their shortlists—but adding only one might not do the trick and could even backfire. If you cannot include more than one woman, keep groups homogenous. Creating token members is in nobody's interest.[25]

Finally, when you design a team, adhere to some basic principles that have been shown to enhance performance. Teams should not be too large. Several studies suggest that ideal teams consist of four to six members with high cognitive and low value diversity. And more important, do not fall prey to the problem of "groupthink." Not only do team members tend to favor information supporting their initial views, but confirming evidence also makes them more confident—without increasing accuracy. Make it a point to seek challenging information and create inclusive processes that help you benefit from the diversity represented in your team.[26]

Designing Gender Equality—Create the Conditions for Collective Intelligence

- Combine average ability with complementary diversity of perspectives and expertise to maximize team performance.
- Include a critical mass of each subgroup in teams to avoid tokenism.
- Create inclusive group processes to allow for diverse perspectives to be contributed and heard, for example, by introducing unanimity rules or political correctness norms.

12

Shaping Norms

In 2011, the UK Behavioral Insights Team sent more than 100,000 letters to British citizens reminding them that they had not yet paid their taxes. Often dubbed the "Nudge Unit," the Behavioral Insights Team was created in 2010 at No. 10 Downing Street to use behavioral insights to improve how government works. The letters sent were identical but for one short paragraph, the difference sometimes consisting of one sentence only. A first group of recipients read that "nine out of ten people pay their taxes on time." A second group received a slightly amended version of this sentence: "Nine out of ten people in the UK pay their taxes on time." And a third group saw the following two sentences: "Nine out of ten people in the UK pay their taxes on time. You are currently in the very small minority of people who have not paid us yet." Others either received no additional message or an altogether different one that reminded them that paying taxes was important for the provision of public services. The third letter was the winner: it generated tax revenue of more than $3 million in less than a month. The team was intrigued and ran more experiments, all confirming that messages that have the most impact tell readers about what others do and point out that you are the outlier.

Sharing such information establishes social norms. Generally, people want to run with the herd. Dozens of field experiments, similar to the one described above, establish this fact. Contrary to traditional economic theory, people do not vote when nobody else is voting. Think about this. In a rational world, we would expect people to be especially interested in voting as the odds increase that their vote would prove decisive. But this is not how it works. People copy others. They are more likely to vote when voter turnout is high and stay home when it is not. Similarly, people are more likely to lower their energy use, donate money in support of public radio, or recycle when informed that most people are also doing these things. People are "conditionally cooperative" and are more likely to contribute to public goods when others do so as well.[1]

People are even more likely to accept a job offer when informed that most others have done so in the past. In a field experiment involving thousands of recent college graduates who were accepted to teach in an underperforming school in the Teach for America program, the admitted were more likely to say yes when the offer letter mentioned the high fraction of people who had accepted the offer in the previous year. They were also more likely to follow through on their acceptance and still be working in the job half a year later.

These studies suggest that we can turn descriptive norms, what many people are already doing, into prescriptive norms just by telling people about them. What is becomes what should be. People are generally more likely to adopt a behavior if they know that most others are already doing it. We sometimes refer to this as *herding behavior*: the behavior of others, the herd, informs us as to what is normal, appropriate, or beneficial to do. And we then do likewise.

An early powerful demonstration of this was run in a parking lot. The researchers put flyers on people's windshields as well as on the ground. They were interested in learning what fraction of the people finding a flyer on their car windows would toss it on the floor as opposed to either keeping it or disposing of it properly. As you would expect, people were much more likely to throw their flyer on the ground if the parking lot was already littered. Robert Cialdini, one of the authors of this study, went on to explore the impact of such norms in many different contexts. One of the more troubling findings is that people also do more bad things if others do them as well. In one study, he and collaborators wished to find out how to discourage visitors to Arizona's Petrified Forest National Park from removing the petrified wood. They found that posting signs emphasizing that many others had stolen some made people more likely to do the same.[2]

In Spring 2013, I shared these insights with the UK Department for Business, Innovation, and Skills, then led by Secretary Vince Cable. The team I met with worked on increasing gender diversity on corporate boards in the United Kingdom without reliance on quotas. They were inspired by the work of the Behavioral Insights Team and eager to apply some of their findings to gender. They were also in a hurry as they were trying to help companies follow through on the goals set in the so-called Davies Report, written by Lord Davies of Abersoch. Following an independent review into the number of women on corporate boards launched in February 2011, Lord Davies recommended that UK listed companies in the FTSE 100 set a minimum target for

25 percent female board member representation by 2015. Lord Davies said: "Over the past 25 years the number of women in full-time employment has increased by more than a third and there have been many steps towards gender equality in the workplace, with flexible working and the Equal Pay Act, however, there is still a long way to go. Currently 18 FTSE 100 companies have no female directors at all and nearly half of all FTSE 250 companies do not have a woman in the boardroom. Radical change is needed in the mindset of the business community if we are to implement the scale of change that is needed."

Similarly, Theresa May, then home secretary and minister for women and equality, commented: "Women make up more than half of the population, but account for just 12.5 per cent of FTSE 100 directors. Lord Davies' report is an important step forward in understanding why this is and what can be done about it, and I shall be considering his findings very carefully."[3]

The illustration on the cover of the report graphically made this point. But was this smart messaging? Based on insights about the relevance of norms in other domains made by the director of the Behavioral Insights Team, David Halpern, I was skeptical. Was it really smart to focus on the small minority that women represented? Couldn't this data point become self-fulfilling, suggesting that this state of affairs is the norm? After all, when it comes to gender we are up against views that are likely more strongly held than those about littering, voting, or tax collection. In an analysis of attitudes espoused in the World Values Surveys of 1990, 1995, and 1999, for example, Nicole Fortin found that across twenty-five OECD countries, women were less likely to be employed outside of the home in countries where a majority agreed with the statement, "When jobs are scarce, men should

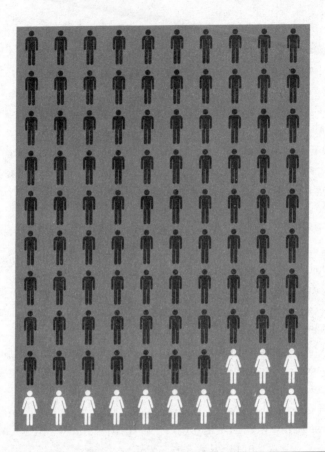

Representing the fraction of women on corporate boards

have more right to a job than women." Around the world, perceptions of men as breadwinners and women as homemakers still matter a lot.[4]

I suggested the Department of Business, Innovation, and Skills run a field experiment to evaluate the effectiveness of these communication strategies. Maybe they worked just fine. Perhaps norms did not play the same role in the gender domain as they did in other domains, and focusing on the fact that most companies and most countries had very few women leaders did not hurt the cause. Or, alternatively, perhaps there was something useful to be learned about encouraging gender diversity. What if instead of describing the small fraction of female corporate directors, messages focused on the large fraction of companies with gender-diverse boards? In fact, I brought an image created by Kerry Conley of the Women and Public Policy Program to the meeting to illustrate what this could look like.

The department never ran the study. My suggestion was crowded out by other felt imperatives. I did note, however, that in 2013, Secretary Cable no longer focused on the small share of women on boards but instead said: "Today 94 of the FTSE 100 companies count women on their boards as do over two thirds of all FTSE 350 companies."[5]

By the end of 2015, the FTSE 100 companies had more than 25 percent female directors on their boards. A success story? Mostly. The best answer is an enthusiastic yes with a little caveat. The achievement certainly is a huge success. After years of very little movement, the United Kingdom was able to more than double the fraction of women on its corporate boards—all without coercion. Much work went into making this happen, by the government, the private sector, and by nongovernmental organizations such as the 30% Club, devoted to increasing the fraction of female directors on FTSE 100 boards to 30 percent.[6]

The caveat relates to what was learned in the process. Unfortunately, the department never ran a controlled trial, so we will never know what the impact of the reframed communication was. Did focusing people's attention on the new norm of having gender

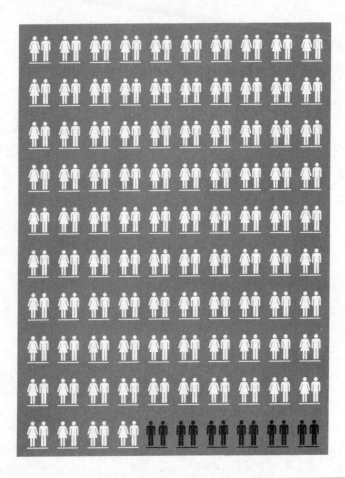

Representing the fraction of gender-diverse corporate boards

diverse boards matter, or was Britain's big step forward attributable to some of the many additional interventions used?

While we will never quite know, my colleagues and I could not let the question rest without some sort of a research-based answer. Short of a field experiment, we brought the question to the lab—and were shocked by what we found. We had a first set of student subjects play the role of "employer" and asked them to hire a team of five people for a math and a verbal task. We chose these tasks, stereotypically associated with men and women, on purpose as we wanted to see whether a norm nudge could correct stereotypical behavior. This first set of employers was the norm creator. We ran various sessions and then informed a second set of "employers" of what experimental participants in a previous session had done.

It turns out that when this new set of employers had no information on what choices others had made, male employers tended to choose slightly stereotypically, with about 60 percent choosing majority-male teams for the math task and majority-female teams for the verbal task. Female employers went with a 50:50 split on both tasks, on average. When we informed them about a session where most employers had chosen majority-female teams for both math and verbal tasks, men reacted by choosing *fewer* women. Under that condition, about 70 percent chose majority-male teams, in both the math and the verbal tasks! The nudge had moved them in the wrong direction and cost women 10 percentage points in the math task and 30 percentage points in the verbal task. In contrast, when we informed male employers about a session where most employers had chosen majority-male teams, not much happened. Neither did anything happen for female employers. On average, women pretty much chose male and female employees equally, independent of the information provided.[7]

Such male defense of the status quo is not unprecedented. After all, we are in a zero-sum world. Increasing the fraction of one gender in a team means decreasing the share of the other gender—unless one can make the team bigger. Deutsche Telekom was one of the first large companies, and the first DAX-30 company, to introduce a gender quota for its middle and senior management. On March 15, 2010, it announced that by the end of 2015, it wanted to have 30 percent women in its middle and senior ranks. As has happened in other companies with gender diversity goals, many men were not excited about this prospect. They saw, quite literally, their slice of the middle and upper management pie shrinking in front of their eyes. German journalists wrote about "discrimination of men," the "battle of the sexes," and asked "where to put the men."[8]

Thus, male resistance to interventions favoring women is real, whether in the laboratory, in corporate offices, and, maybe, even in board rooms. Aaron Dhir, in his 2015 book, *Challenging Boardroom Homogeneity*, argues that gender diversity norms, while often espoused in theory, have not become a reality in most board rooms yet. He is more optimistic about the United Kingdom. The UK government appears to have been able to play the role of a "norm entrepreneur," a term coined by Cass Sunstein in 1996. Without relying on legally mandated gender representation on boards, it has been able to move the needle.

Norm entrepreneurs build on latently available notions of right and wrong, even if people treat such notions more as theoretical concerns rather than guidelines determining their actions. Dhir believes that the United States could be fertile ground for norm entrepreneurship around diversity. He reports on the many businesses that supported the US Supreme Court's 2003 decision to uphold the University of Michigan Law School's affirmative action policy in *Grutter v. Bollinger*. The firms filed an amicus curiae brief arguing that American businesses needed to have access to a diverse talent pool to compete in an increasingly global world with ever-growing diversity. A few years later, many of the same firms submitted another brief in *Fisher v. University of Texas at Austin*, basically repeating their earlier arguments and stating that the case for diversity had become even more compelling.[9]

Norm entrepreneurship can help these organizations embrace diversity not just as a principle but also as a practice. Invoking what others do appears to be more likely to work at resetting norms the less people perceive the consequences as zero-sum. Organizations need to find ways to increase the pie, for example, by increasing the size of executive committees or boards, an approach that many Norwegian companies opted for when they had to comply with the quota of having 40 percent female directors. The *fixed-pie mentality* is a well-known barrier to creative problem solving. How people see competition matters. If people perceive every additional person joining the labor force as a threat, they will be less welcoming of new entrants, including women. In her analysis of the relationship between people's attitudes and women's workforce participation, Fortin finds that in countries where men had a more favorable view of competition, women's employment rates were higher.[10]

Nevertheless, some constraints are real, and choices have to be made. Men who have been standing in line for the next top job will not be excited about additional competition from women. That this is so should strike us as neither surprising nor new. Those who benefit from existing practices and norms generally do not cheer when barriers to entry for new competitors are lowered; monopolies and cartels rarely go quietly. But ignoring those concerns can backfire, as the research on intergroup threat suggests. In the worst case, increasing women's economic independence has led to a surge in domestic violence, evidence from Bangladesh and India suggests. Thus, when changing norms, taking both winners and losers into account is the prudent and the prag-matic approach.[11]

One such approach is reaping the benefits that can come from people comparing themselves with others. This means copying others, yes, but it also implies competing with others. Take Opower, a company based in the United States, as an example. I have immediate experience with their intervention, being the re-cipient and beneficiary of it. Opower has our utility company, National Grid, send our household a personalized Home En-ergy Report that compares my family's energy consumption with how much my neighbors consume.

We are currently doing quite well, outperforming our neigh-bors. But this was not always the case. When we got our first report, we were in the worst category. This, we decided, was unaccept-able. We had our roof insulated and solar panels installed. In addition, we now follow the "Energy Saving Tips" provided by Opower, keep our house warmer in the summer, and wear an ad-ditional sweater in the winter. The latter steps in particular were simple things, and all the changes we embraced substantially decreased our energy use and helped us save money. In the United States, seventy utility companies have implemented Opower pro-grams and more than 8 million households are in their experi-mental populations. This has made Opower one of my favorite examples of a successful design when giving a talk about the power of norms. Invariably, someone in the audience has been subject to this intervention.

In fact, my family and many others have truly been "subjects." Opower has conducted a number of field experiments, using both treatment and control groups. On average, their interventions have significant short-term and long-term effects, decreasing en-

❄ **Last Winter Comparison** | You used **36% less** natural gas than your efficient neighbors.

Your usage last winter: Dec '13–Mar '14

YOU — 750 Therms*

Efficient Neighbors — 1,180

All Neighbors — 1,674

How you did last winter:

▶ **GREAT** ☺ ☺
Good ☺
More than average

* Therms: Standard unit of measuring heat energy

Who are your Neighbors?

■ **All Neighbors:** Approximately 100 occupied nearby homes that are similar in size to yours (avg 4,871 sq ft) and have gas heat

■ **Efficient Neighbors:** The most efficient 20 percent from the "All Neighbors" group

Last 12 Months Neighbor Comparison

You used **36% less** natural gas than your neighbors. This saves you about **$1,810** per year.

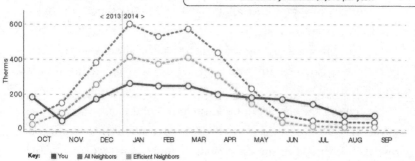

O-Power Personalized Home Energy Reports, comparing household use to that of the neighbors

ergy use even after households have received the mailing and leading to a lower level of consumption after the program has been discontinued.[12]

But, as almost always occurs when researching behavioral insights, Opower's interventions do not work equally well with all subjects or all the time. Some studies have found the Opower intervention can lead to backlash among households holding more conservative views, causing these homes to increase their energy consumption. Others report a boomerang effect, where people increased their usage after learning that they were consuming less than average. This reminds me of the *moral licensing effect* we discussed in Chapter 2, where people who have (or just believe they have) done something good feel licensed to do something bad. I have watched this unfold in my own house. Since joining the ranks of better-than-average energy users in our neighborhood, my husband has gotten into the habit of reminding the rest of us (who are not so great at turning off lights) that we should not feel licensed to misbehave only because we decreased our use of air conditioning.[13]

Accepting the caveats of backlash and moral licensing, Opower's intervention is cheap and effective. It stands atop a wealth of research. By making the appropriate comparisons, we can focus people's attention on specific aspects of a problem. Imagine you are a development officer wishing to increase donations to your charity. You must design a flyer (or email blast) to past contributors. What do you draw the recipients' attention to? You would likely focus on what people have contributed in the past, maybe creating tiers (as many organizations do) that indicate whether people have given at the gold, silver, or bronze level. Certainly, you would not rank people in terms of how much they kept for themselves or how much they still have left over after having donated. A simple laboratory experiment confirmed this. Participants were placed in a dictator game, where individuals were given a certain amount of money that they were to divide as they wished between themselves and an anonymous person. Researchers found that people gave substantially more in a "generosity tournament," where they were ranked publicly from most to least generous, as compared to an "earnings tournament," where they were ranked based on how much they had kept for themselves. In brief, social comparisons matter—on almost anything that we can measure—but we have to focus people's attention on the outcome that we care about.

Exploring this further, Richard Zeckhauser and I became interested in whether people also take fairness clues from others. We ran a modified version of the ultimatum game introduced in Chapter 11. It turns the dictator game described above into a bargaining game where the proposer can offer the receiver a sum of money which she can accept or reject. If she rejects it, however, all the money is lost, including the amount that the proposer was hoping to keep for himself. If the receiver accepts, the deal stays as proposed. When Richard and I told all participants that we would inform the receivers of the average amount given by the proposers before they had to make their accept/reject decision, proposers converged on a norm. In our case, this was an equal split. Proposers feared that receivers would punish deviations from what others did, and they were right.[14]

Making public and visible how well a company or country does in terms of gender equality compared to others might also promote convergence on a new norm. Indeed, a number of organizations now provide social comparisons or explicit rankings based on gender equality. In 2006, the World Economic Forum (WEF) launched its annual Global Gender Gap Report measuring the existing gender gaps in four categories: economic participation and opportunity (pay, participation, and leadership), political empowerment (representation), education (access), and health and survival (life expectancy and sex ratio at birth). Since then, the WEF has annually published a report measuring how the gaps are changing over time. It ranks countries on their overall performance, as well as on how well they do in all four categories. Over nine years, the Nordic countries have been leading the pack with Iceland having closed the overall gap by 87.3 percent (with 100 percent indicating gender equality) as of 2013. Generally, Middle Eastern and North African countries have fared worst, with Yemen having closed only 51.2 percent of the overall gap.

Saadia Zahidi of the WEF and the lead author of the report explains: "The notion that gender equality is not only the right thing to do, but the smart thing is a fairly new mindset that did not exist in the public consciousness even five years ago." Klaus Schwab, the founder and chairman of the WEF, adds: "Achieving gender equality is obviously necessary for economic reasons. Only those economies who have full access to all their talent will remain competitive and will prosper. But even more important, gender equality is a matter of justice. As a humanity, we also have the obligation to ensure a balanced set of values."[15]

Related country reports and rankings, each with a slightly different focus and methodology, have since been created by the World Bank, the United Nations Development Program (UNDP), the OECD, and the European Institute for Gender Equality, among others. While what facets of gender equality they measure and track differ—some focus on gaps between men and women, for example, in economic opportunity, and others look at absolute rates, for example, in terms of workforce participation; some cover outcomes, such as compensation, and others measure input variables, such as laws; some include measures of violence and others of access to finance—they all generally come to similar conclusions: gender equality is quite advanced in the Scandinavian countries while the nations of the Middle East, North Africa, and Sub-Saharan Africa have the longest way to go.

- In 2009, the World Bank started to collect data on *Women, Business, and the Law*, which analyzes the legal differentiations on the basis of gender in 143 economies around the world. The report covers six areas in relation to gender: accessing institutions, using property, getting a job, providing incentives to work, building credit, and going to court. Based on the 2014 report, a seventh area, protecting women from violence, has recently been added for 100 economies.
- In 2009, the OECD's Development Center published its first Social Institutions and Gender Index (SIGI), which provides a composite index of gender inequality. The measure uses five subindices to calculate this score: discriminatory family code, restricted physical integrity, son bias, restricted resources and assets, and restricted civil liberties.
- In 2010, the UNDP launched its Gender Inequality Index (GII), which is a composite measure that calculates differences in the distribution of achievements between women and men across countries. The measure uses three dimensions to calculate this score: (1) reproductive health measured

by maternal mortality ratio and adolescent birth rates; (2) empowerment measured by proportion of parliamentary seats occupied by females and proportion of adult females and males aged 25 years and older with at least some secondary education; and (3) labor market participation rates.

- In 2013, the European Institute for Gender Equality launched its Gender Equality Index report, where it documents the position of the European Union in terms of gender equality. It ranks EU countries based on their gender gaps in several sub-categories including work, money, knowledge, time, health, power, violence, and other intersecting inequalities.

Judith Kelley of Duke and Beth Simmons of Harvard argue that rankings have become an effective instrument of "soft power" in international governance, including on some of the biggest challenges of our time such as human trafficking. Countries which have been included in the annual US *Trafficking in Persons Report* or have been placed on the "watch list" are more likely to criminalize trafficking. Corporations have also been found to respond to ratings, for example, with respect to their impact on the environment. Researchers evaluated how several hundred firms reacted to the ratings issued by a well-known social rating agency. The poorly performing companies improved their performance after the ratings became public while companies that were never rated or did better in the initial evaluation did not change.[16]

Mike Luca of Harvard Business School and his collaborators demonstrated the impact of rankings on students' application decisions. Improvements in a college's rank on *US News and World Report* Best College Rankings immediately translate into a larger number of applications. Interestingly enough, however, the authors only find this effect when the magazine presents the colleges ordered by rank. When the colleges are listed alphabetically, with their rank included in the body copy describing the institution, no effect on applications could be detected. Only easily understandable and highly visible comparisons mattered, something gender equality designers hoping to influence behavior need to keep in mind. A final but important consideration is this: precisely because people and organizations care about their relative standing, rankings may motivate attempts at manipulation. Ben Edelman and Ian Larkin, for example, show that when people fall behind, they may engage in deception to boost their rank.[17]

Laws and regulations can work in a similar fashion. Just as learning about what others do can make us want to follow the herd or even outperform it, learning what is approved or sanctioned, either formally by law or informally by social norms, also provides information on what acceptable behavior is. The law, thus, often goes beyond deterrence; it also has an "expressive function." Even if the expected cost of violating the law is too small to actually deter, people may take a law as a signal for what the social norm regarding a certain behavior is.

Take jaywalking. Growing up in Switzerland, where people only cross the street when the light tells them to, I used not to jaywalk. Then I moved to Cambridge, Massachusetts, and watched in disbelief how most everyone (but the tourists) crossed the streets in Harvard Square with complete disregard for the colors on the traffic lights. Eventually, I started doing the same—although to this day, I always check whether there are any children about and, if I am walking with someone, wait to see what he or she is doing. Clearly, jaywalking norms in Switzerland and in Cambridge are very different. I doubt that the likelihood of being fined or the size of the fine dramatically differ, so the difference in behavior lies elsewhere. Economists would say the two places have settled on two different equilibria, a jaywalking and a nonjaywalking one. Without an intervention, it is unlikely that the norms in either place would change. A habitual jaywalker might be incredulous: no intervention is going to disrupt so ingrained a habit, one that verges, for some, on a perceived right. Odds are, however, that jaywalker isn't also a smoker.

In the United States, smoking in public was quite common until relatively recently. But then, legislation translated an emerging shift in the public's views into something concrete. Nonsmokers who wanted others to refrain from smoking, particularly anywhere near them, now had the moral authority to do so. Social norms were changing from a smoking to a nonsmoking equilibrium, constantly being reinforced by people's increasing willingness to sanction deviations. Similar arguments may apply to large differences across locations in compliance with laws and regulations governing speeding, shoplifting, unethical behavior in organizations, or riding public transportation without paying. Laws and regulations activate informal systems of control. They change how we interpret actions. For example, the National Hockey League's requirement that players wear helmets completely reframed the discussion as to what was proper, acceptable, and to be encouraged. Wearing a helmet, which had been considered a sign of weakness or even unmanliness, now became the norm.[18]

Title IX, one of the landmark laws in the United States, offers another example of the power of regulation to set new norms with far-reaching consequences. Signed into law on June 23, 1972, by President Richard Nixon, Title IX prohibits gender discrimination in any federally funded education program or activity. It is best known for opening doors for girls and women who wished to compete in sports, but it has nine other provisions that influenced norms well outside of sports, including protecting students from sexual harassment, providing equal access to higher education, math, and the sciences, and fair treatment for pregnant and parenting students. Specifically, the law mandates: "No person in the United States shall, on the basis of sex, be excluded from participation in, be denied the benefits of, or be subjected to discrimination under any education program or activity receiving Federal financial assistance."

Before it passed, fewer than 300,000 girls had access to high school sports in the United States. Today, it is estimated that more than 3 million girls participate. Given the central role athletics plays in American educational culture, this is a massive shift. Interestingly, the law's advocates had an inkling of what was to come and deliberately kept it quiet. Celebrating the fortieth anniversary of the law in 2012, a documentary, *Sporting Chance*, tells how Title IX came to be. Bernice Sandler, an American women's rights activist who worked with Edith Green, congresswoman from Oregon, and Birch Bayh, senator from Indiana—two of its key proponents—recalls in the film how Green wanted to avoid drawing too much attention to the law as she feared that if people understood its potential to promote social change they might oppose it: "I don't want you to lobby. Because if you lobby, people will ask questions about this bill, and they will find out what it would really do." Sandler continues: "And she was absolutely right. It was quite a big break that no one was watching."

The impact of Title IX only became apparent a few years after it passed when it started to trigger proposed amendments, including an attempt to exempt "money-making" sports from Title IX, various Supreme Court cases, and a host of political actions. Condoleezza Rice, former US secretary of state, recalled how Title IX overturned social norms in her former hometown of Birmingham, Alabama, then the most segregated big city in the United States. She spoke about "the tremendous explosion of opportunity for young women on the playing field." And off it. "So, I very often think of Title IX as trying to do away with discrimination but really, being about giving opportunity."[19]

Many rules serve expressive functions that often go unexamined. They can informally sanction and reward behavior, which in turn can prove a liability. Take the example of Lee Iacocca, president of the Ford Motor Company from 1970 to 1978, the year he was fired. Iacocca has been described as the driving force behind the Ford Pinto. In 1977, allegations were raised that the Pinto's structural design was compromised, creating a fire hazard. In 1978, 1.5 million of the subcompacts were recalled to install fuel-tank protection. In *The Ford Pinto Case*, their case study on applied ethics taught in many business schools, Douglas Birsch and John Fielder report that safety concerns were not the norm at Ford: "Iacocca was fond of saying, 'Safety doesn't sell.'" Coming from the top, that sent a strong message about company values and what is rewarded and what sanctioned, formally and informally.[20]

What companies live and breathe matters, likely more than any written corporate codes of conduct. Norm entrepreneurs in organizations and in public policy promote behaviors by harnessing people's desire to imitate, compete, and gain social approval. Perhaps the most encouraging testimonial to the powers of norm entrepreneurship is the UK government. Its success at more than doubling the share of female board members without relying on quotas should be a clarion call to others.

Designing Gender Equality—Become a Norm Entrepreneur

- Make others' successes increasing gender diversity salient.
- Use rankings to motivate people to compete on gender equality.
- Use rules, laws, and codes of conduct to express norms.

13

Increasing Transparency

Hungry tourists in Los Angeles, or perhaps longtime residents visiting a new neighborhood, face three restaurants they have never eaten at before. In the door of one, easily visible, is a white piece of paper with a large letter C on it. A quick closer glance and black letters, smaller, above the C read, "Sanitary Inspection Grade." Its close neighbor has a letter B posted on its door. And beside it, the third restaurant has a letter A in its window. Assuming our hungry visitors are broadly agnostic about whether they eat Chinese or Japanese or Italian, and pricing is roughly equivalent across all three choices, which restaurant do you think they enter?

That is the power of transparency. Consider a different example. When you last booked an airplane ticket online, did you read the disclosure statement? If you are like most everyone else, you did not. Instead, you just checked the appropriate box acknowledging that you were okay with the company's policies. If I asked you what fraction of consumers you imagine read the privacy disclosures on websites, you would probably guess that it is small. But would you have thought that it is only 3 percent, as a research study suggests? We do not do much better reading warning labels on products themselves, according to a review of about 400 studies. Most consumers ignore them. So, why do we—governments, companies, consumers—bother?[1]

For starters, some companies overestimate the influence disclosure requirements have on consumers. Known as the *spotlight effect,* we tend to have an exaggerated expectation of others' awareness of our actions. In addition, companies know that it sometimes takes only a few active consumers or consumer groups to raise concerns, making a wider public pay attention. Consequently, not only do companies often respond quickly to initial concerns, they take disclosure requirements seriously, even when they know only a small percentage of consumers give them much time and attention. When the European Union and the United States mandated energy efficiency labels on appliances, for example, manufacturers started immediately to innovate, offering more energy-efficient products even before consumers began to demand different kinds of appliances.[2]

At the same time, disclosure requirements too often do not reach their potential. Poorly designed or implemented, their influence is blunted. A few behavioral design principles can help, and sometimes spectacularly so. The more salient and visible information is, the more likely people are to notice. The easier it is for consumers to read disclosures, from the size of the typeface to how simple and direct the language, the more likely consumers will read it. And the more information is put into a comparative context—"with this car you save $1,850 in fuel costs over five years compared to the average new vehicle"—the more people are able to understand it. The same behavioral rules discussed in Chapter 6 for people evaluations apply whenever we need to process information, particularly when the information is complex or unfamiliar. To increase the chances that we process it accurately, information needs to be salient, simple, and in comparative context.

This is why, at least to a behavioral economist, the energy labels on appliances and cars sold in the United States qualify as beautiful. The information is provided comparatively so that customers can calibrate, for example, the operating cost of a specific car relative to others. In addition, complicated metrics such as MPG—miles per gallon—have been replaced by better ones. Why? Because linear metrics are simpler than nonlinear ones. Miles per gallon is nonlinear: one gallon is saved per 100 miles if the MPG changes from ten to eleven or from thirty-three to fifty. Gallons per hundred miles, or GPhM, gives customers a better sense of what is going on. In this car, you go one hundred miles and you consume this many gallons; in another car, it's more, or less. GPhM is linearly related to consumption and cost.

For example, the 2015 Toyota Prius is a hybrid vehicle that runs on gasoline with a suggested retail price of about $24,000 to $30,000. The average gallons per 100 miles are 2.1, an average estimate based on six vehicles. If you have a Toyota Prius, the EPA reports that you save $4,500 in fuel costs over five years compared to the average new vehicle.[3] Salient, simple, and comparative.

One of the most convincing advocates for simplification is Cass Sunstein, formerly head of the Office of Information and Regulatory Affairs, also known as America's "Regulatory Czar" under President Barack Obama. His wonderful book *Simpler*, published shortly after he left office, uses examples of many of the simplifications he helped oversee and provides helpful guidelines on how we can simplify our communications and make them more effective. These include a number of disclosure requirements "designed to protect students, consumers, and investors by ensuring that they "know before they owe." The Credit Card Accountability, Responsibility and Disclosure Act of 2009, for example, requires clear disclosure of annual percentage rates and finance charges, and advance notice of changes. Your monthly credit card statements now include a "minimum payment warning" explaining how long it would take you to pay off the card by submitting just the minimum and how much this would cost. To make customers even smarter about debt, Mike Luca argued that this transparency should be extended from paper copies to online statements. He shows how easily credit card companies could create an online tool that would help customers understand the long-term implications of different payment amounts.[4]

Sunstein was also involved in helping Americans rethink what they eat. For a great many reasons, the government wished Americans to be healthier than not, and encouraging more Americans to eat healthier food seemed, well, low-hanging fruit. Except for many years it wasn't. Since 1992 the US Department of Agriculture had used a food pyramid to help Americans understand how many fruits and vegetables to eat as compared to, say, meats. It turns out the pyramid did not work well for most people. In their book *Switch*, Chip and Dan Heath didn't mince words: the pyramid's message is "opaque . . . , confuses and demoralizes." Sunstein was in a position to do something about it. Accordingly, the Obama administration searched for a better image. And sometimes, simple really means simple: the pyramid was out and in its place was a dinner plate. Unevenly quartered to recommend a healthy balance of vegetables, fruit, protein, and grains, it also showed a nearby glass representing dairy. The government's MyPlate image is a great example of effectively transparent information. Unlike the pyramid, MyPlate is a mirror to your own plate, and the ease of comparison—perhaps you are used to seeing half of your plate taken up with steak rather than the suggested slightly less than a quarter—is immediate. And revelatory. As a yogurt lover, I confess to being a bit shocked by how small the dairy cup is.[5]

MyPlate is not the only much-celebrated example of successful disclosure to encourage healthier eating. Recall our visitors weighing dining choices who opened this chapter. Public displays of hygiene ratings in restaurants have proven a highly effective intervention in transparency. In January 1998, Los Angeles's Department of Health Services decided that going forward restaurants would be required to post a grade card (with letter grades A, B, or C) in their windows indicating how the department had rated them during their most recent hygiene inspection. The result was dramatically improved hygiene in all city restaurants. Due to the salience, simplicity, and easy comparability of the information displayed, patrons started to pay attention to restaurants' hygiene. The number of foodborne illnesses decreased, both because people switched from lower-quality to higher-quality restaurants and because restaurants improved their sanitation. Over time, health inspection ratings increased citywide.

The next leap forward in eating confidently at a new restaurant might come with data analytics. Today, many cities have websites or apps where consumers can learn about how well their favorite restaurants did on their hygiene inspections. New York has an app called ABCEats and San Francisco collaborates with the review website Yelp to make restaurant health information accessible to the public. Indeed, making use of the large amounts of data created through customer reviews, researchers are now able to build algorithms that predict restaurant quality. According to Mike Luca and Yejin Choi, their statistical model based solely on customer reviews is able to discriminate with more than 80 percent accuracy between restaurants you likely want to avoid and restaurants with no history of unsanitary conditions.[6]

Information disclosure can make us healthier, safer, wiser, and more responsible. It has the potential of reaping large benefits at relatively low cost, it remains an attractive tool for policy makers and regulators, and it is now increasingly being used to make organizations more diverse. A tool is only as useful as it is well designed, of course. An unimpressive effort was initiated by the Securities and Exchange Commission in 2010. The SEC ruled that companies had to disclose how they considered diversity when they selected their boards. Specifically, the rule requires public companies to disclose "whether diversity is a factor in considering candidates for nomination to the board of directors, how diversity is considered in that process, and how the company assesses the effectiveness of its policy for considering diversity."

By now, you likely can guess why this approach isn't effective. It fails on salience, its message is opaque, and there is zero effort at comparative insight. Here's a simple suggestion: if you are going to advocate for diversity, be prepared to define it, simply. The SEC did not. Indeed, the only saving grace of their effort was the transparency of its ambition: the new rules, the SEC said, were "not intended to steer behavior." Unsurprisingly, they did not. Aaron Dhir finds in his study that companies frequently did not include demographic factors when considering diversity. Instead, they defined diversity in terms of directors' prior experiences. While the exclusion of identity-based factors has raised concerns, including from a number of large institutional investors, Dhir remains skeptical that the SEC rule will have any noticeable impact on gender or other demographic diversity on US corporate boards.

Most other countries that have adopted disclosure requirements have offered specific definitions of diversity. For example, the Code of Corporate Governance in Singapore specifies that "the board committees should comprise directors who as a group provide an appropriate balance and diversity of skills, experience, gender and knowledge of the company." In 2014, the Singaporean Diversity Task Force regarding Women on Boards issued a report detailing specific recommendations on how to increase diversity on boards, including the publication of rankings.

Some countries have gone further, adopting a *comply-or-explain* approach. Regulators provide guidance on what they consider good policy, organizational practices, and even outcomes, and ask companies to either comply or publicly disclose why they did not. For example, corporate governance codes in Germany, the Netherlands, and the United Kingdom apply this approach, setting standards for boards' audit and compensation committees. The disclosed information helps investors, proxy advisors, and shareholders evaluate a board's decisions, actions, and outcomes and take appropriate action.

With the comply-or-explain approach, the government in effect sets a soft default for companies. It defines what it considers to be the desired course of affairs and asks companies opting out of them to explain why. While not restricting choices, such soft defaults create a reference point that people dislike leaving. And they leverage our inertia, with people and organizations avoiding or delaying change that might be costly and painful. *Default setting* is a powerful instrument in a behavioral designer's toolbox. When opting out is required to change the status quo, the enrollment rate in retirement savings plans has been shown to be up to almost 40 percentage points higher in opt-out than in opt-in plans.[7]

An increasing number of countries are now using the comply-or-explain approach to promote gender diversity. The Australian Securities Exchange, for example, asks companies to report annually their diversity policies and degree of diversity. They must not only report the fraction of female employees overall, but also the number of women in senior positions and on a company's board of directors. Finally, they must spell out their overall goals regarding gender diversity and to what degree they have met them. Similarly, in Canada, the Ontario Securities Commission introduced comply-or-explain rules in 2014 that required companies listed on the Toronto Stock Exchange to annually disclose:

- "whether the issuer has a written policy regarding the representation of women on the board and if not, why not;
- whether its board or nominating committee considered the level of representation of women in the director identification and selection process and if not, why not;
- whether the issuer considers the representation of women in executive positions when making executive appointments and if not, why not;
- whether the issuer has targets for the representation of women on its board and in executive positions, and the annual and cumulative progress in achieving such targets, and where there are no targets, why not; and
- the number and proportion of women on the board and in executive positions of the company and each of its major subsidiaries."

Spurred by the Davies Report of 2011, which I introduced in the previous chapter, the United Kingdom has likely gone the farthest, using disclosure requirements toward successfully reaching its target of 25 percent female directors by the end of 2015. In 2015, there were no all-male boards left among the FTSE 100 companies, which is a first in the history of the London Stock Exchange. In the same year, more than 90 percent of the FTSE 250 companies were gender diverse, whereas in 2011, more than half of these boards were male only. In 2013, the Netherlands followed suit and set a 30 percent goal for both corporate supervisory and executive boards, specifying that at least 30 percent of the seats should be held by women. If a company fails to meet this goal, it must explain why and what actions it plans to take to meet the goal in the future.[8]

Disclosure requirements are popular in part because they help people make more informed decisions without limiting their autonomy. It is left up to shareholders, investors, analysts, and the public to decide how to use the disclosed information. Those unconcerned about gender may disregard it while those who care about the inclusion of both sexes in decision making and leadership may act on it. However, we know little about whether, how, or to what degree gender diversity disclosure is working to promote diversity. These provisions were recently introduced and were often accompanied by additional interventions, making it impossible to tease apart the particular relevance of disclosures. Also, specific disclosure rules vary greatly across the countries that have adopted them. One comparative fact, however, stands out. In the United States, where the disclosure requirements were unspecific and "not intended to steer behavior," the share of female directors has moved little in recent years, with 16.1 percent female directors in 2011 and 19.2 percent in 2014. It is hard to imagine that the United Kingdom was able to surpass the United States in that same time frame without the Davies Report and the evaluative transparency that comes with disclosures.[9]

Still, the question remains: does disclosure work? Disclosure in other domains, sometimes based on randomized controlled trials, offers insights and caveats. One facet of the US Patient Protection and Affordable Care Act of 2010 sheds useful light. Most of us declare ourselves for gender equality, and nearly all employers would assure us that their desire and intent is to hire the most talented employees. It is not unlike the majority of us who agree that eating healthily is a good thing. But when offered a choice between French fries and salad as a side, many of us select the fries— much like the employer who, confronted with a choice between a more qualified candidate and one who shares his love of baseball, goes with "fit" instead of "ability."

The Affordable Care Act tries to address this disconnect between good intentions and bad actions by mandating that calorie information be disclosed on the menu boards of chain restaurants with twenty or more locations. The evidence of the impact of calorie disclosure, however, is mixed. Even for the well-intentioned, it is hard to get disclosure right, and even when information meets the behavioral requirements of simplicity, salience, and comparability, it does not always change everyone's behavior. Christina Roberto of Yale University and colleagues summarize the evidence on calorie disclosure as follows: "The documented effects of menu labeling on consumer and restaurant industry behavior suggest that menu labeling will likely encourage some consumers to eat more healthfully some of the time, and the policy is likely an important first step toward improving the public's eating habits."

As the wording suggests, the effects proved modest overall and seemed to vary depending on the customer. Indeed, research found that women, normal-weight individuals, socio-demographically advantaged groups, and customers in some but not in other chain restaurants were more responsive to calorie information. In addition, similar to the hygiene findings, the channels of greatest influence might work through the restaurants rather than the customers. One study examining menu offerings in fast food restaurants between 2005 and 2011, during which calorie disclosure was introduced in a number of municipalities, found that menu offerings changed. Chain restaurants in communities where calorie information was posted included healthier choices than the same chain restaurants residing in areas where labeling was not required.

Also, not all labels are created equally. Behavioral design features matter, especially when it comes to comparisons. A systematic review of experimental and quasi-experimental studies testing the impact of disclosing calories to consumers found no impact when only calorie information was provided. In contrast, when that information was put into a context people could understand, they started to consume fewer calories. Knowing that a burrito contains 1,000 calories is one thing; knowing that the recommended daily caloric intake for an average adult is 2,000 calories puts that first number in context. Similar positive effects were reported when the information was made more salient and simpler to interpret, for example, by using the colors made familiar by traffic lights—green, yellow, and red—to indicate whether one should go ahead and consume, pause and consider, or stop and make different choices.

Overall, simply disclosing nutritional information has little to no effect, and when rendered salient, clear, and comparative, that information has modest positive effects for some people. Even so, where is the harm? Disclosures seem to influence corporate behavior. It is a relatively cheap intervention. And giving customers at least the option of a more informed choice is good, right? Right, except for the potential of it backfiring. One could well imagine that the moral licensing effect discussed earlier could also apply here. People might well compensate for picking a healthier main course by also picking the chocolate cake instead of the apple for dessert.

Similarly, corporate boards might feel that by having disclosed how effective they consider their diversity efforts to be, as the SEC rule requires in the United States, they have done their job and can thereafter worry about other things. Indeed, there is some evidence that suggests in some circumstances disclosures benefit the person asked to disclose. Researchers have found that people judge others who have just lied as behaving more ethically if they had disclosed beforehand that they had an incentive to lie. Similarly, people were more likely to trust others who disclosed a potential conflict of interest.[10]

These findings should make us vigilant, but they should not hold us back from advocating for more transparency. They suggest that we must be aware of potential backlash effects and work to mitigate them, starting with holding people accountable for their actions. On this front, the United States has taken an aggressive stance. On April 8, 2014, President Obama not only prohibited federal contractors from punishing employees who discuss their salaries, as mentioned in Chapter 3, but went a step further. Though federal law and the Equal Pay Act of 1963 state that employers cannot compensate men and women differently for the same work, enforcement of this mandate has proven difficult. The National Equal Pay Task Force, created by the president in 2010, found that the absence of wage data broken down by sex and race was one of the main culprits. To address this, a 2014 Presidential Memorandum required federal contractors to submit summary data to the Department of Labor on employee compensation stratified by sex and race. Several other countries, for example Australia, Austria, Belgium, and the United Kingdom, have likewise passed laws that emphasize the importance of transparency in decreasing gender gaps in pay, promotion, and workforce composition, going so far as to ask employers to produce action plans if they are found to have fallen short.[11]

We need to help companies overcome the intention-action gap. Information disclosure, smartly designed, can help organizations act on their virtuous intentions to treat men and women equally and provide both equal opportunities. Providing simple, salient, and comparative information helps. Timing also matters. For example, people tend to respond more strongly to positive information that comes as an unexpected surprise. To illustrate the point, consider a simple online experiment examining how to increase productivity. Three groups of data entry workers were offered a low wage rate, a high wage rate, or a low wage rate that was followed by the high wage rate after the workers had accepted the low offer. This pleasant surprise led to an increase in productivity of 20 percent compared to the other two groups, including the high wage rate group where incentives were identical.[12]

The introduction of a specific target might have helped the United Kingdom meet its goal of increasing the share of women on corporate boards to 25 percent. Other organizations, such as the 30% Club, suggest that high but achievable aspirations can be powerful nudges. Much research in the realm of negotiations, for example, suggests that aspiration setting matters. Similar to setting personal goals, corporate targets may mobilize resources and focus attention. Because of this, they are not uncontroversial. As we have seen, setting targets in zero-sum contexts—making 30 percent of the executive suite women when the overall number of executive-suite positions isn't increased—can invite backlash from men. Others argue that women will be hurt by any real or perceived protected status. Yet others raise more general concerns: performance targets can increase stress, lead to fudged data, and undermine trust. While more research is needed to tease these various concerns apart and evaluate the impact of diversity targets, many organizations continue to announce them. Examples span all sectors and include the Bank of England, Bayer, BMW, Daimler Chrysler, Deloitte, Deutsche Telekom, KPMG, Lloyds Bank, Louis Vuitton, Merck, and Qantas, among others, with targets typically focusing on adding women to senior management or corporate boards and numbers as ambitious as 45 percent.[13]

Recent insights on goal setting suggest that organizations currently introducing long-term targets might well be advised to set smaller, interim goals. Setting sub-goals has been found to have positive effects by increasing a sense of accomplishment, interest in a task, and persistence in achieving it. Related work has shown that setting smaller, achievable goals has helped people save more effectively and pay off their debts. They worked particularly well when people had a single savings goal instead of pursuing multiple goals simultaneously. One simple illustration of the effectiveness of sub-goals was provided by Dan Ariely, author of the illuminating book *Predictably Irrational*, and Klaus Wertenbroch. They asked one set of students to proofread three essays in three weeks, another group to proofread one essay each week over the course of three weeks, and a final group to set their own schedule. The group with sub-goals—one essay each week over the three week period—outperformed the groups with one final goal only, both in terms of timeliness and in terms of accuracy. Not only did they get more of the work done, but the quality of their work was better. Furthermore, when given the option, students generally imposed sub-goals on themselves.[14]

Public accountability matters. Holding organizations accountable by asking them to "explain" when they have not "complied" is another lever that helps people follow through on their good intentions. In fact, the literature on accountability suggests that people charged with evaluating others are less likely to rely on stereotypes if they have to explain their choices.

In one experiment conducted in Israel, female students at a teachers' college were asked to evaluate an essay written by an eighth grader on "an interesting event that happened to me." Everyone received the same essay, and everyone was informed that such evaluations were an essential part of a teacher's job. Each was told to evaluate the essay's literary merits on a scale from 1 to 100. However, one group of evaluators was informed that the student's ethnic origin was Ashkenazi (originally from Europe or America) and another group was informed that the author was Sephardi (originally from Asia or Africa); a final group was told nothing about the author's ethnicity. Finally, to examine the impact of accountability on ratings, the researchers told half of the student teachers rating the essay that the study they were participating in was intended to assess their evaluative ability and that they would have to publicly explain their assessment. In addition, they would eventually be able to compare their evaluation with that of an experienced teacher. In contrast, the other half of the student teachers were told that the purpose of the study was to better understand differences in evaluation styles. Like in other research, the ethnic origin of the teachers rating the essay did not matter. However, the writer's identity proved highly significant. Generally, essays that had an Ashkenazi name were evaluated more favorably than those with a Sephardi name—with one exception: when raters knew they were to be held publicly accountable for their evaluations, the pro-Ashkenazi bias disappeared.

Generally, accountability is more likely to attenuate bias when people confront an audience that is well informed, interested in accuracy, and has a legitimate reason to probe. Put simply, it works because people care about what others think. There are two important caveats. First, accountability works better when people know beforehand that they will be held accountable. Otherwise, they might become defensive and try to rationalize their behavior rather than improve their procedures. Second, and this is a tall order, in an ideal world people would not know their evaluators' views beforehand. The more they know, the more they are tempted to superficially conform to what they believe the audience wants to hear, without actually scrutinizing their arguments or changing underlying processes to make them better. However, while a theoretical ideal, I doubt that this is practicable in most organizational settings. Instead, organizations have found other ways to make sure that talk is not cheap.[15]

In their otherwise depressing review of the efficacy of diversity training programs, Frank Dobbin and colleagues found accountability to be one of the most important mechanisms related to the diversity of the labor force. Assigning responsibility for managing diversity to taskforces, diversity officers, or some similar committee was strongly associated with an increase in workforce diversity, including in the fraction of women. To better understand why accountability was related to an increase in diversity but diversity training was not, the authors conducted a number of interviews in a subset of the firms they originally studied in Atlanta, Boston, San Francisco, and Chicago. Human resource and line managers reported that taskforces and diversity officers were good at identifying problems as well as at suggesting remedies. And they held them accountable, acting as their conscience, monitoring whether managers followed through with agreed-upon initiatives. But these were not always formal reviews. Rather, one study suggests that accountability can work even when no one is formally assigned to review behavior. One reason talk is not cheap is because most of the people most of the time do not like to lie.[16]

An ingenious study examining voting behavior suggests how and why. During the 2010 midterm congressional elections, which historically see abysmal turnouts, Stefano DellaVigna, John List, Ulrike Malmendier, and Gautam Rao set out to find what the value of voting was to someone who thought others would ask if they'd bothered to vote. It turns out the answer is about $10 to $15. That is the amount of money people were willing to spend to be able to honestly tell others that they had voted. This insight suggests that managers do not need to answer to a formal taskforce to be nudged by accountability; just a belief that they might have to answer to someone can do the trick.[17]

People care about what others think, and so do companies. This is the power of transparency. It enables everyone to make more informed choices, whether by buying a particular car because of its energy efficiency, by paying down debt more quickly because of the long-term consequences, or by working for or investing in a company that is more diverse and pays more equitably. Holding organizations accountable through disclosure and comply-or-explain approaches can make compliance the soft default. And the more behaviorally smart the shared information, the more likely it is going to move the needle toward increased transparency and gender equality.

Designing Gender Equality—Behaviorally Informed Disclosure and Accountability

- Make information salient, simple, and comparable.
- Set both long-term targets and specific, short-term, achievable goals.
- Hold people and organizations accountable for their follow-through.

Designing Change

If I could send you off with one big takeaway, it would be this: we can reduce gender inequality. We will use all we know about how the mind works, how biases influence decisions and outcomes, and how behavioral design can alter these. We can effect this change not in a matter of decades but in a matter of years. Even good design cannot solve all our problems. But behavioral design is the most useful and underutilized tool we have. Truth be told, we collectively can do this only if you take part.

I wrote *What Works* to give you the research-based insights, the confidence, and the practical advice necessary for designing your own changes at work or school. In this last chapter, I want to make it easier still. Let me start by introducing an acronym that may help you remember the promise of DESIGN.

D: for data
E: for experiment
SIGN: for signpost

Good behavioral design starts with data. How many men and women has your company hired and promoted, to what positions and at what salaries, over the past five years? Are boys and girls in your school gaining proficiency at reading, staying the same, or becoming less proficient? How many of the portraits in your organization's lobby or conference rooms are of women, and how many are of men?

Armed with data, a behavioral designer must experiment. You do not start off in a design-free environment. In that sense, you are already participating in an experiment, just unknowingly and without the benefit of having a control group available. When you design your experiment, do so knowingly and responsibly. Adhere to the ethical standards set by entities such as the Institutional Review Boards (IRBs) overseeing experimentation at universities.[1]

Experiment with new signposts—on restaurant doors, in interview protocols, or on office walls—that use insights about human behavior to point people in more desirable directions. Remember the hotel key cards that automatically turn room lights on and off? Find signposts that, like these keys, make it easy for our biased minds to make unbiased choices. Do not focus on changing minds—the very purpose of signposts is to help us find the way without having to memorize or even think much about it.

So in brief: collect data to understand whether and why there is gender inequality; experiment with what might close gender gaps; and informed by behavioral insights to create signposts, nudge behavior toward more equality. Finally, be sure to let colleagues know that in embracing DESIGN, they are joining an increasing number of governments, corporations, schools, and universities that, responding to the promise of behavioral insights to change behavior for good, have done the same.

Consider savings. Millions have been added to people's retirement accounts in Denmark, New Zealand, the United Kingdom, the United States, and elsewhere through auto-enrollment, automatic employer contributions, active choice, and Save More Tomorrow plans where employees commit future rather than present earnings to savings accounts. To put this in perspective, recall the evidence from Denmark discussed in the first chapter. Every dollar of government expenditure on subsidies led to an increase in savings by one cent—but the United States keeps spending about $100 billion and the United Kingdom about $30 billion per year on subsidies.

There are many more success stories. In the United Kingdom, the Behavioral Insights Team has helped increase the poor's university enrollment rates by 25 percent with pre-filled application forms, increased payment of taxes by up to 16 percent by reminding taxpayers of the prevalent norms, and encouraged healthy eating by having employees make their choices ahead of time. It has done so through data collection, experimentation, and careful evaluation, as David Halpern's insightful 2015 book, *Inside the Nudge Unit*, explains. The recently established What Works institutes in the United Kingdom provide practitioners with actionable intelligence ranging from how to enhance educational attainment in schools to how to boost local growth. Building on these successes in other areas, the time is right to address gender equality.[2]

Many other countries have launched initiatives similar to the UK's Behavioral Insights Team, including Australia, Austria, Denmark, Finland, Germany, Guatemala, Mexico, the Netherlands, Norway, Singapore, South Africa, Sweden, and the United States. And so have international organizations. The World Bank's flagship report, the *World Development Report,* was devoted to behavioral insights; it launched a Global Insights Initiative in 2015. President Jim Yong Kim writes: "The promise of this approach to decision making and behavior is enormous, and its scope of application is extremely wide . . . This year's *World Development Report* . . . introduces an important new agenda for the development community going forward." Berkeley, Carnegie Mellon, Chicago, Harvard, Princeton, and the University of Pennsylvania, among other universities, are at the forefront of behavioral insights. At Harvard, the Behavioral Insights Group that I co-chair with Max Bazerman is located at the Kennedy School's Center for Public Leadership because applying behavioral insights is a key leadership skill. A good leader is a behavioral designer.[3]

Leaders need to do many things. Most fundamentally, leaders need followers. Political leaders are well advised to take note of research by Todd Rogers and his colleagues on how to increase voter turnout. Barack Obama and Prime Minister Narendra Modi did, and it served them well. Helping voters make plans on when to vote and how to get there and reminding them that most others are voting, too, increases turnout, more so than the traditional strategies used, and at very low cost.[4]

Another important leadership task is to find talent. The police force in the United Kingdom substantially increased the talent pool by adopting a friendlier tone and asking people a simple question before they took the entry exam: Why do you want to join the police and why does it matter to your community? Hearing a different tone and being nudged to think about what motivated them increased the pass rate of minority group applicants by 50 percent. Making a small change that had a big impact required no more than the insights and experimentation of a few creative thinkers at the UK Behavioral Insights Team.

Finally, a leader will want to motivate people to give it their best, both in terms of how much value they produce and how they behave. Consider another subtle design based on research by Scott Wiltermuth and Francesca Gino: people work harder when rewards are grouped into categories. The same bonuses, for example, two all-expenses-paid vacations, feel different when they come from two different "buckets." When two goals are set, people work harder to achieve the second goal when the incentives—two free trips—are labeled differently. Though the trips can be identical, if people first work for the "blue bucket" trip and then have a shot at the "red bucket" trip, more than three times as many people continue to work hard to achieve the second goal. Even after earning a trip from the blue bucket, people feel that they would be "missing out" if they did not also try for a trip from the red bucket.

Good leadership does not end with productivity. Leaders must also make and promote ethical choices. Much insight has been gained on the blind spots that keep us from doing the right thing in the emerging field of behavioral ethics. The same design principles apply. To overcome the tension between what we want and what we know we should do, locking in our future choices today helps us control not only our retirement savings and our calorie consumption, but also our moral decisions. We are more likely to do what is right when the choices will be implemented in the distant future rather than today or tomorrow. A leader-designer, thus, will not make structural changes overnight, but instead, for example, secure a commitment to roll out a new structured interview protocol in a few months.[5]

Among corporations, few have gone further to embrace DESIGN principles than Google. Like most tech companies, Google has a long way to go in terms of gender equality. But data led Google to introduce employee training to identify unconscious bias. After reading the evidence, Laszlo Bock, head of Google's People Operations, started to wonder how bias might play out at Google: "This is a pretty genteel environment, and you don't usually see outright manifestations of bias," he said. "Occasionally you'll have some idiot do something stupid and hurtful, and I like to fire those people." He suspected that most of the manifestations of biases at Google were happening behind closed doors, hidden to most, even to the employees influenced by them. And, indeed, after taking the Implicit Association Test, he reported: "Suddenly you go from being completely oblivious to going, 'Oh my god, it's everywhere.'"[6]

The IAT, https://implicit.harvard.edu, is just one of the tools you can use to start the diagnosis. Another one is EDGE, www .edge-cert.org. Once you understand both your own data and what is going on in your organization and needs fixing, you can move on to experimentation. For a summary of what has already been learned, I recommend the Gender Action Portal, http://gap.hks.harvard.edu/. The Women and Public Policy Program's free online platform allows you to search for user-friendly summaries of scientific evidence—based on experiments in the field and the laboratory—on what works to close gender gaps in economic opportunity, political participation, health, and education. If your concern is potential bias in your hiring, I recommend you try out a tool such as Applied, www .beapplied.com, which allows you to easily employ a more structured approach.[7]

You don't have to wait. You can begin designing immediately. I have offered you thirty-six research-grounded design suggestions in this book. As you get ready to try some of them, let me summarize some key design principles, focusing on the four areas that we have covered in this book: training, talent management, school and work, and diversity. These become useful shorthand aspirations as you introduce any single or several designs.

1. *Training:* Move from "training" to "capacity building."
2. *Talent Management:* Move from "intuition" to "data" and "structure."
3. *School and Work:* Move from an "uneven" to an "even playing field."
4. *Diversity:* Move from a "numbers game" to the "conditions for success."

Let me end on a final example, one from my backyard, Boston, in which the Women and Public Policy Program (wappp.hks.harvard.edu) has been heavily involved. On April 9, 2013, Boston's then mayor, Thomas Menino, established the Women's Workforce Council, composed of leaders from across business, government, nonprofits, and academia. The council's mission is to help "close the gender wage gap and remove the visible and invisible barriers to women's advancement in today's working world." It produced a report outlining what companies, agencies, and not-for-profit organizations could be doing to reduce the gender wage gap, and a compact, titled "100% Talent," that organizations could sign, declaring that they were willing to try out at least three research-based interventions and let researchers evaluate their impact. As I write this book, fifty companies have signed the compact, and the council is in the midst of collaborating with the firms on data collection. Many of these companies are collecting and analyzing their data by gender for the first time. A huge success for the Women's Workforce Council, it is also the beginning of a journey that will allow these firms to use proven designs to fix what is broken.[8]

Companies, universities, and governments from around the world have begun a quest to design gender equality. We can move the needle toward a fairer and better world today. Now it is up to you.

Notes

The Promise of Behavioral Design

1. Claudia Goldin and Cecilia Rouse, "Orchestrating Impartiality: The Impact of 'Blind' Auditions on Female Musicians," *American Economic Review* 90 (2000): 715–741. The relative share of male and female musicians in ten of the highest-budgeted orchestras in the United States has increased at a modest rate from 2004 to 2013, and while the fraction of Asian musicians has substantially increased, the share of African American and Hispanic musicians remains at around one to two percent: League of American Orchestras, 2015: *Orchestra Statistical Report, Fiscal Years 2004–2013* (Anisha Asundi Diversity Request 2004–2013), League of American Orchestras, New York City. Unpublished dataset, cited with permission. For a discussion, see Jutta Allmendinger, J. Richard Hackman, and Erin V. Lehman, "Life and Work in Symphony Orchestras," *Musical Quarterly* 80, no. 2 (1996): 194–219; "Vienna Philharmonic's Conservatism Has Exposed It to Unsettling Truths," *Guardian,* March 11, 2013, sec. Music, http://www.theguardian.com/music/2013/mar/11/vienna -philharmonic-history.

2.   Chia-Jung Tsay, "Sight over Sound in the Judgment of Music Performance," *Proceedings of the National Academy of Sciences USA* 110, no. 36 (2013): 14580–14585.

3.   Shai Danziger, Jonathan Levav, and Liora Avnaim-Pesso, "Extraneous Factors in Judicial Decisions," *Proceedings of the National Academy of Sciences USA* 108 (2011): 6889–6892; Keren Weinshall-Margel and John Shapard, "Overlooked Factors in the Analysis of Parole Decisions," *Proceedings of the National Academy of Sciences USA* 108 (2011): E833; Shai Danziger, Jonathan Levav, and Liora Avnaim-Pesso, reply to Weinshall-Margel and Shapard: "Extraneous Factors in Judicial Decisions Persist," *Proceedings of the National Academy of Sciences USA* 108 (2011): E834. The order in which people appear before those who evaluate them has been shown to matter in many different domains, including, to go back to our opening example, in music competitions, where one surprising insight was that it does not pay to go first: Victor A. Ginsburgh and Jan C. van Ours, "Expert Opinion and Compensation: Evidence from a Musical Competition," *American Economic Review* 93, no. 1 (2003): 289–296.

4.   Richard H. Thaler and Cass R. Sunstein, *Nudge: Improving Decisions About Health, Wealth, and Happiness,* revised and expanded edition (New York: Penguin Books, 2009); Raj Chetty, John N. Friedman, Søren Leth-Petersen, and Torben Heien Nielsen, "Active vs. Passive Decisions and Crowd-Out in Retirement Savings Accounts: Evidence from Denmark," *Quarterly Journal of Economics* 129 (2014): 1141–1219; Gregory M. Walton, "The New Science of Wise Psychological Interventions," *Psychological Science* 23 (2014): 73–82.

5.   Pedro Bordalo, Katherine Coffman, Nicola Gennaioli, and Andrei Shleifer, "Stereotypes" (Working Paper, Harvard University, Cambridge, MA, May 2015), http://scholar.harvard.edu/shleifer/publications/stereotypes.

6.   Chang-Tai Hsieh, Erik Hurst, Charles I. Jones, and Peter J. Kienow, "The Allocation of Talent and U.S. Economic Growth" (National Bureau of Economic Research [NBER] Working Paper, January 2013), http://www.nber.org/papers/w18693.

7. US Central Intelligence Agency, "Country Comparison: Total Fertility Rate," *The World Factbook,* https://www.cia.gov/library /publications/the-world-factbook/rankorder/2127rank.html.

8. Marc Teignier and David Cuberes, "Aggregate Costs of Gender Gaps in the Labor Market: A Quantitative Estimate" (Social Science Research Network [SSRN] Scholarly Paper, February 10, 2014), http://papers .ssrn.com/abstract=2405006; *Closing the Gender Gap: Act Now* (OECD Publishing, 2012), http://www.oecd-ilibrary.org/social-issues -migration-health/close-the-gender-gap-now_9789264179370-en; Groundbreakers (Ernst & Young, 2009), www.ey.com; "The Economic Power of Women's Empowerment, Keynote Speech by Christine Lagarde, Managing Director, International Monetary Fund" (International Monetary Fund, September 8, 2015), https://www.imf .org/external/np/speeches/2014/091214.htm; Stephen J. Ceci, Donna K. Ginther, Shulamit Kahn, and Wendy M. Williams, "Women in Academic Science: A Changing Landscape," *Psychological Science in the Public Interest* 15 (2014): 75–141; Ina Ganguli, Ricardo Hausmann, and Martina Viarengo, "Closing the Gender Gap in Education: What Is the State of Gaps in Labour Force Participation for Women, Wives and Mothers?" *International Labour Review* 153, no. 2 (2014): 173–207.

9. Esther Duflo and Christopher Udry, "Intrahousehold Resource Allocation in Cote d'Ivoire: Social Norms, Separate Accounts and Consumption Choices" (NBER Working Paper, May 2004), http://www.nber.org/papers/w10498; Anita Williams Woolley, Christopher F. Chabris, Alex Pentland, Nada Hashmi, and Thomas W. Malone, "Evidence for a Collective Intelligence Factor in the Performance of Human Groups," *Science* 330 (2010): 686–688.

10. For an excellent discussion, see Esther Duflo, "Women Empowerment and Economic Development," *Journal of Economic Literature* 50 (2012): 1051–1079. The macro-evidence comes with a caveat: most analyses are based on correlations that help us understand to what degree women's empowerment and economic returns are related but do not allow us to tease apart the channels of influence. The micro-evidence typically is based on experiments that

allow us to make causal inferences but beg the question of generalizability. Clearly, gender equality and economic development are closely interrelated, but development will not automatically help women advance nor will women's advancement automatically induce economic progress.

11. Marie Vlachová and Lea Biason, eds., "Women in an Insecure World: Violence against Women, Facts, Figures and Analysis (Geneva Center for the Demographic Control of Armed Forces, UNICEF, September 2005), http://www.unicef.org/emerg/files/women_insecure_world .pdf; "The Worldwide War on Baby Girls," *Economist*, March 4, 2010, http://www.economist.com/node/15636231; Rohini Pande, "Keeping Women Safe," *Harvard Magazine*, September 8, 2015, http://harvardmagazine.com/2015/01/keeping-women-safe; Nicholas D. Kristof and Sheryl WuDunn, "The Women's Crusade," *New York Times,* August 17, 2009, http://www.nytimes.com/2009/08 /23/magazine/23Women-t.html; Valerie M. Hudson and Andrea M. den Boer, *Bare Branches: The Security Implications of Asia's Surplus Male Population* (Cambridge: MIT Press, 2005).

12. Robert Jensen, "Do Labor Market Opportunities Affect Young Women's Work and Family Decisions? Experimental Evidence from India," *Quarterly Journal of Economics* 127 (2012): 753–792.

13. I concur with the conclusions reached in a meta-analysis on interventions aimed at changing gender stereotypes: "at this stage, it is still not possible to determine conclusively whether the male and the female stereotypes are equally susceptible to interventions, given the dearth of studies in which researchers have attempted to alter only the male stereotype." Alison P. Lenton, Martin Bruder, and Constantine Sedikides, "A Meta-analysis on the Malleability of Automatic Gender Stereotypes," *Psychology of Women Quarterly* 33 (2009): 183–196. For a discussion of men who are falling behind, see: "The Weaker Sex," *Economist,* March 7, 2015, http://www.economist.com/news /international/21645759-boys-are-being-outclassed-girls-both-school -and-university-and-gap; "Nature plus Nurture," *Economist,* March 7, 2015, http://www.economist.com/news/leaders/21645734-girls-do

-better-boys-school-and-university-both-can-still-improvesometimes; "The Weaker Sex," *Economist,* May 30, 2015, http://www.economist .com/news/leaders/21652323-blue-collar-men-rich-countries-are -trouble-they-must-learn-adapt-weaker-sex, quotation on p. 9.

14. Richard F. Martell, David M. Lane, and Cynthia Emrich, "Male-Female Differences: A Computer Simulation," *American Psychologist* 51 (1996): 157–158.

15. Sheryl Sandberg, *Lean In: Women, Work, and the Will to Lead* (New York: Knopf, 2013).

16. I am a nonexecutive director on the board of Credit Suisse Group AG.

1. Unconscious Bias Is Everywhere

1. Kathleen L. McGinn and Nicole Tempest, "Heidi Roizen" (Harvard Business School Case Collection, January 2000, Revised April 2010), http://www.hbs.edu/faculty/Pages/item.aspx?num=26880.

2. See, e.g., Laurie A. Rudman and Peter Glick, "Prescriptive Gender Stereotypes and Backlash Toward Agentic Women," *Journal of Social Issues* 57 (2001): 743–762; Alice H. Eagly, Anne E. Beall, and Robert Sternberg, *The Psychology of Gender, Second Edition* (New York: The Guilford Press, 2005); Madeline E. Heilman and Elizabeth Parks-Stamm, "Gender Stereotypes in the Workplace: Obstacles to Women's Career Progress," in *Social Psychology of Gender,* vol. 24, *Advances in Group Processes* (Emerald Group Publishing Limited, 2007), 47–77; Victoria L. Brescoll and Eric Luis Uhlmann, "Can an Angry Woman Get Ahead? Status Conferral, Gender, and Expression of Emotion in the Workplace," *Psychological Science* 19, no. 3 (2008): 268–275.

3. Robert W. Livingston, Ashleigh Shelby Rosette, and Ella F. Washington, "Can an Agentic Black Woman Get Ahead? The Impact of Race and Interpersonal Dominance on Perceptions of Female Leaders," *Psychological Science* 23, no. 4 (2012): 354–358; Robert W. Livingston and Nicholas A. Pearce, "The Teddy-Bear Effect: Does Having a Baby Face Benefit Black Chief Executive Officers?"

Psychological Science 20, no. 10 (2009): 1229–1236; for a broader discussion of what has been referred to as the stereotype of the "angry black woman," see Melissa V. Harris-Perry, *Sister Citizen: Shame, Stereotypes, and Black Women in America* (New Haven: Yale University Press, 2013). For a discussion of additive vs. intersecting models of gender and race, including Asian, Hispanic and Native Americans, see Valerie Purdie-Vaughns and Richard P. Eibach, "Intersectional Invisibility: The Distinctive Advantages and Disadvantages of Multiple Subordinate-Group Identities," *Sex Roles* 59 (2008): 377–391; for gender profiles, see Adam D. Galinsky, Erika V. Hall, and Amy J. C. Cuddy, "Gendered Races Implications for Interracial Marriage, Leadership Selection, and Athletic Participation," *Psychological Science* 24, no. 4 (2013): 498–506; Erika V. Hall, Adam D. Galinsky, and Katherine W. Phillips, "Gender Profiling: A Gendered Race Perspective on Person–Position Fit," *Personality and Social Psychology Bulletin* 41, no. 6 (2015): 853–868.

4.   Amy J. C. Cuddy, Susan T. Fiske, Virginia S. Y. Kwan, Peter Glick, Stéphanie Demoulin, Jacques-Philippe Leyens, Michael Harris Bond, Jean-Claude Croizet, Naomi Ellemers, Ed Sleebos, Tin Tin Htun, Hyun-Jeong Kim, Greg Maio, Judi Perry, Kristina Petkova, Valery Todorov, Rosa Rodríguez-Bailón, Elena Morales, Miguel Moya, Marisol Palacios, Vanessa Smith, Rolando Perez, Jorge Vala, and Rene Ziegler, "Stereotype Content Model across Cultures: Towards Universal Similarities and Some Differences," *British Journal of Social Psychology* 48, no. 1 (2009): 1–33; Amy J. C. Cuddy, Elizabeth Baily Wolf, Peter Glick, Susan Crotty, Jihye Chong, and Michael I. Norton, "Men as Cultural Ideals: Cultural Values Moderate Gender Stereotype Content," *Journal of Personality and Social Psychology* 109, no. 4 (2015): 622–635.

5.   Katherine L. Milkman, Modupe Akinola, and Dolly Chugh, "What Happens Before? A Field Experiment Exploring How Pay and Representation Differentially Shape Bias on the Pathway into Organizations," *Journal of Applied Psychology* 100, no. 6 (2015): 1678–1712.

6. For bias in science faculty, see Corinne A. Moss-Racusin, John F. Dovidio, Victoria L. Brescoll, Mark J. Graham, and Jo Handelsman, "Science Faculty's Subtle Gender Biases Favor Male Students," *Proceedings of the National Academy of Sciences USA* 109 (2012): 16474–16479; for bias and arithmetic tasks, see Ernesto Reuben, Paola Sapienza, and Luigi Zingales, "How Stereotypes Impair Women's Careers in Science," *Proceedings of the National Academy of Sciences USA* 111 (2014): 4403–4408.

7. Laurie A. Rudman, "Self-Promotion as a Risk Factor for Women: The Costs and Benefits of Counterstereotypical Impression Management," *Journal of Personality and Social Psychology* 74 (1998): 629–645; Laurie A. Rudman and Peter Glick, "Feminized Management and Backlash toward Agentic Women: The Hidden Costs to Women of a Kinder, Gentler Image of Middle Managers," *Journal of Personality and Social Psychology* 77 (1999): 1004–1010; Madeline E. Heilman, Aaron S. Wallen, Daniella Fuchs, and Melinda M. Tamkins, "Penalties for Success: Reactions to Women Who Succeed at Male Gender-Typed Tasks," *Journal of Applied Psychology* 89 (2004): 416–427; Alice H. Eagly and Linda L. Carli, *Through the Labyrinth: The Truth about How Women Become Leaders* (Boston: Harvard Business Review Press, 2007); Amy J. C. Cuddy, Susan T. Fiske, and Peter Glick, "When Professionals Become Mothers, Warmth Doesn't Cut the Ice," *Journal of Social Issues* 60 (2004): 701–718.

8. For a review of the literature concerning field experiments on gender, sometimes referred to as audit or correspondence studies, and their critics, see Ghazala Azmat and Barbara Petrongolo, "Gender and the Labor Market: What Have We Learned from Field and Lab Experiments?" (CEP Occasional Paper, Centre for Economic Performance, LSE, 2014), https://ideas.repec.org/p/cep/cepops/40.html; for evidence on racial prejudice from audit studies, see, e.g., Devah Pager, Bruce Western, and Bart Bonikowski, "Discrimination in a Low-Wage Labor Market: A Field Experiment," *American Sociological Review* 74 (2009): 777–799.

9. For the segment on the Heidi/Howard study on the Anderson Cooper show, see http://ac360.blogs.cnn.com/2013/03/12/how-are -powerful-women-perceived/; Wendy M. Williams and Stephen J. Ceci, "National Hiring Experiments Reveal 2:1 Faculty Preference for Women on STEM Tenure Track," *Proceedings of the National Academy of Sciences USA* 112 (2015): 5360–5365.

10. Eagly and Carli, *Through the Labyrinth*; Marianne Bertrand and Kevin Hallock, "The Gender Gap in Top Corporate Jobs," *Industrial and Labor Relations Review* 55 (2001): 3–21; Francine Blau and Jed DeVaro, "New Evidence on Gender Differences in Promotion Rates: An Empirical Analysis of a Sample of New Hires," *Industrial Relations* 46 (2007): 511–550. For a 2015 report by Lean In and McKinsey, see: http://womenintheworkplace.com/.

11. Ina Ganguli, Ricardo Hausmann, and Martina Viarengo, "Gender Differences in Professional Career Dynamics: New Evidence from a Global Law Firm" (Working Paper, Harvard University).

12. M. Ena Inesi and Daniel M. Cable, "When Accomplishments Come Back to Haunt You: The Negative Effect of Competence Signals on Women's Performance Evaluations," *Personnel Psychology* 68 (2014): 615–657; for an early review, see Robert L. Dipboye, "Some Neglected Variables in Research on Discrimination in Appraisals," *Academy of Management Review* 10 (1985): 116–127.

13. Kim M. Elsesser and Janet Lever, "Does Gender Bias against Female Leaders Persist? Quantitative and Qualitative Data from a Large-Scale Survey," *Human Relations* 64 (2011): 1555–1578; Ashleigh Shelby Rosette and Robert W. Livingston, "Failure Is Not an Option for Black Women: Effects of Organizational Performance on Leaders with Single versus Dual-Subordinate Identities," *Journal of Experimental Social Psychology* 48 (2012): 1162–1167; Paul Milgrom and John Roberts, *Economics, Organization and Management* (Englewood Cliffs, NJ: Prentice Hall, 1992), quotation on p. 344.

14. Marc Mangel and Francisco J. Samaniego, "Abraham Wald's Work on Aircraft Survivability," *Journal of the American Statistical Association* 79 (1984): 259–267.

15. United States, National Aeronautics and Space Administration and Presidential Commission on the Space Shuttle Challenger Accident, "Report to the President: Actions to Implement the Recommendations of the Presidential Commission on the Space Shuttle Challenger Accident" (Washington, D.C.: National Aeronautics and Space Administration, 1986), http://history.nasa .gov/rogersrep/actions.pdf; Jack W. Brittain and Sim Sitkin, "Carter Racing" (revised 2000), http://www.deltaleadership.com/case -studies.php.

16. "U.S. Department of Commerce Women's History Month: March 2015," *US Census Bureau News,* February 26, 2015, https://www .census.gov/content/dam/Census/newsroom/facts-for-features/2015 /cb15ff-05_womens_history.pdf; Ian Ayres and Peter Siegelman, "Race and Gender Discrimination in Bargaining for a New Car," *American Economic Review* 85 (1995): 304–321; "statistical discrimination" was first identified by Kenneth J. Arrow, "The Theory of Discrimination," in *Discrimination in Labor Markets,* by Orley Ashenfelter and Albert Rees (Princeton: Princeton University Press, 1973), 3–33, and Edmund S. Phelps, "The Statistical Theory of Racism and Sexism," *American Economic Review* 62 (1972): 659–661.

17. Hundreds of studies have identified a "child salary penalty" for women in the labor market as a whole, while at the same time identifying a marriage and child premium for men: see Michelle J. Budig and Paula England, "The Wage Penalty for Motherhood," *American Sociological Review* 66 (2001): 204–225; Jane Waldfogel, "The Effect of Children on Women's Wages," *American Sociological Review* 62 (1997): 209–217. Much of this child penalty has been attributed to weekly hours, gaps in careers, and occupational choices that accommodate flexibility with hours worked: see Claudia Goldin, "A Grand Gender Convergence: Its Last Chapter," *American Economic Review* 104 (2014): 1091–1119. Jennifer H. Lundquist, Joya Misra, and KerryAnn O'Meara, "Parental Leave Usage by Fathers and Mothers at an American University," *Fathering* 10 (2012): 337–363, found that the

overwhelming majority of faculty taking advantage of parental leave (72 percent) were women. Steven E. Rhoads and Christopher H. Rhoads, "Gender Roles and Infant/Toddler Care: Male and Female Professors on the Tenure Track," *Journal of Social, Evolutionary, and Cultural Psychology* 6 (2012): 13–31, surveyed 181 married tenure-track faculty working at institutions with paid parental-leave policies who had children under the age of two. They found that 69 percent of women took parental leave but only 12 percent of men. Colleen Flaherty Manchester, Lisa Leslie, and Amit Kramer, "Is the Clock Still Ticking? An Evaluation of the Consequences of Stopping the Tenure Clock," *ILR Review* 66, no. 1, Cornell University, 2013, http://digitalcommons.ilr.cornell.edu/ilrreview/vol66/iss1/1, found that faculty who took leave at a midwestern research university were paid less. See also Robert Drago, Carol L. Colbeck, Kai Dawn Stauffer, Amy Pirretti, Kurt Burkum, Jennifer Fazioli, Gabriela Lazzaro, and Tara Habasevich, "The Avoidance of Bias against Caregiving: The Case of Academic Faculty," *American Behavioral Scientist* 49 (2006): 1222–1247, who found that women faculty (in Chemistry and English) engaged in "bias avoidance" to hide family commitments, such as by not taking parental leave or stopping the tenure clock.

18. Kate Antonovics and Brian G. Knight, "A New Look at Racial Profiling: Evidence from the Boston Police Department," *Review of Economics and Statistics* 91 (2009): 163–177; "Racial Profiling and Traffic Stops," National Institute of Justice, http://www.nij.gov/topics/law-enforcement/legitimacy/pages/traffic-stops.aspx.

19. "PISA 2012 Results: The ABC of Gender Equality in Education: Aptitude, Behaviour, Confidence," Organisation for Economic Co-operation and Development (OECD), http://www.oecd.org/pisa/keyfindings/pisa-2012-results-gender.htm; Luigi Guiso, Ferdinando Monte, Paola Sapienza, and Luigi Zingales, "Culture, Gender, and Math," *Science* 320 (2008): 1164–1165; Curtis R. Price, "Gender, Competition, and Managerial Decisions," *Management Science* 58 (2012): 114–122.

20. For the reversal of the gender gap in mathematics, see Guiso et al., "Culture, Gender, and Math"; Pedro Bordalo, Katherine Coffman, Nicola Gennaioli, and Andrei Shleifer, "Stereotypes" (Working Paper, Harvard University, May 2015), http://scholar.harvard.edu /shleifer/publications/stereotypes; for representativeness, Daniel Kahneman and Amos Tversky, "Subjective Probability: A Judgment of Representativeness," in *The Concept of Probability in Psychological Experiments*, ed. Carl-Axel S. Staël von Holstein (Dordrecht: Springer Netherlands, 1972), 25–48.

21. Gordon W. Allport, *The Nature of Prejudice* (Cambridge, MA: Addison-Wesley, 1954); Susan T. Fiske and Steven L. Neuberg, "A Continuum of Impression Formation, from Category-Based to Individuating Processes: Influences of Information and Motivation on Attention and Interpretation," in *Advances in Experimental Social Psychology*, ed. Mark P. Zanna, vol. 23 (Waltham, MA: Academic Press, 1990), 1–74; Henri Tajfel, "Cognitive Aspects of Prejudice," *Journal of Social Issues* 25 (1969): 79–97; Henri Tajfel and Michael Billic, "Familiarity and Categorization in Intergroup Behavior," *Journal of Experimental Social Psychology* 10 (1974): 159–170; Michael I. Norton, Joseph A. Vandello, and John M. Darley, "Casuistry and Social Category Bias," *Journal of Personality and Social Psychology* 87 (2004): 817–831.

22. Mahzarin R. Banaji and Anthony G. Greenwald, *Blindspot: Hidden Biases of Good People* (New York: Delacorte Press, 2013). For the relationship between IAT-sexism and laughing at sexist jokes, see Robert Lynch, "It's Funny Because We Think It's True: Laughter Is Augmented by Implicit Preferences," *Evolution and Human Behavior* 31 (2010): 141–148. For the speed with which we make these associations, see Nalini Ambady and Robert Rosenthal, "Half a Minute: Predicting Teacher Evaluations from Thin Slices of Nonverbal Behavior and Physical Attractiveness," *Journal of Personality and Social Psychology* 64, no. 3 (1993): 431–441.

23. Ernesto Reuben, Pedro Rey-Biel, Paola Sapienza, and Luigi Zingales, "The Emergence of Male Leadership in Competitive Environments,"

Journal of Economic Behavior & Organization, Gender Differences in Risk Aversion and Competition 83 (2012): 111–117.

24. Nicholas D. Kristof and Sheryl WuDunn, *Half the Sky: Turning Oppression into Opportunity for Women Worldwide* (New York: Knopf, 2009). See also www.halftheskymovement.org/.

25. Orley Ashenfelter and Timothy Hannan, "Sex Discrimination and Product Market Competition: The Case of the Banking Industry," *Quarterly Journal of Economics* 101 (1986): 149–173.

26. "The Social Capitalist: Heidi Roizen," My Greenlight, http://mygreenlight.com/system/files/private/coaching/social_capitalist _transcript_-_heidi_roizen.pdf?token=LbR9yvD4YfNqXkqtFW3S.

2. De-Biasing Minds Is Hard

1. "Byrnes, Byrnes & Townsend: Case and Simulation," *Harvard Business Review,* https://hbr.org/product/byrnes-byrnes-townsend-case-and -simulation/395135-PDF-ENG; "Patriot National Insurance Co.: Case and Simulation," *Harvard Business Review,* https://hbr.org /product/patriot-national-insurance-co-case-and-simulation/395134 -PDF-ENG. The student data was analyzed and made available to me in 1999 by Hannah Riley Bowles and James Robinson.

2. Linda Babcock and George Loewenstein, "Explaining Bargaining Impasse: The Role of Self-Serving Biases," *Journal of Economic Perspectives* 11 (1997): 109–126. Amos Tversky and Daniel Kahneman, "Rational Choice and the Framing of Decisions," *Journal of Business* 59 (1986): 251–278, are not optimistic that judgmental biases correct themselves with experience over time. Linda Babcock, Xianghong Wang, and George Loewenstein, "Choosing the Wrong Pond: Social Comparisons in Negotiations that Reflect a Self-Serving Bias," *Quarterly Journal of Economics* 111 (1996): 1–19. For bias awareness and stereotype reactance, see, for example, Laura J. Kray, Leigh Thompson, and Adam Galinsky, "Battle of the Sexes: Gender Stereotype Confirmation and Reactance in Negotiations," *Journal of Personality and Social Psychology* 80 (2001): 942; see also Richard P.

Larrick, "Debiasing," in *Blackwell Handbook of Judgment and Decision Making*, ed. Derek J. Koehler and Nigel Harvey (Blackwell Publishing Ltd, 2004), 316–338, and Max Bazerman and Don A. Moore, *Judgment in Managerial Decision Making*, 7th edition (Hoboken, NJ: Wiley, 2008) for a discussion.

3. For naive realism, see Lee Ross and Andrew Ward, "Naive Realism in Everyday Life: Implications for Social Conflict and Misunderstanding," in *Values and Knowledge*, ed. Edward S. Reed, Elliot Turiel, and Terrance Brown (Sussex: Psychology Press, 2013). Emily Pronin, Daniel Y. Lin, and Lee Ross, "The Bias Blind Spot: Perceptions of Bias in Self Versus Others," *Personality and Social Psychology Bulletin* 28 (2002): 369–381; Emily Pronin, Thomas Gilovich, and Lee Ross, "Objectivity in the Eye of the Beholder: Divergent Perceptions of Bias in Self Versus Others," *Psychological Review* 111 (2004): 781–799; for the halo effect, see Christopher G. Wetzel, Timothy D. Wilson, and James Kort, "The Halo Effect Revisited: Forewarned Is Not Forearmed," *Journal of Experimental Social Psychology* 17 (1981): 427–439; for racial stereotypes, see John F. Dovidio and Samuel L. Gaertner, "Changes in the Expression and Assessment of Racial Prejudice," in *Opening Doors: Perspectives on Race Relations in Contemporary America*, ed. Harry J. Knopke et al. (Tuscaloosa: University of Alabama Press, 1991), 119–148.

4. On awareness having no effect, see Do-Yeong Kim, "Voluntary Controllability of the Implicit Association Test (IAT)," *Social Psychology Quarterly* 66 (2003): 83–96; on suppression not working, see Adam D. Galinsky and Gordon B. Moskowitz, "Perspective-Taking: Decreasing Stereotype Expression, Stereotype Accessibility, and In-Group Favoritism," *Journal of Personality and Social Psychology* 78 (2000): 708–724; Carol T. Kulik, Elissa L. Perry, and Anne C. Bourhis, "Ironic Evaluation Processes: Effects of Thought Suppression on Evaluations of Older Job Applicants," *Journal of Organizational Behavior* 21 (2000): 689–711; Irene V. Blair, Jennifer E. Ma, and Alison P. Lenton, "Imagining Stereotypes Away: The Moderation of Implicit Stereotypes through Mental Imagery," *Journal of Personality and Social Psychology* 81

(2001): 828–841; Giulio Boccato, Vincent Yzerbyt, and Olivier Corneille, "Another Look at the New Look: The Moderating Impact of Stereotypic Beliefs on the Delboeuf Illusion," *TPM-Testing, Psychometrics, Methodology in Applied Psychology* 14 (2007): 151–163; for the meta-analysis, see Alison P. Lenton, Martin Bruder, and Constantine Sedikides, "A Meta-Analysis on the Malleability of Automatic Gender Stereotypes," *Psychology of Women Quarterly* 33 (2009): 183–196. For avoidance tactics and race, see Evan P. Apfelbaum, Samuel R. Sommers, and Michael I. Norton, "Seeing Race and Seeming Racist? Evaluating Strategic Colorblindness in Social Interaction," *Journal of Personality and Social Psychology* 95 (2008): 918–932.

5. On awareness having no effect on, for example, hindsight bias, see Baruch Fischhoff, "Perceived Informativeness of Facts," *Journal of Experimental Psychology: Human Perception and Performance* 3 (1977): 349–358; Baruch Fischhoff, "Debiasing," in *Judgment under Uncertainty* (Cambridge: Cambridge University Press, 1982).

6. Elizabeth Levy Paluck and Donald P. Green, "Prejudice Reduction: What Works? A Review and Assessment of Research and Practice," *Annual Review of Psychology* 60 (2009): 339–367; quotation on p. 356. The 2005 study is Eboni G. Price, Mary Catherine Beach, Tiffany L. Gary, Karen A. Robinson, Aysegul Gozu, Ana Palacio, Carole Smarth, Mollie Jenckes, Carolyn Feuerstein, Eric B. Bass, Neil R. Powe, and Lisa A. Cooper, "A Systematic Review of the Methodological Rigor of Studies Evaluating Cultural Competence Training of Health Professionals," *Academic Medicine* 80 (2005): 578–586.

7. For the field experiment with children, see Melissa A. Houlette, Samuel L. Gaertner, Kelly M. Johnson, Brenda S. Banker, Blake M. Riek, and John F. Dovidio, "Developing a More Inclusive Social Identity: An Elementary School Intervention," *Journal of Social Issues* 60 (2004): 35–55.

8. Alexandra Kalev, Frank Dobbin, and Erin Kelly, "Best Practices or Best Guesses? Assessing the Efficacy of Corporate Affirmative Action

and Diversity Policies," *American Sociological Review* 71 (2006): 589–617; Frank Dobbin, Alexandra Kalev, and Erin Kelly, "Diversity Management in Corporate America," *Contexts* 6 (2007): 21–27.

9. For cognitive overload and ego depletion, see, for example, Mark Muraven, Dianne M. Tice, and Roy F. Baumeister, "Self-Control as a Limited Resource: Regulatory Depletion Patterns," *Journal of Personality and Social Psychology* 74 (1998): 774–789.

10. For the Taiwan study, see Wen-Bin Chiou, Chao-Chin Yang, and Chin-Sheng Wan, "Ironic Effects of Dietary Supplementation: Illusory Invulnerability Created by Taking Dietary Supplements Licenses Health-Risk Behaviors," *Psychological Science* 22 (2011): 1081–1086. For moral licensing after having endorsed Obama, see Daniel A. Effron, Jessica S. Cameron, and Benoît Monin, "Endorsing Obama Licenses Favoring Whites," *Journal of Experimental Social Psychology* 45 (2009): 590–593. For gender bias and moral licensing, see Emilio J. Castilla and Stephen Benard, "The Paradox of Meritocracy in Organizations," *Administrative Science Quarterly* 55 (2010): 543–676. For the cost of diversity training, see Fay Hansen, "Diversity's Business Case Doesn't Add Up," *Workforce* 4 (2003): 28. For the meta-analysis, Lenton, Bruder, and Sedikides, "A Meta-Analysis on the Malleability of Automatic Gender Stereotypes."

11. Babcock and Loewenstein, "Explaining Bargaining Impasse: The Role of Self-Serving Biases"; Max H. Bazerman and Margaret A. Neale, "Heuristics in Negotiation: Limitations to Effective Dispute Resolution," in *Judgment and Decision Making: An Interdisciplinary Reader*, ed. H. R. Arkes and K. R. Hammond (New York: Cambridge University Press, 1986), 311–321; Adam D. Galinsky and Gordon B. Moskowitz, "Perspective-Taking: Decreasing Stereotype Expression, Stereotype Accessibility, and In-Group Favoritism," *Journal of Personality and Social Psychology* 78 (2000): 708–724; Victoria M. Esses and John F. Dovidio, "The Role of Emotions in Determining Willingness to Engage in Intergroup Contact," *Personality and Social Psychology Bulletin* 28 (2002): 1202–1214; Paluck and Green, "Prejudice Reduction." For the intervention in India, see Ritwik

Banerjee and Nabanita Datta Gupta, "Awareness Programs and Change in Taste-Based Caste Prejudice," *PLOS ONE* 10 (2015): 1–17; quotation on p. 5.

12. For consider-the-opposite strategies, see Charles G. Lord, Mark R. Lepper, and Elizabeth Preston, "Considering the Opposite: A Corrective Strategy for Social Judgment," *Journal of Personality and Social Psychology* 47 (1984): 1231–1243. For a discussion, see Larrick, "Debiasing"; Linda Babcock, George Loewenstein, and Samuel Issacharoff, "Creating Convergence: Debiasing Biased Litigants," *Law & Social Inquiry* 22 (1997): 913–925; Babcock and Loewenstein, "Explaining Bargaining Impasse"; Calvin K. Lai, Maddalena Marini, Steven A. Lehr, Carlo Cerruti, Jiyun-Elizabeth L. Shin, Jennifer A. Joy-Gaba, Arnold K. Ho, Bethany A. Teachman, Sean P. Wojcik, Spassena P. Koleva, Rebecca S. Frazier, Larisa Heiphetz, Eva E. Chen, Rhiannon N. Turner, Jonathan Haidt, Selin Kesebir, Carlee Beth Hawkins, Hillary S. Schaefer, Sandro Rubichi, Giuseppe Sartori, Christopher M. Dial, N. Sriram, Mahzarin R. Banaji, and Brian A. Nosek, "Reducing Implicit Racial Preferences: I. A Comparative Investigation of 17 Interventions," *Journal of Experimental Psychology: General* 143, no. 4 (2014): 1765–1785; for *consider-the-counterstereotype* and gender, see the meta-analysis by Lenton, Bruder, and Sedikides, "A Meta-Analysis on the Malleability of Automatic Gender Stereotypes."

13. On statistical reasoning and stereotypes, see Mark Schaller, Charles H. Asp, Michelle Ceynar Roseil, and Stephen J. Heim, "Training in Statistical Reasoning Inhibits the Formation of Erroneous Group Stereotypes," *Personality and Social Psychology Bulletin* 22 (1996): 829–844.

14. Irving Janis, *Groupthink: Psychological Studies of Policy Decisions and Fiascoes*, 2nd edition (Boston: Cengage Learning, 1982); Cass R. Sunstein and Reid Hastie, *Wiser: Getting Beyond Groupthink to Make Groups Smarter* (Boston: Harvard Business Review Press, 2014).

15. For the wisdom of crowds, see James Surowiecki, *The Wisdom of Crowds*, reprint edition (New York: Anchor, 2005). For aggregation

rules, see Reid Hastie and Tatsuya Kameda, "The Robust Beauty of Majority Rules in Group Decisions," *Psychological Review* 112 (2005): 494–508. For a discussion of the crowd-within approaches, see Jack B. Soll, Katherine L. Milkman, and John W. Payne, "A User's Guide to Debiasing," in *Handbook of Judgment and Decision Making*, ed. Gideon Keren and George Wu (Malden: Wiley Blackwell, 2015), vol. 2, 924–951.

16. Elizabeth Levy Paluck, "Reducing Intergroup Prejudice and Conflict Using the Media: A Field Experiment in Rwanda," *Journal of Personality and Social Psychology* 96 (2009): 574–587.

17. Kurt Lewin, "Group Decision and Social Change," in *Readings in Social Psychology*, ed. Eugene L. Hartley and Theodore M. Newcomb (New York: Henry Holt and Company, 1947); Bazerman and Moore, *Judgment in Managerial Decision Making*.

18. For the relevance of process, and in particular, having voice in the process, see E. Allan Lind and Tom R. Tyler, *The Social Psychology of Procedural Justice* (New York: Springer, 1988), and Bruno S. Frey, Matthias Benz, and Alois Stutzer, "Introducing Procedural Utility: Not Only What, but Also How Matters," *Journal of Institutional and Theoretical Economics* (JITE) (2004): 377–401.

19. Evan P. Apfelbaum, Nicole M. Stephens, and Ray E. Reagans, "Beyond One-Size Fits-All: Tailoring Diversity Approaches to the Representation of Social Groups" (Working Paper, MIT, 2015), quotation on p. 4. For earlier work on teams and organizational diversity, see Robin J. Ely and David A. Thomas, "Cultural Diversity at Work: The Effects of Diversity Perspectives on Work Group Processes and Outcomes," *Administrative Science Quarterly* 46 (2001): 229–273.

3. Doing It Yourself Is Risky

1. Iris Bohnet and Hannah Riley Bowles, "Introduction," *Negotiation Journal* 24 (2008): 389–392.

2. Hannah Riley Bowles, Linda Babcock, and Lei Lai, "Social Incentives for Gender Differences in the Propensity to Initiate Negotiations:

Sometimes It Does Hurt to Ask," *Organizational Behavior and Human Decision Processes* 103 (2007): 84–103; Hannah Riley Bowles and Michele Gelfand, "Status and the Evaluation of Workplace Deviance," *Psychological Science* 21 (2010): 49–54.

3. Linda Babcock and Sara Laschever, *Women Don't Ask: The High Cost of Avoiding Negotiation—and Positive Strategies for Change* (New York: Bantam, 2003); Fiona Greig, "Propensity to Negotiate and Career Advancement: Evidence from an Investment Bank That Women Are on a 'Slow Elevator,'" *Negotiation Journal* 24 (2008): 495–508.

4. Jenny Säve-Söderbergh, "Are Women Asking for Low Wages? Gender Differences in Wage Bargaining Strategies and Ensuing Bargaining Success" (Working Paper Series, Swedish Institute for Social Research, 2007), https://ideas.repec.org/p/hhs/sofiwp/2007_007.html; David Blackaby, Alison L. Booth, and Jeff Frank, "Outside Offers and the Gender Pay Gap: Empirical Evidence from the UK Academic Labour Market," *Economic Journal* 115 (2005): 81–107.

5. Jennifer Lawrence, "Why Do I Make Less Than My Male Co-Stars?" *Lenny*, October 13, 2015, http://us11.campaign-archive1.com/?u=a5b04a26aae05a24bc4efb63e&id=64e6f35176&e=fe292e1416#wage.

6. Hannah Riley Bowles, Linda Babcock, and Kathleen L. McGinn, "Constraints and Triggers: Situational Mechanics of Gender in Negotiation," *Journal of Personality and Social Psychology* 89 (2005): 951–965; Andreas Leibbrandt and John A. List, "Do Women Avoid Salary Negotiations? Evidence from a Large-Scale Natural Field Experiment," *Management Science* 61 (2014): 2016–2024.

7. Laszlo Bock, *Work Rules! Insights from Inside Google that Will Transform How You Live and Lead* (New York: Twelve, 2015). Francesca Gino, Caroline Ashley Wilmuth, and Alison Wood Brooks, "Compared to Men, Women View Professional Advancement as Equally Attainable, but Less Desirable," *Proceedings of the National Academy of Sciences USA* 112 (2015): 12354–12359.

8. Laura A. Liswood, *The Loudest Duck: Moving Beyond Diversity While Embracing Differences to Achieve Success at Work* (Hoboken: Wiley, 2009).

9. "Hannah Riley Bowles on Katie Couric's 'Lean In' Panel Discussion," WAPPP Wire, May 1, 2013, http://wapppwire.blogspot.com/2013/05/hannah-riley-bowles-on-katie-couric-in.html.

10. Bowles, Babcock, and McGinn, "Constraints and Triggers," 951–965.

11. Hanna Bäck, Marc Debus, and Jochen Müller, "Who Takes the Parliamentary Floor? The Role of Gender in Speech-Making in the Swedish Riksdag," *Political Research Quarterly* 67 (2014): 504–518; Victoria L. Brescoll, "Who Takes the Floor and Why: Gender, Power, and Volubility in Organizations," *Administrative Science Quarterly* 56 (2011): 622–641.

12. Katherine Baldiga Coffman, "Evidence on Self-Stereotyping and the Contribution of Ideas," *Quarterly Journal of Economics* 129 (2014): 1625–1660.

13. Bowles, Babcock, and McGinn, "Constraints and Triggers," 951–965; Emily T. Amanatullah and Michael W. Morris, "Negotiating Gender Roles: Gender Differences in Assertive Negotiating Are Mediated by Women's Fear of Backlash and Attenuated When Negotiating on Behalf of Others," *Journal of Personality and Social Psychology* 98 (2010): 256–267. Jens Mazei, Joachim Hüffmeier, Philipp Alexander Freund, Alice F. Stuhlmacher, Lena Bilke and Guido Hertel, "A Meta-Analysis on Gender Differences in Negotiation Outcomes and Their Moderators," *Psychological Bulletin* 141 (2015): 85–104 also found gender differences to be decreasing with experience.

14. Kristina A. Diekmann, " 'Implicit Justifications' and Self-Serving Group Allocations," *Journal of Organizational Behavior* 18 (1997): 3–16; Marianne Bertrand, Emir Kamenica, and Jessica Pan, "Gender Identity and Relative Income within Households," *Quarterly Journal of Economics* 130 (2015): 571–614; Tara Watson and Sara McLanahan, "Marriage Meets the Joneses: Relative Income, Identity, and Marital Status," *Journal of Human Resources* 46 (2011): 482–517; Ina Ganguli, Ricardo Hausmann, and Martina Viarengo, "Marriage, Education and Assortative Mating in Latin America," *Applied Economics Letters* 21 (2014): 806–811.

15. Nava Ashraf, "Spousal Control and Intra-Household Decision Making: An Experimental Study in the Philippines," *American Economic Review* 99 (2009): 1245–1277.

16. Christopher Udry, "Gender, Agricultural Production, and the Theory of the Household," *Journal of Political Economy* 104 (1996): 1010–1046; Esther Duflo and Christopher Udry, "Intrahousehold Resource Allocation in Cote d'Ivoire: Social Norms, Separate Accounts and Consumption Choices" (NBER Working Paper, May 2004), http://www.nber.org/papers/w10498; Alberto Alesina, Paola Giuliano, and Nathan Nunn, "On the Origins of Gender Roles: Women and the Plough," *Quarterly Journal of Economics* 128 (2013): 469–530.

17. Nava Ashraf, Corinne Low, Kathleen McGinn, and Remy Mukonka, "Negotiating a Better Future," Harvard Business School Profile, 2012, http://www.hbs.edu/faculty/Profile%20Files/GN_OnePage_9 -18-12_67dedee3-ef8b-467f-88e3-80097232ecf5.pdf.

18. Alice F. Stuhlmacher and Eileen Linnabery, "Gender and Negotiation: A Social Role Analysis," *Handbook of Research on Negotiation* (Northampton: Edward Elgar Publishing, 2013), 221–248; Maria Konnikova, "Lean Out: The Dangers for Women Who Negotiate," *New Yorker*, June 10, 2014, http://www.newyorker.com/science/maria -konnikova/lean-out-the-dangers-for-women-who-negotiate.

19. Claudia Goldin, *Understanding the Gender Gap: An Economic History of American Women* (New York: Oxford University Press, 1992); Francine D. Blau and Lawrence M. Kahn, "Gender Differences in Pay," *Journal of Economic Perspectives* 14 (2000): 75–99; Claudia Goldin and Lawrence F. Katz, "The Power of the Pill: Oral Contraceptives and Women's Career and Marriage Decisions" (NBER Working Paper, February 2000), http://www.nber.org/papers/w7527; Marianne Bertrand, Claudia Goldin, and Lawrence F. Katz, "Dynamics of the Gender Gap for Young Professionals in the Financial and Corporate Sectors," *American Economic Journal: Applied Economics* 2 (2010): 228–255.

20. Anne-Marie Slaughter, *Unfinished Business: Women Men Work Family* (New York: Random House, 2015); Najy Benhassine, Florencia

Devoto, Esther Duflo, Pascaline Dupas, and Victor Pouliquen, "Turning a Shove into a Nudge? A 'Labeled Cash Transfer' for Education" (NBER Working Paper, 2013), https://ideas.repec.org/p /nbr/nberwo/19227.html.

21. Department of Labor, "OFCCP News Release: Rule to Improve Pay Transparency for Employees of Federal Contractors Proposed by US Labor Department," http://www.dol.gov/opa/media/press/ofccp /OFCCP20141696.htm; "Valerie Jarrett: Wage 'Transparency' Will Help Employers 'Avoid Lawsuits,'" *CNS News*, April 8, 2014, http://www.cnsnews.com/news/article/susan-jones/valerie-jarrett -wage-transparency-will-help-employers-avoid-lawsuits.

4. Getting Help Only Takes You So Far

1. Robin J. Ely, Herminia Ibarra, and Deborah Kolb, "Taking Gender into Account: Theory and Design for Women's Leadership Development Programs" (Harvard Business School, September 1, 2011), http://www.hbs.edu/faculty/Pages/item.aspx?num=41610. For more information on the survey, see Andrea Gutmann and Petra Seisl, "WoMENizing: Eine empirische Studie zum Themenfeld Frauen und Karriere," January 2014, http://www.plan-ag.net/uploads/index_64 _230630819.pdf; quotation from "Mentoring für Frauen: Was bringt die Frauenförderung?" *Die Zeit*, March 2015, sec. Beruf, http://www .zeit.de/karriere/beruf/2014-12/frauen-foerder-programme -wirksamkeit/komplettansicht; "Why Leadership-Development Programs Fail," McKinsey & Company, http://www.mckinsey.com /insights/leading_in_the_21st_century/why_leadership-development _programs_fail; Harrison Monarth, "Evaluate Your Leadership Development Program," *Harvard Business Review*, January 22, 2015, https://hbr.org/2015/01/evaluate-your-leadership-development -program.

2. Frank Dobbin and Alexandra Kalev, "The Origins and Effects of Corporate Diversity Programs" (Rochester, NY: Social Science Research Network, 2013), http://papers.ssrn.com/abstract=2274946.

3. See Donna K. Ginther and Shulamit Kahn, "Women in Economics: Moving Up or Falling Off the Academic Career Ladder?" *Journal of Economic Perspectives* 18 (2004): 193–214; the mentoring program was analyzed in Francine D. Blau, Janet M. Currie, Rachel T. A. Croson, and Donna K. Ginther, "Can Mentoring Help Female Assistant Professors? Interim Results from a Randomized Trial," *American Economic Review* 100 (2010): 348–352.

4. Tammy D. Allen, Lillian T. Eby, Mark L. Poteet, Elizabeth Lentz, and Lizzette Lima, "Career Benefits Associated with Mentoring for Protegés: A Meta-Analysis," *Journal of Applied Psychology* 89 (2004): 127–136; David L. DuBois, Bruce E. Holloway, Jeffrey C. Valentine, and Harris Cooper, "Effectiveness of Mentoring Programs for Youth: A Meta-Analytic Review," *American Journal of Community Psychology* 30 (2002): 157–197; Lillian T. Eby, Tammy D. Allen, Sarah C. Evans, and Thomas Ng, "Does Mentoring Matter? A Multidisciplinary Meta-Analysis Comparing Mentored and Non-Mentored Individuals," *Journal of Vocational Behavior,* Mentoring, 72, no. 2 (April 2008): 254–267; "The Chronicle of Evidence-Based Mentoring," http://chronicle.umbmentoring.org/.

5. Herminia Ibarra, Nancy M. Carter, and Christine Silva, "Why Men Still Get More Promotions than Women," *Harvard Business Review,* September 2010, https://hbr.org/2010/09/why-men-still-get-more-promotions-than-women; on arguing for sponsorship, see Sylvia Ann Hewlett, *Forget a Mentor, Find a Sponsor: The New Way to Fast-Track Your Career* (Boston: Harvard Business Review Press, 2013).

6. Nancy R. Baldiga and Katherine Baldiga Coffman, "Lab Evidence on the Effects of Sponsorship on Competitive Preferences" (Working Paper, 2015), https://drive.google.com/file/d/0B2fD6UtLe0bcb VZmLUtxNjQxNms/view.

7. Iris Bohnet and Farzad Saidi, "Informational Differences and Performance: Experimental Evidence" (Working Paper, Harvard Kennedy School of Government, Cambridge, MA, 2015): http://wappp.hks .harvard.edu/files/wappp/files/informational_differences_and _performance_0.pdf; for religion-based networks and their impact on

trust among Jewish diamond dealers, Yoram Ben-Porath, "The F-Connection: Families, Friends, and Firms and the Organization of Exchange," *Population and Development Review* 6, no. 1 (1980): 1–30; for country-of-origin or same-language social networks facilitating job seeking, see Per-Anders Edin, Peter Fredriksson, and Olof Åslund, "Ethnic Enclaves and the Economic Success of Immigrants— Evidence from a Natural Experiment," *Quarterly Journal of Economics* 118 (2003): 329–357; for business relationships, see C. Kirabo Jackson and Henry S. Schneider, "Do Social Connections Reduce Moral Hazard? Evidence from the New York City Taxi Industry," *American Economic Journal: Applied Economics* 3 (2011): 244–267; and for participation in welfare and social programs, see Marianne Bertrand, Erzo F. P. Luttmer, and Sendhil Mullainathan, "Network Effects and Welfare Cultures," *Quarterly Journal of Economics* 115 (2000): 1019–1055, and David N. Figlio, Sarah Hamersma, and Jeffrey Roth, "Information Shocks and the Take-Up of Social Programs," *Journal of Policy Analysis and Management* (July 1, 2015): 1–25.

8. Herminia Ibarra, "Homophily and Differential Returns: Sex Differences in Network Structure and Access in an Advertising Firm," *Administrative Science Quarterly* 37 (1992): 422–447; Herminia Ibarra, "Network Assessment Exercise: Executive Version, *Harvard Business Review*," https://hbr.org/product/network-assessment -exercise-executive-version/497003-PDF-ENG; Dobbin and Kalev, "The Origins and Effects of Corporate Diversity Programs."

9. "New Campaign Encourages Men to Take Up Flexible Work Patterns," NewsComAu, http://www.news.com.au/lifestyle /parenting/new-campaign-encourages-men-to-take-up-flexible-work -patterns/story-fnet08ui-1227323658455; "Equilibrium Challenge," http://equilibriumchallenge.com.au/; *The Workplace Gender Equality Agency*, www.wgea.gov.au/; "Teilzeitmann," TeilzeitKarriere, http://www.teilzeitkarriere.ch/teilzeitmann.html; "Sensitising Men and Companies," NRP 60 Gender Equality, http://www.nfp60.ch/E /knowledge-transfer-and-communication/in-focus/Pages/_xc _project_part_time_man.aspx.

10. George Loewenstein, "Out of Control: Visceral Influences on Behavior," *Organizational Behavior and Human Decision Processes* 65 (1996): 272–292; Todd Rogers and Max H. Bazerman, "Future Lock-in: Future Implementation Increases Selection of 'Should' Choices," *Organizational Behavior and Human Decision Processes* 106 (2008): 1–20; for active choice and 401(k) enrollment, see Gabriel D. Carroll, James J. Choi, David Laibson, Brigitte C. Madrian, and Andrew Metrick, "Optimal Defaults and Active Decisions," *Quarterly Journal of Economics* 124 (2009): 1639–1674; Richard Thaler and Shlomo Benartzi, "Save More Tomorrow: Using Behavioral Economics to Increase Employee Saving," *Journal of Political Economy* 112 (2004): S164–187; Richard H. Thaler, *Misbehaving: The Making of Behavioral Economics* (New York: W.W. Norton & Company, 2015); for pre-committing to going to the gym, see Stefano DellaVigna and Ulrike Malmendier, "Paying Not to Go to the Gym," *American Economic Review* 96 (2006): 694–719; for pre-commitment and nutrition, see Brian Wansink, *Slim by Design: Mindless Eating Solutions for Everyday Life* (New York: William Morrow, 2014); "stickK," http://www.stickk.com/; Richard H. Thaler and Cass R. Sunstein, *Nudge: Improving Decisions About Health, Wealth, and Happiness,* revised and expanded edition (New York: Penguin Books, 2009).

11. Abhijit Banerjee, Esther Duflo, Rachel Glennerster, and Cynthia Kinnan, "The Miracle of Microfinance? Evidence from a Randomized Evaluation," *American Economic Journal: Applied Economics* 7 (2015): 22–53.

12. For the evidence on business training in India, see Erica Field, Seema Jayachandran, and Rohini Pande, "Do Traditional Institutions Constrain Female Entrepreneurship? A Field Experiment on Business Training in India," *American Economic Review* 100 (2010): 125–129; for an excellent overview of the evidence on financial capacity building, see "Enhancing Financial Capability and Behavior in Low- and Middle-Income Countries," World Bank, http://documents .worldbank.org/curated/en/2014/01/19770351/enhancing-financial -capability-behavior-low—middle-income-countries.

13. For simplicity in the Dominican Republic, see Alejandro Drexler, Greg Fischer, and Antoinette Schoar, "Keeping It Simple: Financial Literacy and Rules of Thumb," *American Economic Journal: Applied Economics* 6 (2014): 1–31; Sendhil Mullainathan and Eldar Shafir, *Scarcity: The New Science of Having Less and How It Defines Our Lives* (New York: Picador, 2014). For personalized training in India, see Fenella Carpena, Shawn Cole, Jeremy Shapiro, and Bilal Zia, "The ABCs of Financial Literacy—Experimental Evidence on Attitudes, Behavior and Cognitive Biases" (Poverty Action Lab Working Paper): https://www.povertyactionlab.org/sites/default/files/Improving%20Financial%20Capabilities%202.pdf.

14. Edwin A. Locke, Gary P. Latham, Ken J. Smith, and Robert E. Wood, *A Theory of Goal Setting and Task Performance* (Englewood Cliffs, NJ: Prentice Hall College, 1990); for the importance of the goals, see Dilip Soman and Min Zhao, "The Fewer the Better: Number of Goals and Savings Behavior," *Journal of Marketing Research* 48, no. 6 (2011): 944–957.

15. Lisa D. Ordóñez, Maurice E. Schweitzer, Adam D. Galinsky, and Max H. Bazerman, "Goals Gone Wild: The Systematic Side Effects of Overprescribing Goal Setting," *Academy of Management Perspectives* 23, no. 1 (2009): 6–16; Daniel J. Simons and Christopher F. Chabris, "Gorillas in Our Midst: Sustained Inattentional Blindness for Dynamic Events," *Perception* 28, no. 9 (1999): 1059–1074; Max H. Bazerman and Dolly Chugh, "Decisions without Blinders," *Harvard Business Review* 84, no. 1 (January 2006): 88–97.

16. For plan making and voting, see David W. Nickerson and Todd Rogers, "Do You Have a Voting Plan?: Implementation Intentions, Voter Turnout, and Organic Plan Making," *Psychological Science* 21, no. 2 (2010): 194–199; for exercise, see Sarah Milne, Sheina Orbell, and Paschal Sheeran, "Combining Motivational and Volitional Interventions to Promote Exercise Participation: Protection Motivation Theory and Implementation Intentions," *British Journal of Health Psychology* 7 (2002): 163–184; for flu shot take-up, see Katherine L. Milkman, John Beshears, James J. Choi, David Laibson,

and Brigitte C. Madrian, "Using Implementation Intentions Prompts to Enhance Influenza Vaccination Rates," *Proceedings of the National Academy of Sciences USA* 108 (2011): 10415–10420; and for meeting deadlines, see Utpal M. Dholakia, Richard P. Bagozzi, and Lisa Klein Pearo, "A Social Influence Model of Consumer Participation in Network- and Small-Group-Based Virtual Communities," *International Journal of Research in Marketing* 21 (2004): 241–263.

17. For feedback and goal-setting, see Lawrence J. Becker, "Joint Effect of Feedback and Goal Setting on Performance: A Field Study of Residential Energy Conservation," *Journal of Applied Psychology* 63 (1978): 428–433; for networking in Uganda, see Kathryn Vasilaky and Kenneth Leonard, "As Good as the Networks They Keep? Expanding Farmer's Social Networks Using Randomized Encouragement in Rural Uganda" (Working Paper, Princeton University, 2014), http://paa2011.princeton.edu/papers/111216; for networking in India, see Benjamin Feigenberg, Erica Field, and Rohini Pande, "The Economic Returns to Social Interaction: Experimental Evidence from Microfinance," *Review of Economic Studies* 80 (2013): 1459–1483; Emily Breza and Arun G. Chandrasekhar, "Social Networks, Reputation And Commitment: Evidence From A Savings Monitors Experiment" (NBER Working Paper, May 2015), http://http://www.nber.org/papers/w21169; for a discussion more generally, see World Development Report 2015: Mind, Society and Behavior (Washington, DC: World Bank Reports, 2015), https://openknowledge.worldbank.org/handle/10986/20597.

5. Applying Data to People Decisions

1. To learn more, see the Wharton People Analytics conference, organized by Adam Grant and Cade Massey of the Wharton School: http://www.peopleanalyticsconference.com/.

2. "The World Factbook," Central Intelligence Agency, https://www.cia.gov/library/publications/the-world-factbook/rankorder/2095rank.html.

3. Viktor Mayer-Schönberger and Kenneth Cukier, *Big Data: A Revolution that Will Transform How We Live, Work, and Think* (Boston: Eamon Dolan/Mariner Books, 2014); Sasha Issenberg, *The Victory Lab: The Secret Science of Winning Campaigns* (New York: Broadway Books, 2013); Benedict Carey, " 'Dream Team' of Behavioral Scientists Advised Obama Campaign," *New York Times,* November 12, 2012, http://www.nytimes.com/2012/11/13/health /dream-team-of-behavioral-scientists-advised-obama-campaign.html; "Are Indian Companies Making Enough Sense of Big Data?" (LiveMint, July 23, 2014), http://www.livemint.com/Industry /bUQo8xQ3gStSAy5II9lxoK/Are-Indian-companies-making -enough-sense-of-Big-Data.html.

4. An evaluation of a parental leave program in Quebec, in which in contrast to other Canadian provinces, fathers enjoy an individual, nontransferable right to parental leave, a five-week "daddy quota," proved Google right. Using data from time-diaries, it finds a jump of 250 percent in fathers' participation in the program and a long-term increase in how much time they spend at home. Interestingly, the quota worked even if it did not change a binding constraint for fathers. Labeling it as "daddy-only" produced a behavioral response compelling fathers to take the leave and changing how fathers and mothers spend their time, reducing the typical sex specialization. See Ankita Patnaik, "Reserving Time for Daddy: The Short and Long-Run Consequences of Fathers' Quotas" (SSRN Scholarly Paper, Rochester, NY, January 15, 2015), http://papers.ssrn.com /abstract=2475970.

5. Laszlo Bock, *Work Rules!: Insights from Inside Google That Will Transform How You Live and Lead* (New York: Twelve, 2015); Farhad Manjoo, "The Happiness Machine," *Slate,* January 21, 2013, http://www.slate .com/articles/technology/technology/2013/01/google_people _operations_the_secrets_of_the_world_s_most_scientific_human .single.html. For research on happiness and, specifically, on how money translates into happiness, see Elizabeth Dunn and Michael Norton, *Happy Money: The Science of Happier Spending* (New York:

Simon & Schuster, 2014); Daniel Gilbert, *Stumbling on Happiness* (New York: Vintage, 2007). For experimental evidence on savings, see John Beshears, James J. Choi, David Laibson, and Brigitte C. Madrian, "Simplification and Saving," *Journal of Economic Behavior & Organization* 95 (2013): 130–145; Brigitte C. Madrian and Dennis F. Shea, "The Power of Suggestion: Inertia in 401(k) Participation and Savings Behavior," *Quarterly Journal of Economics* 116 (2001): 1149–1187.

6.   Janice Fanning Madden, "Performance-Support Bias and the Gender Pay Gap among Stockbrokers," *Gender & Society* 26 (2012): 488–518.

7.   For the 2009 report, see "A Study on the Status of Women Faculty In Science at MIT," 2009, http://web.mit.edu/fnl/women/women.html; for the 2011 report: "A Report on the Status of Women Faculty in the Schools of Science and Engineering at MIT, 2011," http://newsoffice .mit.edu//sites/mit.edu.newsoffice/files/documents/women-report -2011.pdf; Kate Zernike, "The Reluctant Feminist," *New York Times,* April 8, 2001, sec. Education, http://www.nytimes.com/2001/04/08 /education/08ED-FEMI.html; Cathy Young, "Sex and Science," *Salon,* April 12, 2001, http://www.salon.com/2001/04/12/science_women/.

8.   "EDGE Is the Global Business Certification for Gender Equality," EDGE, http://www.edge-cert.org/; "World Bank Group to Seek Key Certification on Workplace Equality," World Bank, http://www .worldbank.org/en/news/feature/2015/03/11/world-bank-group-to -seek-key-certification-on-workplace-equality.

9.   For gender bias in comments in performance reviews, see this illuminating article (not based on a random sample) by Kieran Snyder, "The Abrasiveness Trap: High Achieving Men and Women Are Described Differently in Reviews," *Fortune,* August 26, 2014, http://fortune.com/2014/08/26/performance-review-gender-bias/; Emilio J. Castilla, "Gender, Race, and Meritocracy in Organizational Careers," *Academy of Management Proceedings* no. 1 (2005): G1–6; Emilio J. Castilla and Stephen Benard, "The Paradox of Meritocracy in Organizations," *Administrative Science Quarterly* 55 (2010): 543–676; Benoît Monin and Dale T. Miller, "Moral Credentials and the Expression of Prejudice," *Journal of Personality and Social Psychology* 81

(2001): 33–43; Maura A. Belliveau, "Engendering Inequity? How Social Accounts Create vs. Merely Explain Unfavorable Pay Outcomes for Women," *Organization Science* 23 (2011): 1154–1174.

10. Claudia Goldin, *Understanding the Gender Gap: An Economic History of American Women* (New York: Oxford University Press, 1992); Ulrike Muench, Jody Sindelar, Susan H. Busch, and Peter I. Buerhaus, "Salary Differences between Male and Female Registered Nurses in the United States," *JAMA* 313 (2015): 1265–1267.

11. For Australia's work on the gender pay gap: "Australia's Gender Equality Scorecard," Workplace Gender Equality Agency, Australian Government, https://www.wgea.gov.au/sites/default/files/2013-14 _summary_report_website.pdf. For a report on the United States' gender pay gap: "The Simple Truth about the Gender Pay Gap: 2015 Edition," American Association of University Women, http://www .aauw.org/files/2015/02/The-Simple-Truth_Spring-2015.pdf. For a report on the gender pay gap in the European Union: "Gender Pay Gap Statistics—Statistics Explained," EuroStat, European Union, http://ec.europa.eu/eurostat/statistics-explained/index.php/Gender _pay_gap_statistics; and for a report on the gender wage gap in OECD countries see "Gender Wage Gap," OECD, http://www.oecd .org/gender/data/genderwagegap.htm.

12. The literature on the gender pay gap is vast. I have found the following articles particularly helpful: Claudia Goldin and Solomon Polachek, "Residual Differences by Sex: Perspectives on the Gender Gap in Earnings," *American Economic Review* 77 (1987): 143–151; Francine D. Blau and Lawrence M. Kahn, "Understanding International Differences in the Gender Pay Gap," *Journal of Labor Economics* 21 (2003): 106; Francine D. Blau and Lawrence M. Kahn, "The US Gender Pay Gap in the 1990s: Slowing Convergence," *Industrial & Labor Relations Review* 60 (2006): 45–66; Wiji Arulampalam, Alison L. Booth, and Mark L. Bryan, "Is There a Glass Ceiling over Europe? Exploring the Gender Pay Gap across the Wage Distribution," *Industrial & Labor Relations Review* 60 (2007): 163–186; Heather Antecol, Anneke Jong, and Michael Steinberger, "The

Sexual Orientation Wage Gap: The Role of Occupational Sorting and Human Capital," *Industrial and Labor Relations Review* 61 (2008): 518–543; Shelley J. Correll, Stephen Benard, and In Paik, "Getting a Job: Is There a Motherhood Penalty?" *American Journal of Sociology* 112 (2007): 1297–1339; Alexandra Killewald, "A Reconsideration of the Fatherhood Premium: Marriage, Coresidence, Biology, and Fathers' Wages," *American Sociological Review* 78 (2013): 96–116.

13. D. Brian McNatt, "Ancient Pygmalion Joins Contemporary Management: A Meta-Analysis of the Result," *Journal of Applied Psychology* 85 (2000): 314–322.

14. Lisa L. Shu, Nina Mazar, Francesca Gino, Dan Ariely, and Max H. Bazerman, "Signing at the Beginning Makes Ethics Salient and Decreases Dishonest Self-Reports in Comparison to Signing at the End," *Proceedings of the National Academy of Sciences USA* 109 (2012): 15197–15200.

15. On formal rules and gender pay gaps in fixed and in variable pay: Marta M. Elvira and Mary E. Graham, "Not Just a Formality: Pay System Formalization and Sex-Related Earnings Effects," *Organization Science* 13 (2002): 601–617; Barbara F. Reskin and Debra Branch McBrier, "Why Not Ascription? Organizations' Employment of Male and Female Managers," *American Sociological Review* 65 (2000): 210–233 find that large employers with formal personnel procedures have more women in management. In a longitudinal study, James N. Baron, Michael T. Hannan, Greta Hsu, and Özgecan Koçak, "In the Company of Women: Gender Inequality and the Logic of Bureaucracy in Start-Up Firms," *Work and Occupations* 34 (2007): 35–66 find that more women work in such firms six years later; on Google, see Bock, *Work Rules!*

16. Some studies have found that evaluators tend to inflate their ratings and be too lenient with their direct reports, and they also constrain the range of ratings, decreasing variance. Rankings do not guard against favoritism, and the system can be gamed by rotating top performance across years, with losers in one year turning into winners in the next. Generally, rankings tend to work better when used for larger groups and where they do not crowd out cooperation among

employees. For a discussion of performance management, see Elaine D. Pulakos and Ryan S. O'Leary, "Why Is Performance Management Broken?" *Industrial and Organizational Psychology* 4 (2011): 146–164, and James N. Baron and David M. Kreps, "Chapter 10: Performance Evaluation," in *Strategic Human Resources: Frameworks for General Managers* (New York: Wiley, 1999).

17. Iwan Barankay, "Rank Incentives Evidence from a Randomized Workplace Experiment" (under revision, University of Pennsylvania, Wharton School of Business, July 7, 2012). For a meta-analysis of psychology studies about feedback, see Avraham N. Kluger and Angelo DeNisi, "The Effects of Feedback Interventions on Performance: A Historical Review, a Meta-Analysis, and a Preliminary Feedback Intervention Theory," *Psychological Bulletin* 119 (1996): 254–284.

18. Charles Duhigg, "How Companies Learn Your Secrets," *New York Times,* February 16, 2012, http://www.nytimes.com/2012/02/19 /magazine/shopping-habits.html; David Lazer, Ryan Kennedy, Gary King, and Alessandro Vespignani, "The Parable of Google Flu: Traps in Big Data Analysis," *Science* 343 (2014): 1203–1205.

19. Paul E. Meehl, *Clinical Versus Statistical Prediction: A Theoretical Analysis and a Review of the Evidence* (Northvale, NJ: Echo Point Books & Media, 1954). See also the discussion in Daniel Kahneman, *Thinking, Fast and Slow,* reprint edition (New York: Farrar, Straus and Giroux, 2013); and for a review of the evidence, see Colin F. Camerer and Eric J. Johnson, "The Process-Performance Paradox in Expert Judgment—How Can Experts Know so Much and Predict so Badly?" in *Toward a General Theory of Expertise: Prospects and Limits,* ed. K. Anders Ericsson and Jacqui Smith (Cambridge: Cambridge University Press, 1991), 195–217.

20. Philip E. Tetlock, *Expert Political Judgment: How Good Is It? How Can We Know?* (Princeton, NJ: Princeton University Press, 2006); Michael Lewis, *Moneyball: The Art of Winning an Unfair Game* (New York: W.W. Norton & Company, 2004).

21. On forecasting accuracy: Robert Fildes, Paul Goodwin, Michael Lawrence, and Konstantinos Nikolopoulos, "Effective Forecasting and

Judgmental Adjustments: An Empirical Evaluation and Strategies for Improvement in Supply-Chain Planning," *International Journal of Forecasting* 25 (2009): 3–23; on algorithm aversion, see Berkeley J. Dietvorst, Joseph P. Simmons, and Cade Massey, "Algorithm Aversion: People Erroneously Avoid Algorithms after Seeing Them Err," *Journal of Experimental Psychology* 144 (2015): 114; on overcoming algorithm aversion, see Berkeley J. Dietvorst, Joseph P. Simmons, and Cade Massey, "Overcoming Algorithm Aversion: People Will Use Algorithms If They Can (Even Slightly) Modify Them" (SSRN Scholarly Paper, Rochester, NY, June 11, 2015), http://papers.ssrn.com/abstract=2616787. For a review of the evidence on forecasting, see Michael Lawrence, Paul Goodwin, Marcus O'Connor, and Dilek Önkal, "Judgmental Forecasting: A Review of Progress over the Last 25 Years," *International Journal of Forecasting* 22 (2006): 493–518.

6. Orchestrating Smarter Evaluation Procedures

1. The quote from Chew Ee Tien comes from this article: "A Tip for Policy-Making: Nudge, Not Shove," Challenge: Approaching the Public Service Differently, http://www.challenge.gov.sg/print/cover-story/a-tip-for-policy-making-nudge-not-shove; for additional examples of how Singapore has been using behavioral insights to inform policy-making, see Donald Low, *Behavioural Economics and Policy Design: Examples from Singapore* (Singapore: World Scientific Publishing Company, 2011).

2. Amos Tversky and Daniel Kahneman, "Evidential Impact of Base Rates," in *Judgment under Uncertainty*, ed. Daniel Kahneman, Paul Slovic, and Amos Tversky (Cambridge: Cambridge University Press, 1982); Amos Tversky and Daniel Kahneman, "Extensional versus Intuitive Reasoning: The Conjunction Fallacy in Probability Judgment," *Psychological Review* 90 (1983): 293–315; Marianne Bertrand and Sendhil Mullainathan, "Are Emily and Greg More Employable Than Lakisha and Jamal? A Field Experiment on Labor Market Discrimination," *American Economic Review* 94 (2004): 991–1013.

3. Iris Bohnet, Alexandra van Geen, and Max Bazerman, "When Performance Trumps Gender Bias: Joint vs. Separate Evaluation," *Management Science*, September 29, 2015, http://dx.doi.org/10.1287 /mnsc.2015.2186; for the prevalence of joint and separate hiring strategies: Paul Oyer and Scott Schaefer, "Personnel Economics: Hiring and Incentives" (NBER Working Paper, May 2010), http://www.nber.org/papers/w15977; Jos van Ommeren and Giovanni Russo, "Firm Recruitment Behaviour: Sequential or Non-Sequential Search?" *Oxford Bulletin of Economics and Statistics* 76 (2014): 432–455; "Executive Masters in Leadership Capstone Project" (Georgetown University McDonough School of Business & Penn Schoen Berland, Jonathan Gardener), http://msb.georgetown.edu /document/1242764748554/Favoritism+Research+McDonough +School+of+Business.pdf; for gender attitudes in math and verbal tasks, see Isabelle Plante, Manon Théorêt, and Olga Eizner Favreau, "Student Gender Stereotypes: Contrasting the Perceived Maleness and Femaleness of Mathematics and Language," *Educational Psychology* 29 (2009): 385–405; Curtis R. Price, "Gender, Competition, and Managerial Decisions," *Management Science* 58 (2011): 114–122. The evidence on actual performance differences between the genders is mixed: Luigi Guiso, Ferdinando Monte, Paola Sapienza, and Luigi Zingales, "Culture, Gender, and Math," *Science* 320 (2008): 1164–1165; OECD, "The ABC of Gender Equality in Education, PISA" (OECD Publishing, 2015), http://www.oecd-ilibrary.org/education /the-abc-of-gender-equality-in-education_9789264229945-en.

4. "Best Practices for Conducting Faculty Searches," Harvard University Office of the Senior Vice Provost, Faculty Development and Diversity, http://www.faculty.harvard.edu/sites/default/files/Best%20 Practices%20for%20Conducting%20Faculty%20Searches%2C%20 Harvard%20FD%26D%202014_V1.0.pdf; Daniel Read and George Loewenstein, "Diversification Bias: Explaining the Discrepancy in Variety Seeking Between Combined and Separated Choices," *Journal of Experimental Psychology: Applied* 1 (1995): 34–49; Itamar Simonson, "The Effect of Purchase Quantity and Timing on Variety-Seeking

Behavior," *Journal of Marketing Research* 27 (1990): 150–162; Itamar Simonson and Russell S. Winer, "The Influence of Purchase Quantity and Display Format on Consumer Preference for Variety," *Journal of Consumer Research* 19 (1992): 133–138.

5. Lauren A. Rivera, "Hiring as Cultural Matching: The Case of Elite Professional Service Firms," *American Sociological Review* 77 (2012): 999–1022.

6. "When Doctors Make Bad Calls," *Globe and Mail,* February 24, 2012, http://www.theglobeandmail.com/life/health-and-fitness /when-doctors-make-bad-calls/article549084/.

7. On attractiveness and cooperation, see James Andreoni and Ragan Petrie, "Beauty, Gender and Stereotypes: Evidence from Laboratory Experiments," *Journal of Economic Psychology* 29 (2008): 73–93; on attractiveness and puzzle-solving, see Markus M. Mobius and Tanya S. Rosenblat, "Why Beauty Matters," *American Economic Review* 96 (2006): 222–235. On the beauty premium for men but not for women, see Bradley J. Ruffle and Ze'ev Shtudiner, "Are Good-Looking People More Employable?" (SSRN Research Paper, Social Science Research Network, February 5, 2014), http://papers.ssrn.com/abstract=1705244; Daniel S. Hamermesh, *Beauty Pays: Why Attractive People Are More Successful* (Princeton: Princeton University Press, 2013). Also see Daniel S. Hamermesh and Jeff E. Biddle, "Beauty and the Labor Market," *American Economic Review* 84 (1994): 1174–1194. For a review of studies examining the relationship between candidate looks and election outcomes, see Michaela Wänke, Jakub Samochowiec, and Jan Landwehr, "Facial Politics: Political Judgment Based on Looks," in *Social Thinking and Interpersonal Behavior,* ed. Joseph P. Forgas, Klaus Fiedler, and Constantine Sedikides (New York: Psychology Press, 2012); for ratings of US presidents, see William J. Ridings, *Rating the Presidents: A Ranking of US Leaders, from the Great and Honorable to the Dishonest and Incompetent,* revised edition (New York: Citadel, 2000); for a discussion of whether attractiveness is a credible signal for effectiveness, see the discussion in the *Economist*: "To Those That Have, Shall Be Given," *Economist,* December 19, 2007; and see related

research in Maryanne Fisher and Anthony Cox, "The Influence of Female Attractiveness on Competitor Derogation," *Journal of Evolutionary Psychology* 7 (2009): 141–155.

8. Luc Behaghel, Bruno Crépon, and Thomas Le Barbanchon, "Unintended Effects of Anonymous Résumés," *American Economic Journal: Applied Economics* 7 (2015): 1–27. In addition to the orchestra study by Goldin and Rouse discussed earlier, for studies finding the opposite (including in France), namely that anonymous procedures benefit members of traditionally disadvantaged groups, see Olaf Aslund and Oskar N. Skans, "Do Anonymous Job Application Procedures Level the Playing Field?" *Industrial and Labor Relations Review* (2012): 82–107; Emmanuel Duguet, Yannick L'Horty, Dominique Meurs, and Pascale Petit, "Measuring Discriminations: An Introduction," *Annals of Economics and Statistics* 99 (2010): 5–14.

9. Richard A. DeVaul, Faith Jervey, James A. Chappell, Patricia Carver, Barbara Short, and Stephen O'Keefe, "Medical School Performance of Initially Rejected Students," *JAMA* 257, no. 1 (1987): 47–51; quotation on p. 48.

10. Scott Highhouse, "Stubborn Reliance on Intuition and Subjectivity in Employee Selection," *Industrial and Organizational Psychology* 1 (2008): 333–334; DeVaul, Jervey, Chappell, Carver, Short, and O'Keefe, "Medical School Performance," quotation on p. 51.

11. For the meta-analysis, see Frank L. Schmidt and John E. Hunter, "The Validity and Utility of Selection Methods in Personnel Psychology: Practical and Theoretical Implications of 85 Years of Research Findings," *Psychological Bulletin* 124 (1998): 262–274; for the value of referrals, see Stephen V. Burks, Bo Cowgill, Mitchell Hoffman, and Michael Housman, "The Value of Hiring through Employee Referrals," *Quarterly Journal of Economics* 130 (2015): 805–839. Referrals appear to be most valuable when coming from your best employees, as people tend to refer people like themselves. Jason Dana, Robyn Dawes, and Nathanial Peterson, "Belief in the Unstructured Interview: The Persistence of an Illusion," *Judgment and Decision Making* 8 (2013): 512–520; Robyn Dawes, *Everyday*

Irrationality: How Pseudo-Scientists, Lunatics, and the Rest of Us Systematically Fail to Think Rationally (Boulder, CO: Westview Press, 2002). For seeing patterns in random data, see Thomas Gilovich, *How We Know What Isn't So: The Fallibility of Human Reason in Everyday Life* (New York: Free Press, 1993).

12. Lauren A. Rivera, "Hiring as Cultural Matching: The Case of Elite Professional Service Firms," *American Sociological Review* 77 (2012): 999–1022; for structured interviews, see Barbara F. Reskin and Debra Branch McBrier, "Why Not Ascription? Organizations' Employment of Male and Female Managers," *American Sociological Review* 65 (2000): 210–233.

13. Atul Gawande, *The Checklist Manifesto: How to Get Things Right* (New York: Picador, 2011).

14. Hal Arkowitz and Scott O. Lilienfeld, "Why Science Tells Us Not to Rely on Eyewitness Accounts," *Scientific American,* January 8, 2009, http://www.scientificamerican.com/article/do-the-eyes-have-it/.

15. Daniel Kahneman, Paul Slovic, and Amos Tversky, eds., *Judgment Under Uncertainty: Heuristics and Biases* (Cambridge: Cambridge University Press, 1982); Daniel Kahneman, Barbara L. Fredrickson, Charles A. Schreiber, and Donald A. Redelmeier, "When More Pain Is Preferred to Less: Adding a Better End," *Psychological Science* 4, no. 6 (1993): 401–405. For anchoring and willingness to pay, see Dan Ariely, *Predictably Irrational: The Hidden Forces that Shape Our Decisions,* revised and expanded edition (New York: Harper Perennial, 2010).

16. Irving Janis, *Groupthink: Psychological Studies of Policy Decisions and Fiascoes* (Boston: Cengage Learning, 1982); Cass R. Sunstein and Reid Hastie, *Wiser: Getting Beyond Groupthink to Make Groups Smarter* (Boston: Harvard Business Review Press, 2014).

17. Sunstein and Hastie, *Wiser.*

18. To learn more about Applied, visit www.beapplied.com, about GapJumpers, visit www.gapjumpers.me, and about Unitive, visit www.unitive.works.

19. For status quo bias, see the seminal paper by William Samuelson and Richard Zeckhauser, "Status Quo Bias in Decision Making," *Journal*

of Risk and Uncertainty 1 (1988): 7–59; and W. Kip Viscusi, Wesley A. Magat, and Joel Huber, "An Investigation of the Rationality of Consumer Valuations of Multiple Health Risks," *RAND Journal of Economics* 18 (1987): 465–479; Boris Groysberg and Deborah Bell, "Talent Management: Boards Give Their Companies an 'F,'" *Harvard Business Review,* May 28, 2013, https://hbr.org/2013/05/talent -management-boards-give.

7. Attracting the Right People

1. Mark Tungate, *Branded Male: Marketing to Men* (London: Kogan Page Limited, 2008), 62–74.
2. Carmen Nobel, "Should Men's Products Fear a Woman's Touch?" (HBS Working Knowledge, Nov 2013), http://hbswk.hbs.edu/item /7149.html.
3. Sandra L. Bem and Daryl J. Bem, "Does Sex-Biased Job Advertising 'Aid and Abet' Sex Discrimination?" *Journal of Applied Social Psychology* 3 (1973): 6–18, quotation on p. 15. The decline in occupational sex segregation in the United States began in the 1960s and proceeded more quickly in the 1970s and 1980s. For an excellent discussion of this, and more generally, the factors contributing to a change in gender inequality over time, see Francine D. Blau, Mary Brinton, and David Grusky, eds., *The Declining Significance of Gender?* (New York: Russell Sage Foundation, 2006).
4. Peter Kuhn and Kailing Shen, "Gender Discrimination in Job Ads: Evidence from China," *Quarterly Journal of Economics* 128 (2013): 287–336.
5. Danielle Gaucher, Justin Friesen, and Aaron C. Kay, "Evidence That Gendered Wording in Job Advertisements Exists and Sustains Gender Inequality," *Journal of Personality and Social Psychology* 101 (July 2011): 109–128.
6. Alvin E. Roth, *Who Gets What—and Why: The New Economics of Matchmaking and Market Design* (Boston: Eamon Dolan/Houghton Mifflin Harcourt, 2015).

7. Frances Trix and Carolyn Psenka, "Exploring the Color of Glass: Letters of Recommendation for Female and Male Medical Faculty," *Discourse & Society* 14 (2003): 191–220.

8. Nava Ashraf, Oriana Bandiera, and Scott Lee, "Do-Gooders and Go-Getters: Career Incentives, Selection, and Performance in Public Service Delivery" (LSE STICERD - Economic Organisation and Public Policy Discussion Papers Series No. 54, July 2015), http://sticerd.lse.ac.uk/dps/eopp/eopp54.pdf; similar evidence was found for public sector positions in Mexico where higher wages also attracted more able applicants as measured by their IQ, personality, and fit for public sector work—see Ernesto Dal Bó, Frederico Finan, and Martín A. Rossi, "Strengthening State Capabilities: The Role of Financial Incentives in the Call to Public Service," *Quarterly Journal of Economics* 128 (2013): 1169–1218.

9. Jeffrey A. Flory, Andreas Leibbrandt, and John A. List, "Do Competitive Workplaces Deter Female Workers? A Large-Scale Natural Field Experiment on Job Entry Decisions," *Review of Economic Studies* 82 (2015): 122–155.

10. Experimental literature studying self-selection into competitive environments: Nabanita Datta Gupta, Anders Poulsen, and Marie Claire Villeval, "Gender Matching and Competitiveness: Experimental Evidence," *Economic Inquiry* 51 (2013): 816–835. Thomas Dohmen and Armin Falk, "Performance Pay and Multidimensional Sorting: Productivity, Preferences, and Gender," *American Economic Review* 101, no. 2 (2011): 556–590, and Muriel Niederle and Lise Vesterlund, "Do Women Shy Away From Competition? Do Men Compete Too Much?" *Quarterly Journal of Economics* 122 (2007): 1067–1101, find that men opt significantly more often for competitive compensation schemes than women. Uri Gneezy, Kenneth Leonard, and John A. List, "Gender Differences in Competition: Evidence from a Matrilineal and a Patriarchal Society," *Econometrica* 77 (2009): 1637–1664, show that the reverse holds in a matrilineal society. Recent studies have shown that the gender gap in self-selection into competition by and large vanishes for

girls attending single-sex schools (Alison L. Booth and Patrick Nolen, "Gender Differences in Risk Behaviour: Does Nurture Matter?" *Economic Journal* 122 [2012]: 56–78) and when the tournament is among teams rather than among individuals (Marie-Pierre Dargnies, "Men Too Sometimes Shy Away from Competition: The Case of Team Competition," *Management Science* 58 [2012]: 1982–2000).

11. Uwe Jirjahn and Gesine Stephan, "Gender, Piece Rates and Wages: Evidence from Matched Employer–Employee Data," *Cambridge Journal of Economics* 28 (2004): 683–704; Claudia Dale Goldin, *Understanding the Gender Gap: An Economic History of American Women* (New York: Oxford University Press, 1992).

12. Claudia Dale Goldin, "A Grand Gender Convergence: Its Last Chapter," *American Economic Review* 104 (2014): 1091–1119.

13. Gabriel D. Carroll, James J. Choi, David Laibson, Brigitte C. Madrian, and Andrew Metrick, "Optimal Defaults and Active Decisions," *Quarterly Journal of Economics* 124 (2009): 1639–1674; James J. Choi, David Laibson, and Brigitte C. Madrian, "Reducing the Complexity Costs of 401(k) Participation Through Quick Enrollment," in *Developments in the Economics of Aging,* ed. David A. Wise (University of Chicago Press, 2009), 57–82.

14. Telstra Home, Careers, https://careers.telstra.com/.

15. Laura Gee, "The More You Know: Information Effects in Job Application Rates by Gender in a Large Field Experiment," Department of Economics Discussion Papers No. 780 (Tufts University, September 2014), http://econpapers.repec.org/paper/tuftuftec/0780.htm.

16. Steven D. Levitt and Stephen J. Dubner, *Think Like a Freak: The Authors of Freakonomics Offer to Retrain Your Brain* (New York: William Morrow, 2014).

17. Corporate Culture Pros, "Corporate Culture Example: Google's Eric Schmidt on Corporate Culture and Hiring," http://www.corporateculturepros.com/2011/07/corporate-culture-example-google-hiring/; Ryan Tate, "Google Couldn't Kill 20 Percent Time Even If It Wanted To," *Wired,* August 2013, http://www.wired.com/2013/08/20-percent-time-will-never-die/ and Laszlo Bock, *Work*

Rules! Insights from Inside Google That Will Transform How You Live and Lead (New York: Twelve, 2015).

18. Izabella Kaminska, "Since You Asked: The Tech Industry and Its Problem with Women," *Financial Times*, February 27, 2015.

19. Boris Groysberg, *Chasing Stars: The Myth of Talent and the Portability of Performance* (Princeton: Princeton University Press, 2012); Boris Groysberg, "How Star Women Build Portable Skills," *Harvard Business Review,* February 2008, https://hbr.org/2008/02/how-star-women -build-portable-skills; Boris Groysberg, Ashish Nanda, and Nitin Nohria, "The Risky Business of Hiring Stars," *Harvard Business Review,* May 2004, https://hbr.org/2004/05/the-risky-business-of -hiring-stars.

20. Chief of Army Lieutenant General David Morrison, Message about Unacceptable Behaviour, YouTube, https://www.youtube.com/watch ?v=QaqpoeVgr8U; see also Julie Baird, "A Timely Halt to the War Within," *Sydney Morning Herald*, June 8, 2013, http://www.smh.com .au/comment/a-timely-halt-to-the-war-within-20130607-2nvl7.html; Mary Gearin, "Army Chief Slams 'Global Disgrace' of Gender Gap," *ABC News*, June 14, 2014, http://www.abc.net.au/news/2014-06-14 /australia-army-chief-delivers-speech-to-summit-on-wartime-rape /5523942; Mary Elizabeth Williams, "This Is How You Talk about Military Sex Abuse," *Salon*, June 13, 2013, http://www.salon.com /2013/06/13/this_is_how_you_talk_about_military_sex_abuse/.

21. Robert Jensen and Emily Oster, "The Power of TV: Cable Television and Women's Status in India," *Quarterly Journal of Economics* 124 (2009): 1057–1094.

8. Adjusting Risk

1. "The Test Prep Industry Is Booming," BloombergView, http://www .bloomberg.com/bw/articles/2014-10-08/sats-the-test-prep-business -is-booming.

2. "SAT Suite of Assessments," SAT Suite of Assessments, https:// collegereadiness.collegeboard.org/.

3. For the mathematics SAT scores, see Daniel Tannenbaum, "Do Gender Differences in Risk Aversion Explain the Gender Gap in SAT Scores? Uncovering Risk Attitudes and the Test Score Gap," (April 2012), http://home.uchicago.edu/~dtannenbaum/Research%20files /tannenbaum_SAT_risk.pdf; for South Africa, see Justine Burns, Simon Halliday, and Malcolm Keswell, "Gender and Risk Taking in the Classroom" (SALDRU Working Paper, Southern Africa Labour and Development Research Unit, University of Cape Town, 2012), https://ideas.repec.org/p/ldr/wpaper/87.html; for Poland, see Michał Krawczyk, "Framing in the Field. A Simple Experiment on the Reflection Effect" (Working Paper, Faculty of Economic Sciences, University of Warsaw, 2011), https://ideas.repec.org/p/war/wpaper /2011-14.html; and for Israel, see Gershon Ben-Shakhar and Yakov Sinai, "Gender Differences in Multiple-Choice Tests: The Role of Differential Guessing Tendencies," *Journal of Educational Measurement* 28 (1991): 23–35; for an analysis on the gender gap in political knowledge: Jeffery J. Mondak and Mary R. Anderson, "The Knowledge Gap: A Reexamination of Gender-Based Differences in Political Knowledge," *Journal of Politics* 66 (2004): 492–512.

4. Katherine Baldiga, "Gender Differences in Willingness to Guess," *Management Science* 60 (2013): 434–448.

5. Ibid.; for reviews of the evidence on gender and willingness to take risks, see Rachel Croson and Uri Gneezy, "Gender Differences in Preferences," *Journal of Economic Literature* 47 (2009): 448–474; Catherine C. Eckel and Philip J. Grossman, "Men, Women and Risk Aversion: Experimental Evidence" in Charles R. Plott and Vernon L. Smith, eds., *Handbook of Experimental Economics Results* (New York: Elsevier, 2008), 1061–1073; for the German study, see Thomas Dohmen, Armin Falk, David Huffman, Uwe Sunde, Jurgen Schupp, and Gert G. Wagner, "Individual Risk Attitudes: Measurement, Determinants, and Behavioral Consequences," *Journal of the European Economic Association* 9 (2011): 522–550; and for the relationship between willingness to take risks and sorting into occupations, Holger Bonin, Thomas Dohmen, Armin Falk, David Huffman, and

Uwe Sunde, "Cross-Sectional Earnings Risk and Occupational Sorting: The Role of Risk Attitudes," *Labour Economics, Education and Risk* 14 (2007): 926–937, and Alan Manning and Farzad Saidi, "Understanding The Gender Pay Gap: What's Competition Got To Do With It?" *Industrial and Labor Relations Review* 63 (2010): 681–698.

6. Sarah A. Fulton, Cherie D. Maestas, L. Sandy Maisel, and Walter J. Stone, "The Sense of a Woman: Gender, Ambition, and the Decision to Run for Congress," *Political Research Quarterly* 59 (2006): 235–248.

7. Barbara Burrell, *A Woman's Place Is in the House: Campaigning for Congress in the Feminist Era* (Ann Arbor: University of Michigan Press, 1996); Jennifer L. Lawless, *Becoming a Candidate: Political Ambition and the Decision to Run for Office* (New York: Cambridge University Press, 2012); Jennifer L. Lawless and Richard L. Fox, *It Still Takes a Candidate: Why Women Don't Run for Office* (New York: Cambridge University Press, 2010); Jennifer L. Lawless and Richard L. Fox, *It Takes a Candidate: Why Women Don't Run for Office* (New York: Cambridge University Press, 2005); Jennifer L. Lawless and Richard L. Fox, "Men Rule: The Continued Under-Representation of Women in US Politics" (Women & Politics Institute, School of Public Affairs, American University, January 2012), https://www.american.edu/spa/wpi/upload/2012-Men-Rule-Report-web.pdf.

8. For gender differences in willingness to take risks in *Who Wants to Be a Millionaire* in Germany, Austria, and Slovenia, see Fedor Daghofer, "Financial Risk-Taking on 'Who Wants to Be a Millionaire': A Comparison between Austria, Germany, and Slovenia," *International Journal of Psychology* 42 (2007): 317–330; and in *Deal or No Deal* in Australia, see Robert Brooks, Robert Faff, Daniel Mulino, and Richard Scheelings, "Deal or No Deal, That Is the Question: The Impact of Increasing Stakes and Framing Effects on Decision-Making under Risk," *International Review of Finance* 9 (2009): 27–50; on *El Jugador*, see Robin M. Hogarth, Natalia Karelaia, and Carlos Andrés Trujillo, "When Should I Quit? Gender Differences in Exiting Competitions," *Journal of Economic Behavior & Organization*, Gender Differences in Risk Aversion and Competition, 83 (2012): 136–150.

9. John Coates, *The Hour Between Dog and Wolf: Risk Taking, Gut Feelings and the Biology of Boom and Bust* (New York: Penguin Press, 2012); on the lottery, see Alexandra Van Geen, Risk in the Background: How Men and Women Respond (Working Paper, Erasmus University, Rotterdam), http://www.erim.eur.nl/fileadmin/erim_content /documents/jmp_vangeen.pdf; on testosterone and willingness to take risks, see Coren L. Apicella, Anna Dreber, and Johanna Mollerstrom, "Salivary Testosterone Change Following Monetary Wins and Losses Predicts Future Financial Risk-Taking," *Psychoneuroendocrinology* 39 (2014): 58–64; on cortisol, see Narayanan Kandasamy, Ben Hardy, Lionel Page, Markus Schaffner, Johann Graggaber, Andrew S. Powlson, Paul C. Fletcher, Mark Gurnell, and John Coates, "Cortisol Shifts Financial Risk Preferences," *Proceedings of the National Academy of Sciences USA* 111 (2014): 3608–3613.

10. Catherine C. Eckel and Sascha C. Füllbrunn, "Thar SHE Blows? Gender, Competition, and Bubbles in Experimental Asset Markets," *American Economic Review* 105 (2015): 906–920, quotation on p. 919; Stefan Palan, "A Review of Bubbles and Crashes in Experimental Asset Markets," *Journal of Economic Surveys—Special Issue: A Collection of Surveys on Market Experiments* 27 (2013): 570–588.

11. Michael Inzlicht and Talia Ben-Zeev, "A Threatening Intellectual Environment: Why Females Are Susceptible to Experiencing Problem-Solving Deficits in the Presence of Males," *Psychological Science* 11 (2000): 365–371; Stephen M. Garcia and Avishalom Tor, "The N-Effect: More Competitors, Less Competition," *Psychological Science* 20 (2009): 871–877.

12. A positive relationship between SAT scores and college achievement has been found by Leonard Ramist, Charles Lewis, and Laura McCamley-Jenkins, "Student Group Differences in Predicting College Grades: Sex, Language, and Ethnic Groups" (ETS Research Report Series no. 1, June 1, 1994), https://research .collegeboard.org/sites/default/files/publications/2012/7 /researchreport-1993-1-student-group-differences-predicting-college -grades.pdf and Nancy W. Burton and Leonard Ramist, "Predicting

Success in College: SAT Studies of Classes Graduating Since 1980" (Collegeboard, January 1, 2001), https://research.collegeboard.org /publications/content/2012/05/predicting-success-college-sat -studies-classes-graduating-1980. On how SAT I scores under-predict women's achievement during the first year of college, see Mary Jo Clark and Jerilee Grandy, "Sex Differences in the Academic Performance of Scholastic Aptitude Test Takers" (ETS Research Report Series 1984, no. 2, 1984), https://www.ets.org /Media/Research/pdf/RR-88-51-Grandy.pdf; for evidence that women perform relatively worse on multiple-choice tests as compared to essay-style tests: Marianne A. Ferber, Bonnie G. Birnbaum, and Carole A. Green, "Gender Differences in Economic Knowledge: A Reevaluation of the Evidence," *Journal of Economic Education* 14 (1983): 24–37; Keith G. Lumsden and Alex Scott, "The Economics Student Reexamined: Male-Female Differences in Comprehension," *Journal of Economic Education* 18 (1987): 365–375; William B. Walstad and Denise Robson, "Differential Item Functioning and Male-Female Differences on Multiple-Choice Tests in Economics," *Journal of Economic Education* 28 (1997): 155–171.

13. Saul Geiser, "Back to the Basics: In Defense of Achievement (and Achievement Tests) in College Admissions" (Research & Occasional Paper Series: CSHE.12.08. Center for Studies in Higher Education, 2008), http://eric.ed.gov/?id=ED502730.

14. Lee Jussim and Kent D. Harber, "Teacher Expectations and Self-Fulfilling Prophecies: Knowns and Unknowns, Resolved and Unresolved Controversies," *Personality and Social Psychology Review* 9 (2005): 131–155.

15. Steven J. Spencer, Claude M. Steele, and Diane M. Quinn, "Stereo-type Threat and Women's Math Performance," *Journal of Experimental Social Psychology* 35 (1999): 4–28; Claude M. Steele, *Whistling Vivaldi: How Stereotypes Affect Us and What We Can Do* (New York: W.W. Norton & Company, 2011); for increased neural activity in part of the affective network involved in processing negative social

information with stereotype threat, see Anne C. Krendl, Jennifer A. Richeson, William M. Kelley, and Todd F. Heatherton, "The Negative Consequences of Threat: A Functional Magnetic Resonance Imaging Investigation of the Neural Mechanisms Underlying Women's Underperformance in Math," *Psychological Science* 19 (2008): 168–175; Nalini Ambady, Margaret Shih, Amy Kim, and Todd L. Pittinsky, "Stereotype Susceptibility in Children: Effects of Identity Activation on Quantitative Performance," *Psychological Science* 12 (2001): 385–390; Vishal K. Gupta, Daniel B. Turban, and Nachiket M. Bhawe, "The Effect of Gender Stereotype Activation on Entrepreneurial Intentions," *Journal of Applied Psychology* 93 (2008): 1053–1061; on placement of demographic boxes on tests, see Kelly Danaher and Christian S. Crandall, "Stereotype Threat in Applied Settings Re-Examined," *Journal of Applied Social Psychology* 38 (2008): 1639–1655; for a discussion of possible interventions, see Geoffrey L. Cohen, Valerie Purdie-Vaughns, and Julio Garcia, "An Identity Threat Perspective on Intervention" in *Stereotype Threat: Theory, Process, and Application,* ed. Michael Inzlicht and Toni Schmader (New York: Oxford University Press, 2011), 280–296.

16. Alison L. Booth and Patrick Nolen, "Gender Differences in Risk Behavior: Does Nurture Matter?" *Economic Journal* 122 (2012): 56–78; Gerald Eisenkopf, Zohal Hessami, Urs Fischbacher, and Heinrich W. Ursprung, "Academic Performance and Single-Sex Schooling: Evidence from a Natural Experiment in Switzerland," *Journal of Economic Behavior & Organization,* Behavioral Economics of Education 115 (2015): 123–143.

17. See William J. Horrey and Christopher D. Wickens, "Examining the Impact of Cell Phone Conversations on Driving Using Meta-Analytic Techniques," *Human Factors: The Journal of the Human Factors and Ergonomics Society* 48 (2006): 196–205, for a meta-analysis of one particularly challenging multi-tasking environment, driving and using a phone, showing that the more attention-demanding tasks you undertake at the same time, the worse you do on each one of them.

For a typical laboratory experiment on multi-tasking, see Joshua S. Rubinstein, David E. Meyer, and Jeffrey E. Evans, "Executive Control of Cognitive Processes in Task Switching," *Journal of Experimental Psychology: Human Perception and Performance* 27 (2001): 763–797. More generally, on the challenges of "noticing," see Christopher Chabris and Daniel Simons, *The Invisible Gorilla: How Our Intuitions Deceive Us* (New York: Harmony, 2011); Max Bazerman, *The Power of Noticing: What the Best Leaders See* (New York: Simon & Schuster, 2014).

18. Nanette Fondas, "First Step to Fixing Gender Bias in Business School: Admit the Problem," *Atlantic Monthly,* September 17, 2013, http://www.theatlantic.com/education/archive/2013/09/first-step-to-fixing-gender-bias-in-business-school-admit-the-problem/279740/; Jodi Kantor, "Harvard Business School Case Study: Gender Equity," *New York Times,* September 7, 2013.

9. Leveling the Playing Field

1. Thomas S. Dee, "A Teacher Like Me: Does Race, Ethnicity, or Gender Matter?" *American Economic Review* 95 (2005): 158–165; Thomas S. Dee, "Teachers and the Gender Gaps in Student Achievement," *Journal of Human Resources* 42 (2007): 528–554.

2. The B4 program comes with a fun blog: "Boys Blokes Books: Because Boys Read, Too," http://boysblokesbooks.edublogs.org/; one program called "Boys, Blokes and Books" was evaluated here: Janet Carroll and Kaye Lowe, "Boys, Blokes and Books: Engaging Boys in Reading," *Australasian Public Libraries and Information Services* 20 (2007): 72; for the OECD report, see *The ABC of Gender Equality in Education,* PISA (OECD Publishing, 2015), http://www.oecd-ilibrary.org/education/the-abc-of-gender-equality-in-education_9789264229945-en; OECD Skills Outlook 2015 (OECD Publishing, 2015), http://www.oecd-ilibrary.org/education/oecd-skills-outlook-2015_9789264234178-en.

3. For more on the scholarship program, see Michael Kremer, Edward Miguel, and Rebecca Thornton, "Incentives to Learn," *Review of*

Economics and Statistics 91 (2009): 437–456; for a cost-effectiveness analysis, see Iqbal Dhaliwal, Esther Duflo, Rachel Glennerster, and Caitlin Tulloch, "Comparative Cost: Effectiveness Analysis to Inform Policy in Developing Countries. A General Framework with Applications for Education" (Poverty Action Lab, December 3, 2012), http://www.povertyactionlab.org/publication/cost-effectiveness; for the original deworming impact evaluation, see Edward Miguel and Michael Kremer, "Worms: Identifying Impacts on Education and Health in the Presence of Treatment Externalities," *Econometrica* 72 (2004): 159–217; Sarah Baird, Joan Hamory Hicks, Michael Kremer, and Edward Miguel, "Worms at Work: Long-Run Impacts of a Child Health Investment" (NBER Working Paper, July 2015), http://www.nber.org/papers/w21428; Michael Kremer and Edward Miguel, "The Illusion of Sustainability," *Quarterly Journal of Economics* 122 (2007): 1007–1065; "School-Based Deworming," The Abdul Latif Jameel Poverty Action Lab, http://www.povertyactionlab.org/scale-ups/school-based-deworming.

4. Bazerman and Moore, *Judgment in Managerial Decision Making*; for the quote on universality, see Dale W. Griffin and Carol A. Varey, "Towards a Consensus on Overconfidence," *Organizational Behavior and Human Decision Processes* 65 (1996): 227–231, quotation on p. 228.

5. Brad M. Barber and Terrance Odean, "Boys Will Be Boys: Gender, Overconfidence, and Common Stock Investment," *Quarterly Journal of Economics* 116 (2001): 261–292; for women's self-confidence in mathematics, see Shelley J. Correll, "Constraints into Preferences: Gender, Status, and Emerging Career Aspirations," *American Sociological Review* 69 (2004): 93–113, and for women's increased likelihood of dropping out of science and engineering majors, see Elaine Seymour and Nancy Hewitt, *Talking About Leaving: Why Undergraduates Leave the Sciences* (Boulder: Westview Press, 2000).

6. For self-serving bias and inflated self-assessments, see Timothy A. Judge, Jeffery A. LePine, and Bruce L. Rich, "Loving Yourself Abundantly: Relationship of the Narcissistic Personality to Self- and Other Perceptions of Workplace Deviance, Leadership, and Task and

Contextual Performance," *Journal of Applied Psychology* 91 (2006): 762–776; Samantha C. Paustian-Underdahl, Lisa Slattery Walker, and David J. Woehr, "Gender and Perceptions of Leadership Effectiveness: A Meta-Analysis of Contextual Moderators," *Journal of Applied Psychology* 99 (2014): 1129–1145. For the impact of self-appraisals on manager evaluations, see Richard Klimoski and Lawrence Inks, "Accountability Forces in Performance Appraisal," *Organizational Behavior and Human Decision Processes* 45 (1990): 194–208.

7. Uri Gneezy, Muriel Niederle, and Aldo Rustichini, "Performance in Competitive Environments: Gender Differences," *Quarterly Journal of Economics* 118 (2003): 1049–1074; Muriel Niederle and Lise Vesterlund, "Do Women Shy Away from Competition? Do Men Compete Too Much?" *Quarterly Journal of Economics* 122 (2007): 1067–1101.

8. Thomas Buser, Muriel Niederle, and Hessel Oosterbeek, "Gender, Competitiveness, and Career Choices," *Quarterly Journal of Economics* 129 (2014): 1409–1447 show that willingness to compete predicts the choice of university track among Dutch students; for the MBA students, see Ernesto Reuben, Paola Sapienza, and Luigi Zingales, "Competitiveness and the gender gap among young business professionals" (Working Paper, Columbia Business School, 2015, http://www.ereuben.net/research/GenderGapCompetitiveness.pdf).

9. For the experiments with the Maasai and Khasi, see Uri Gneezy, Kenneth L. Leonard, and John A. List, "Gender Differences in Competition: Evidence From a Matrilineal and a Patriarchal Society," *Econometrica* 77 (2009): 1637–1664; Anna Dreber, Emma von Essen, and Eva Ranehill, "Outrunning the Gender Gap—Boys and Girls Compete Equally," *Experimental Economics* 14 (2011): 567–582; for the effect of task type on competition, see Christina Günther, Neslihan Arslan Ekinci, Christiane Schwieren, and Martin Strobel, "Women Can't Jump?—An Experiment on Competitive Attitudes and Stereotype Threat," *Journal of Economic Behavior & Organization* 75 (2010): 395–401; Olga Shurchkov, "Under Pressure: Gender Differences in Output Quality and Quantity Under Competition and Time Constraints," *Journal of the European Economic Association* 10 (2012):

1189–1213; Alison L. Booth and Patrick J. Nolen, "Choosing to Compete: How Different Are Girls and Boys?" (IZA Discussion Papers, February 2009), http://ideas.repec.org/p/iza/izadps/dp4027 .html; Muriel Niederle and Lise Vesterlund, "Explaining the Gender Gap in Math Test Scores: The Role of Competition," *Journal of Economic Perspectives* 24 (2010): 129–144.

10. See, for example, the World Economic Forum's Global Gender Gap Reports, 2006–2015: "The Global Gender Gap Report 2015," World Economic Forum, http://reports.weforum.org/global-gender-gap -report-2015/.

11. Timothy N. Cason, William A. Masters, and Roman M. Sheremeta, "Entry into Winner-Take-All and Proportional-Prize Contests: An Experimental Study," *Journal of Public Economics* 94 (2010): 604–611; Seda Ertaç and Balazs Szentes, "The Effect of Information on Gender Differences in Competitiveness: Experimental Evidence" (Koç University-TUSIAD Economic Research Forum Working Paper, Koc University-TUSIAD Economic Research Forum, February 2011), http://econpapers.repec.org/paper/kocwpaper/1104.htm; David Wozniak, William T. Harbaugh, and Ulrich Mayr, "The Menstrual Cycle and Performance Feedback Alter Gender Differences in Competitive Choices," *Journal of Labor Economics* 32 (2014): 161–198.

12. Robert H. Frank and Philip J. Cook, *The Winner-Take-All Society: Why the Few at the Top Get So Much More Than the Rest of Us* (New York: Penguin Books, 1996); Michael Mauboussin, *The Success Equation: Untangling Skill and Luck in Business, Sports, and Investing* (Allston, MA: Harvard Business School Press, 2012).

13. John Gray, *Men Are from Mars, Women Are from Venus: The Classic Guide to Understanding the Opposite Sex* (New York: Harper Paperbacks, 2012); Hanna Rosin, *The End of Men: And the Rise of Women* (New York: Riverhead Hardcover, 2012).

14. For gender equality and values, see Shalom H. Schwartz and Tammy Rubel-Lifschitz, "Cross-National Variation in the Size of Sex Differences in Values: Effects of Gender Equality," *Journal of Personality and Social Psychology* 97 (2009): 171–185. For development and

cognitive abilities, see Daniela Weber, Vegard Skirbekk, Inga Freund, and Agneta Herlitz, "The Changing Face of Cognitive Gender Differences in Europe," *Proceedings of the National Academy of Sciences USA* 111 (2014): 11673–11678; for the relationship between testosterone and risk taking, Anna Dreber and Moshe Hoffman, "Biological Basis of Sex Differences in Risk Aversion and Competitiveness" (Working Paper, UCLA, 2010), http://www.bec.ucla.edu/papers/HoffmanPaper1.pdf; Coren L. Apicella, Anna Dreber, Benjamin Campbell, Peter B. Gray, Moshe Hoffman, and Anthony C. Little, "Testosterone and Financial Risk Preferences," *Evolution and Human Behavior* 29, no. 6 (2008): 384–390; and for the impact of the menstrual cycle on women's willingness to take risks, see Arndt Bröder and Natalia Hohmann, "Variations in Risk Taking Behavior over the Menstrual Cycle: An Improved Replication," *Evolution and Human Behavior* 24 (2003): 391–398.

15. James Andreoni and Lise Vesterlund, "Which Is the Fair Sex? Gender Differences in Altruism," *Quarterly Journal of Economics* 116 (2001): 293–312; Catherine C. Eckel and Philip J. Grossman, "Chapter 57: Differences in the Economic Decisions of Men and Women: Experimental Evidence," in *Handbook of Experimental Economics Results*, ed. Charles R. Plott and Vernon L. Smith, vol. 1 (Elsevier, 2008), 509–519; John A. Rizzo and Richard J. Zeckhauser, "Pushing Incomes to Reference Points: Why Do Male Doctors Earn More?" *Journal of Economic Behavior & Organization* 63 (2007): 514–536; for a review of the evidence on gender differences in other-regarding preferences, see Rachel Croson and Uri Gneezy, "Gender Differences in Preferences," *Journal of Economic Literature* 47 (2009): 448–474.

16. Ceci et al., "Women in Academic Science: A Changing Landscape"; Lise Vesterlund, Linda Babcock, Maria Recalde, and Laurie Weingart, "Breaking the Glass Ceiling with 'No': Gender Differences in Declining Requests for Non-Promotable Tasks" (Working Paper, University of Pittsburgh, 2013), http://www.pitt.edu/~vester/Saying_no.pdf.

10. Creating Role Models

1. Nilanjana Dasgupta and Shaki Asgari, "Seeing Is Believing: Exposure to Counterstereotypic Women Leaders and Its Effect on the Malleability of Automatic Gender Stereotyping," *Journal of Experimental Social Psychology* 40 (2004): 642–658; Ethan G. Loewi, "Painting a New Path at the Kennedy School," *Harvard Crimson,* March 5, 2012, http://www.thecrimson.com/article/2012/3/5 /women-portraits-kennedy-school/; Sapna Cheryan, Victoria C. Plaut, Paul G. Davies, and Claude M. Steele, "Ambient Belonging: How Stereotypical Cues Impact Gender Participation in Computer Science," *Journal of Personality and Social Psychology* 97 (2009): 1045–1060; Ioana M. Latu, Marianne Schmid Mast, Joris Lammers, and Dario Bombari, "Successful Female Leaders Empower Women's Behavior in Leadership Tasks," *Journal of Experimental Social Psychology* 49 (2013): 444–448. Irene V. Blair, Jennifer E. Ma, and Alison P. Lenton, "Imagining Stereotypes Away: The Moderation of Implicit Stereotypes through Mental Imagery," *Journal of Personality and Social Psychology* 81 (2001): 828–841.

2. See the excellent case study on the topic by Rohini Pande, *Women as Leaders: Lessons from Political Quotas In India* (Harvard Kennedy School Case no. 1996, Cambridge, MA, July 18, 2013), https://www.case.hks .harvard.edu/casetitle.asp?caseNo=1996.0.

3. Raghabendra Chattopadhyay and Esther Duflo, "Women as Policy Makers: Evidence from a Randomized Policy Experiment in India," *Econometrica* 72 (2004): 1409–1443; Lori Beaman, Raghabendra Chattopadhyay, Esther Duflo, Rohini Pande, and Petia Topalova, "Powerful Women: Does Exposure Reduce Bias?" *Quarterly Journal of Economics* 124 (2009): 1497–1540; Lakshmi Iyer, Anandi Mani, Prachi Mishra, and Petia Topalova, "The Power of Political Voice: Women's Political Representation and Crime in India," *American Economic Journal: Applied Economics* 4 (2012): 165–193; Lori Beaman, Esther Duflo, Rohini Pande, and Petia Topalova, "Female Leadership Raises Aspirations and Educational Attainment for Girls: A Policy Experiment

in India," *Science* 335 (2012): 582–586; *Gender Equality: The Smart Thing to Do* (Women and Public Policy Program, Harvard Kennedy School, Cambridge, MA, 2011), www.youtube.com/watch?v=hdOcjKsUqOI.

4. Johanna Mollerstrom, "Favoritism Reduces Cooperation" (Working Paper, George Mason University, 2014).

5. Marianne Bertrand, Sandra E. Black, Sissel Jensen, and Adriana Lleras-Muney, "Breaking the Glass Ceiling? The Effect of Board Quotas on Female Labor Market Outcomes in Norway" (NBER Working Paper, June 2014), http://www.nber.org/papers/w20256; David A. Matsa and Amalia R. Miller, "A Female Style in Corporate Leadership? Evidence from Quotas," *American Economic Journal: Applied Economics* 5 (2013): 136–169.

6. Fidan Ana Kurtulus and Donald Tomaskovic-Devey, "Do Female Top Managers Help Women to Advance? A Panel Study Using EEO-1 Records," *ANNALS of the American Academy of Political and Social Science* 639 (2012): 173–197.

7. Melanne Verveer and Kim K. Azzarelli, *Fast Forward: How Women Can Achieve Power and Purpose* (Boston: Houghton Mifflin Harcourt, 2015).

8. Eric P. Bettinger and Bridget Terry Long, "Do Faculty Serve as Role Models? The Impact of Instructor Gender on Female Students," *American Economic Review* 95 (2005): 152–157; Scott E. Carrell, Marianne E. Page, and James E. West, "Sex and Science: How Professor Gender Perpetuates the Gender Gap," *Quarterly Journal of Economics* 125 (2010): 1101–1144. Thomas S. Dee, "Teachers and the Gender Gaps in Student Achievement," *Journal of Human Resources* 42 (2007): 528–554.

9. For a review of same-sex vs. other-sex preferences in candidate evaluation, see Allen I. Huffcutt, "An Empirical Review of the Employment Interview Construct Literature," *International Journal of Selection and Assessment* 19 (2011): 62–81; Manuel F. Bagues and Berta Esteve-Volart, "Can Gender Parity Break the Glass Ceiling? Evidence from a Repeated Randomized Experiment," *Review of Economic Studies* 77 (2010): 1301–1328.

10. For gender roles and adolescents, see George A. Akerlof, "A Theory of Social Custom, of Which Unemployment May Be One Consequence," *Quarterly Journal of Economics* 94 (1980): 749–775; Keith B. Burt and Jacqueline Scott, "Parent and Adolescent Gender Role Attitudes in 1990s Great Britain," *Sex Roles* 46 (2002): 239–245. For men with working moms, see Raquel Fernández, Alessandra Fogli, and Claudia Olivetti, "Mothers and Sons: Preference Formation and Female Labor Force Dynamics," *Quarterly Journal of Economics* 119 (2004): 1249–1299. Nicole M. Fortin, "Gender Role Attitudes and the Labour-Market Outcomes of Women across OECD Countries," *Oxford Review of Economic Policy* 21 (2005): 416–438.

11. Linda Greenhouse, *Becoming Justice Blackmun: Harry Blackmun's Supreme Court Journey* (New York: Times Books, 2006); on Sally Blackmun: Cynthia L. Cooper, "Daughter of Justice Blackmun Goes Public about Roe," *WeNews: Womens Enews.org,* February 29, 2004, http://womensenews.org/story/the-nation/040229/daughter-justice-blackmun-goes-public-about-roe; Adam N. Glynn and Maya Sen, "Identifying Judicial Empathy: Does Having Daughters Cause Judges to Rule for Women's Issues?" *American Journal of Political Science* 59 (2015): 37–54.

12. Ebonya L. Washington, "Female Socialization: How Daughters Affect Their Legislator Fathers' Voting on Women's Issues," *American Economic Review* 98 (2008): 311–332; for the influence of daughters of CEOs: Michael S. Dahl, Cristian L. Dezső, and David Gaddis Ross, "Fatherhood and Managerial Style: How a Male CEO's Children Affect the Wages of His Employees," *Administrative Science Quarterly* 57 (2012): 669–693.

13. See www.heforshe.org and http://malechampionsofchange.com.

11. Crafting Groups

1. Bert D'Espallier, Isabelle Guérin, and Roy Mersland, "Women and Repayment in Microfinance: A Global Analysis," *World Development*

39 (2011): 758–772; Beatriz Armendáriz and Jonathan Morduch, *The Economics of Microfinance*, 2nd edition (Cambridge, MA: The MIT Press, 2010). For an excellent discussion of the determinants and impacts of microfinance, see "Where Credit Is Due," *Abdul Latif Jameel Poverty Action Lab & Innovations for Poverty Action Policy Bulletin,* February 2015, http://www.povertyactionlab.org/publication/where -credit-is-due; a hotly debated issue, to date microfinance has not had the transformative impact on poverty reduction or women's empowerment that many had envisioned. At the same time, additional resources have given the poor more freedom in how to make and use money, thus improving their well-being. In addition, not all microfinance institutions are created equal, and innovations in product design have yielded promising results; Fiona Greig and Iris Bohnet, "Exploring Gendered Behavior in the Field with Experiments: Why Public Goods Are Provided by Women in a Nairobi Slum," *Journal of Economic Behavior & Organization* 70 (2009): 1–9.

2. Felix Oberholzer-Gee, Joel Waldfogel, and Matthew W. White, "Friend Or Foe? Cooperation and Learning in High-Stakes Games," *Review of Economics and Statistics* 92, no. 1 (2010): 179–187.

3. Rachel Croson and Uri Gneezy, "Gender Differences in Preferences," *Journal of Economic Literature* 47 (2009): 448–474; Sarah J. Solnick, "Gender Differences in the Ultimatum Game," *Economic Inquiry* 39 (2001): 189–200.

4. See "News," US Department of Education, http://www.ed.gov/news /pressreleases/2006/10/10242006.html; National Association for Single Sex Public Education, http://www.singlesexschools.org/; for a critique, see Sue Klein, Jennifer Lee, Paige McKinsey, and Charmaine Archer, "Identifying US K-12 Public Schools with Deliberate Sex Segregation" (Feminist Majority Foundation Education Equality Program, December 11, 2014), http://feminist .org/education/pdfs/IdentifyingSexSegregation12-12-14.pdf. See also Patricia B. Campbell and Jo Sanders, "Challenging the System: Assumptions and Data Behind the Push for Single-Sex Schooling,"

in *Gender in Policy and Practice: Perspectives on Single Sex and Coeducational Schooling*, ed. Amanda Datnow and Lea Hubbard (New York: Routledge, 2002).

5. For the Texas study, see Caroline Hoxby, "Peer Effects in the Classroom: Learning from Gender and Race Variation" (NBER Working Paper, August 2000), http://www.nber.org/papers/w7867; for the Israeli study, see Victor Lavy and Analia Schlosser, "Mechanisms and Impacts of Gender Peer Effects at School," *American Economic Journal: Applied Economics* 3 (2011): 1–33; for the study in Spain, see Walter Garcia-Fontes and Antonio Ciccone, "Gender Peer Effects in School, a Birth Cohort Approach" (SSRN Scholarly Paper, Rochester, NY, June 1, 2014), http://papers.ssrn.com/abstract =2501514.

6. Johanne Boisjoly, Greg J. Duncan, Michael Kremer, Dan M. Levy, and Jacque Eccles, "Empathy or Antipathy? The Impact of Diversity," *American Economic Review* 96 (2006): 1890–1905; Bruce Sacerdote, "Peer Effects with Random Assignment: Results for Dartmouth Roommates," *Quarterly Journal of Economics* 116 (2001): 681–704; Daniel A. McFarland, James Moody, David Diehl, Jeffrey A. Smith, and Reuben J. Thomas, "Network Ecology and Adolescent Social Structure," *American Sociological Review* 79 (2014): 1088–1121; Thomas F. Pettigrew and Linda R. Tropp, "A Meta-Analytic Test of Intergroup Contact Theory," *Journal of Personality and Social Psychology* 90 (2006): 751–783.

7. Denise Lewin Loyd, Cynthia S. Wang, Katherine W. Phillips, and Robert B. Lount Jr., "Social Category Diversity Promotes Premeeting Elaboration: The Role of Relationship Focus," *Organization Science* 24 (2013): 757–772; Anita Williams Woolley, Christopher F. Chabris, Alex Pentland, Nada Hashmi, and Thomas W. Malone, "Evidence for a Collective Intelligence Factor in the Performance of Human Groups," *Science* 330 (2010): 686–688.

8. Christopher F. Karpowitz, Tali Mendelberg, and Lee Shaker, "Gender Inequality in Deliberative Participation," *American Political Science*

Review 106 (2012): 533–547, quotation on p. 533; Jack A. Goncalo, Jennifer A. Chatman, Michelle M. Duguid, and Jessica A. Kennedy, "Creativity from Constraint? How the Political Correctness Norm Influences Creativity in Mixed-Sex Work Groups," *Administrative Science Quarterly* 60 (2015): 1–30.

9. Sara Fisher Ellison and Wallace P. Mullin, "Diversity, Social Goods Provision, and Performance in the Firm," *Journal of Economics & Management Strategy* 23 (2014): 465–481.

10. Cristian L. Dezsö and David Gaddis Ross, "Does Female Representation in Top Management Improve Firm Performance? A Panel Data Investigation," *Strategic Management Journal* 33, no. 9 (2012): 1072–1089; Claude Francoeur, Réal Labelle, and Bernard Sinclair-Desgagné, "Gender Diversity in Corporate Governance and Top Management," *Journal of Business Ethics* 81 (2008): 83–95. "The CS Gender 3000: Women in Senior Management" (Credit Suisse Publications, January 2014), http://publications.credit-suisse.com/index.cfm/publikationen -shop/research-institute/the-cs-gender-3000-women-in-senior -management-2/; Andrea Weber and Christine Zulehner, "Female Hires and the Success of Start-Up Firms," *American Economic Review* 100 (2010): 358–361; Sander Hoogendoorn, Hessel Oosterbeek, and Mirjam van Praag, "The Impact of Gender Diversity on the Performance of Business Teams: Evidence from a Field Experiment," *Management Science* 59 (2013): 1514–1528.

11. Boris Groysberg, Jeffrey T. Polzer, and Hillary Anger Elfenbein, "Too Many Cooks Spoil the Broth: How High-Status Individuals Decrease Group Effectiveness," *Organization Science* 22 (2010): 722–737; Scott Page, *The Difference: How the Power of Diversity Creates Better Groups, Firms, Schools, and Societies* (Princeton: Princeton University Press, 2008).

12. Katherine Y. Williams and Charles A. O'Reilly III, "Demography and Diversity in Organizations: A Review of 40 years of Research," in *Research in Organizational Behavior,* ed. Barry M. Staw and Larry L. Cummings (Greenwich, CT: JAI Press, 1981), 77–140; Elizabeth Mannix and Margaret A. Neale, "What Differences Make a Difference? The Promise and Reality of Diverse Teams in Organizations,"

Psychological Science in the Public Interest 6 (2005): 31–55; Robin J. Ely, "A Field Study of Group Diversity, Participation in Diversity Education Programs, and Performance," *Journal of Organizational Behavior* 25 (2004): 755–780; Karen A. Jehn, Gregory B. Northcraft, and Margaret A. Neale, "Why Differences Make a Difference: A Field Study of Diversity, Conflict, and Performance in Workgroups," *Administrative Science Quarterly* 44 (1999): 741–763; Steven Frost, *The Inclusion Imperative: How Real Inclusion Creates Better Business and Builds Better Societies* (London: Kogan Page, 2014); on how to improve team processes, see J. Richard Hackman, *Leading Teams: Setting the Stage for Great Performances* (Boston: Harvard Business School Press, 2002); Amy C. Edmondson, *Teaming: How Organizations Learn, Innovate, and Compete in the Knowledge Economy* (San Francisco: Jossey-Bass, 2012).

13. Michaela Bär, Alexandra Niessen, and Stefan Ruenzi, "The Impact of Work Group Diversity on Performance: Large Sample Evidence from the Mutual Fund Industry" (CFR Working Papers, 2007), http://ideas.repec.org/p/zbw/cfrwps/0716.html.

14. Rosabeth Moss Kanter, "Some Effects of Proportions on Group Life: Skewed Sex Ratios and Responses to Token Women," *American Journal of Sociology* 82 (1977): 965–990; Williams and O'Reilly, "Demography and Diversity in Organizations: A Review of 40 Years of Research." The Queen Bee syndrome was coined in the 1970s and is discussed here: Peggy Drexler, "The Tyranny of the Queen Bee," *Wall Street Journal,* March 6, 2013, http://www.wsj.com/articles/SB10001424127887323884304578328271526080496; evidence on how female "token" group members can inhibit group diversification, either through fear of competitive threat from similar others or through "collective threat," namely the fear that nonperfect similar others could reinforce negative group stereotypes, is presented by Michelle Duguid, "Female Tokens in High-Prestige Work Groups: Catalysts or Inhibitors of Group Diversification?" *Organizational Behavior and Human Decision Processes* 116 (2011): 104–115.

15. Drude Dahlerup, "From a Small to a Large Minority: Women in Scandinavian Politics," *Scandinavian Political Studies* 11 (1988):

275–298; Grant Miller, "Women's Suffrage, Political Responsiveness, and Child Survival in American History," *Quarterly Journal of Economics* 123 (2008): 1287–1327; for the political representation of castes in India, see Rohini Pande, "Can Mandated Political Representation Increase Policy Influence for Disadvantaged Minorities? Theory and Evidence from India," *American Economic Review* 93 (2003): 1132–1151; for a discussion, see Jane Mansbridge, "Should Blacks Represent Blacks and Women Represent Women? A Contingent 'Yes,'" *Journal of Politics* 61 (1999): 628–657.

16. Katherine W. Phillips and Damon Phillips, "Nationality Heterogeneity, Performance, and Blau's Paradox: The Case of NHL Hockey Teams, 1988–1998" (Northwestern Kellogg School of Management Working Paper), http://www.kellogg.northwestern.edu/?sc_itemid=%7BE23AD21B-AFBA-4C56-A189-0269121664ED%7D; more generally on fault lines, see Dora C. Lau and J. Keith Murnighan, "Interactions within Groups and Subgroups: The Effects of Demographic Faultlines," *Academy of Management Journal* 48 (2005): 645–659.

17. On procedural fairness, see E. Allan Lind and Tom R. Tyler, *The Social Psychology of Procedural Justice, Critical Issues in Social Justice* (Boston: Springer US, 1988); for an application to democratic decision-making, see Felix Oberholzer-Gee, Iris Bohnet, and Bruno S. Frey, "Fairness and Competence in Democratic Decisions," *Public Choice* 91 (1997): 89–105.

18. Johanna Mollerstrom, "Favoritism Reduces Cooperation" (Working Paper, George Mason University, 2014); Andreas Leibbrandt, Liang Choon Wang, and Cordelia Foo, "Gender Quotas, Competitions and Peer Review: Experimental Evidence on the Backlash against Women" (Working Paper, Monash University, 2015); for Spain, see Manuel F. Bagues and Berta Esteve-Volart, "Can Gender Parity Break the Glass Ceiling? Evidence from a Repeated Randomized Experiment," *Review of Economic Studies* 77 (2010): 1301–1328; for France, see Guillaume R. Fréchette, Francois Maniquet, and Massimo Morelli, "Incumbents' Interests and Gender Quotas," *American Journal*

of Political Science 52 (2008): 891–909; for an excellent review on quotas, see Rohini Pande and Deanna Ford, "Gender Quotas and Female Leadership," https://openknowledge.worldbank.org/handle /10986/9120; Mona Lena Krook, *Quotas for Women in Politics: Gender and Candidate Selection Reform Worldwide* (New York: Oxford University Press, 2009).

19. Stephen J. Ceci, Donna K. Ginther, Shulamit Kahn, and Wendy M. Williams, "Women in Academic Science: A Changing Landscape," *Psychological Science in the Public Interest* 15 (2014): 75–141; Muriel Niederle, Carmit Segal, and Lise Vesterlund, "How Costly Is Diversity? Affirmative Action in Light of Gender Differences in Competitiveness," *Management Science* 59 (2012): 1–16; and Loukas Balafoutas and Matthias Sutter, "Affirmative Action Policies Promote Women and Do Not Harm Efficiency in the Laboratory," *Science* 335 (2012): 579–582. These sources find that affirmative action policies, in which there is a quota for the number of female winners of a tournament, can increase willingness to compete among women; for data on women in STEM, see *Women, Minorities, and Persons with Disabilities in Science and Engineering 2015* (National Science Foundation, National Center for Science and Engineering Statistics, Special Report NSF 15-311, 2015), http://www.nsf.gov /statistics/wmpd/.

20. For a review of the evidence, see Jonathan S. Leonard, "Women and Affirmative Action," *Journal of Economic Perspectives* 3 (1989): 61–75. Roland G. Fryer Jr. and Glenn C. Loury, "Affirmative Action and Its Mythology," *Journal of Economic Perspectives* 19 (2005): 147–162; for the survey on recruitment practices, see David Neumark and Harry J. Holzer, "What Does Affirmative Action Do?" *Industrial and Labor Relations Review* (2000): 240–271; and for a comprehensive analysis of the impact on federal contractors versus noncontractors, see Fidan Ana Kurtulus, "The Impact of Affirmative Action on the Employment of Women and Minorities over Three Decades: 1973– 2003," *Journal of Policy Analysis and Management* (Forthcoming): http://economics.lafayette.edu/files/2011/04/kurtulus.pdf.

21. For a discussion, see the excellent textbook by Mukesh Eswaran, *Why Gender Matters in Economics* (Princeton: Princeton University Press, 2014), 350–354; see also Madeline E. Heilman, Caryn J. Block, and Peter Stathatos, "The Affirmative Action Stigma of Incompetence: Effects of Performance Information Ambiguity," *Academy of Management Journal* 40 (1997): 603–625; and David C. Evans, "A Comparison of the Other-Directed Stigmatization Produced by Legal and Illegal Forms of Affirmative Action," *Journal of Applied Psychology* 88 (2003): 121–130.

22. "German Boardrooms to Introduce Female Quotas," *Telegraph*, November 26, 2014, http://www.telegraph.co.uk/news/worldnews /europe/germany/11255970/German-boardrooms-to-introduce -female-quotas.html.

23. "Gender Diversity and Corporate Performance" (Credit Suisse Research Institute, August 2012), https://publications.credit-suisse.com /tasks/render/file/index.cfm?fileid=88EC32A9-83E8-EB92 -9D5A40FF69E66808; Deborah Rhode and Amanda K. Packel, "Diversity on Corporate Boards: How Much Difference Does Difference Make?" (SSRN Scholarly Paper, Rochester, NY, 2014), http://papers.ssrn.com/abstract=1685615; Miriam Schwartz-Ziv, "Does the Gender of Directors Matter?" (SSRN Scholarly Paper, Rochester, NY, May 2, 2013), http://papers.ssrn.com/abstract=2257867; Alison M. Konrad, Vicki Kramer, and Sumru Erkut, "Critical Mass: The Impact of Three or More Women on Corporate Boards," *Organizational Dynamics* 37 (2008): 145–164; Corinne Post and Kris Byron, "Women on Boards and Firm Financial Performance: A Meta-Analysis," *Academy of Management Journal* 58, no. 5 (2015): 1546–1571.

24. On how the market responded to the introduction of quotas, see Kenneth R. Ahern and Amy K. Dittmar, "The Changing of the Boards: The Impact on Firm Valuation of Mandated Female Board Representation," *Quarterly Journal of Economics* 127 (2012): 137–197; on the impact of quotas on profits, see David A. Matsa and Amalia R. Miller, "A Female Style in Corporate Leadership? Evidence from Quotas," *American Economic Journal: Applied Economics* 5 (2013):

136–169; Renée B. Adams and Patricia Funk, "Beyond the Glass Ceiling: Does Gender Matter?," *Management Science* 58, no. 2 (2011): 219–235 suggest that female board members care more about stakeholders than their male counterparts; Richard J. Hackman, *Leading Teams: Setting the Stage for Great Performance* (Boston: Harvard Business School Press, 2002).

25. Paul R. Sackett, Cathy L. DuBois, and Ann W. Noe, "Tokenism in Performance Evaluation: The Effects of Work Group Representation on Male-Female and White-Black Differences in Performance Ratings," *Journal of Applied Psychology* 76 (1991): 263–267.

26. Cass R. Sunstein and Reid Hastie, *Wiser: Getting Beyond Groupthink to Make Groups Smarter* (Boston: Harvard Business Review Press, 2014); Michael J. Mauboussin and Dan Callahan, "Building an Effective Team: How to Manage a Team to Make Good Decisions" (Credit Suisse, Global Financial Strategies, 2014).

12. Shaping Norms

1. Michael Hallsworth, John A. List, Robert D. Metcalfe, and Ivo Vlaev, "The Behavioralist As Tax Collector: Using Natural Field Experiments to Enhance Tax Compliance" (NBER Working Paper, March 2014), http://www.nber.org/papers/w20007; see also "Fraud, Error and Debt: Behavioural Insights Team Paper" (UK Government: Behavioral Insights Team, Cabinet Office Paper), https://www.gov.uk /government/publications/fraud-error-and-debt-behavioural-insights -team-paper; P. Wesley Schultz, Jessica M. Nolan, Robert B. Cialdini, Noah J. Goldstein, and Vladas Griskevicius, "The Constructive, Destructive, and Reconstructive Power of Social Norms," *Psychological Science* 18 (2007): 429–434; Stephen Coleman, "The Minnesota Income Tax Compliance Experiment: State Tax Results," http://mpra.ub.uni-muenchen.de/4827/; Donna D. Bobek, Robin W. Roberts, and John T. Sweeney, "The Social Norms of Tax Compliance: Evidence from Australia, Singapore, and the United States," *Journal of Business Ethics* 74 (2007): 49–64; Alan S. Gerber and

Todd Rogers, "Descriptive Social Norms and Motivation to Vote: Everyone's Voting and so Should You," *Journal of Politics*, 71, no. 1 (2009): 1–14; Rachel Croson and Jen (Yue) Shang, "Social Influence in Giving: Field Experiments in Public Radio," in *Experimental Approaches to the Study of Charity*, ed. Daniel M. Oppenheimer and Christopher Y. Olivola (New York: Psychology Press, 2011); and more generally, on conditional cooperation, Urs Fischbacher, Simon Gächter, and Ernst Fehr, "Are People Conditionally Cooperative? Evidence from a Public Goods Experiment," *Economics Letters* 71 (2001): 397–404.

2. Lucas Coffman, Clayton R. Featherstone, and Jude Kessler, "Can Social Information Affect What Job You Choose and Keep?" (Working Paper, Abdul Latif Jameel Poverty Action Lab, November 22, 2014), http://www.povertyactionlab.org/evaluation/can -social-information-affect-what-job-you-choose-and-keep-field -experiment-united-states; for the petrified wood study, see Robert B. Cialdini, Linda J. Demaine, Brad J. Sagarin, Daniel W. Barrett, Kelton Rhoads, and Patricia L. Winter, "Managing Social Norms for Persuasive Impact," *Social Influence* 1 (2006): 3–15; for the original parking lot study, see Robert B. Cialdini, Raymond R. Reno, and Carl A. Kallgren, "A Focus Theory of Normative Conduct: Recycling the Concept of Norms to Reduce Littering in Public Places," *Journal of Personality and Social Psychology* 58 (1990): 1015–1026.

3. Both Theresa May's and Lord Davies's quotations can be found in "Women on Boards," UK Government, https://www.gov.uk /government/news/women-on-boards.

4. Nicole M. Fortin, "Gender Role Attitudes and the Labour-Market Outcomes of Women across OECD Countries," *Oxford Review of Economic Policy* 21 (2005): 416–438.

5. "Women on Boards: Two Years On," UK Government, https://www .gov.uk/government/news/women-on-boards-two-years-on.

6. Women on Boards 2015: Fourth Annual Review, Department of Business, Innovation and Skills, UK Government, https://www.gov .uk/government/publications/women-on-boards-2015-fourth-annual

-review. Davies Report Says No More All-Male Boards on FTSE 100, BBC October 29, 2015, www.bbc.com/news/business=34663119.

7. Maliheh Paryavi, Iris Bohnet, and Alexandra van Geen, "Descriptive Norms and Gender Diversity: Reactance from Men" (Harvard Kennedy School Working Paper, 2015).

8. Flora Wisdorff, "Wie Die Telekom Die Frauenquote Erfüllen Will" *Welt Online,* December 3, 2014, sec. Wirtschaft, http://www.welt.de /wirtschaft/article134969155/Wie-die-Telekom-die-Frauenquote -erfuellen-will.html; "Die Frauenquote Bremst Männer Aus," *WirtschaftsWoche,* http://www.wiwo.de/erfolg/management /geschlechterkampf-die-frauenquote-bremst-maenner-aus/6984126 .html.

9. Aaron A. Dhir, *Challenging Boardroom Homogeneity: Corporate Law, Governance, and Diversity* (New York: Cambridge University Press, 2015); "Brief for Amici Curiae 65 Leading American Businesses in Support of Respondents in *Grutter v. Bollinger,* et al.," Leadership Conference on Civil and Human Rights, http://www.civilrights.org /equal-opportunity/legal-briefs/brief-for-amici-curiae-65-leading -american-businesses-in-support-of-respondents-in-grutter-v -bollinger-et-al.html; "*Fisher v. University of Texas,*" Oyez Project at IIT Chicago-Kent College of Law, http://www.oyez.org/cases/2010 -2019/2012/2012_11_34.

10. Fortin, "Gender Role Attitudes and the Labour-Market Outcomes of Women across OECD Countries."

11. Michael A. Koenig, Saifuddin Ahmed, Mian Bazle Hossain, and A. B. M. Khorshed Alam Mozumder, "Women's Status and Domestic Violence in Rural Bangladesh: Individual- and Community-Level Effects," *Demography* 40 (2003): 269–288; Nancy Luke and Kaivan Munshi, "Women as Agents of Change: Female Income and Mobility in India," *Journal of Development Economics* 94 (2011): 1–17.

12. Hunt Allcott, "Social Norms and Energy Conservation," *Journal of Public Economics, Special Issue: The Role of Firms in Tax Systems* 95 (2011): 1082–1095; Hunt Allcott and Todd Rogers, "The Short-Run and Long-Run Effects of Behavioral Interventions: Experimental

Evidence from Energy Conservation," *American Economic Review* 104, no. 10 (2014): 3003–3037.

13. Schultz et al., "The Constructive, Destructive, and Reconstructive Power of Social Norms"; see also Dora L. Costa and Matthew E. Kahn, "Energy Conservation 'Nudges' and Environmentalist Ideology: Evidence from a Randomized Residential Electricity Field Experiment," *Journal of the European Economic Association* 11 (2013): 680–702, who found that Republicans increased their energy usage; but see Allcott, "Social Norms and Energy Conservation" who found no such effect; note that peer social norm information has had negative effects on the academic performance of the lowest-ability students: Scott E. Carrell, Bruce I. Sacerdote, and James E. West, "From Natural Variation to Optimal Policy? The Lucas Critique Meets Peer Effects" (NBER Working Paper, March 2011), http://www.nber.org/papers/w16865; and for savings of unionized employees, see John Beshears, James J. Choi, David Laibson, Brigitte C. Madrian, and Katherine L. Milkman, "The Effect of Providing Peer Information on Retirement Savings Decisions," *Journal of Finance* 70 (2015): 1161–1201.

14. Iris Bohnet and Richard Zeckhauser, "Social Comparisons in Ultimatum Bargaining," *Scandinavian Journal of Economics* 106 (2004): 495–510; John Duffy and Tatiana Kornienko, "Does Competition Affect Giving?" *Journal of Economic Behavior & Organization* 74 (2010): 82–103.

15. World Economic Forum, Global Gender Gap Reports, 2006–2015. See "The Global Gender Gap Report 2006," World Economic Forum, http://www3.weforum.org/docs/WEF_GenderGap_Report _2006.pdf; the Saadia Zahidi quotation can be found in "Why the US Is Losing the Global Fight for Gender Equality," *Fortune,* October 27, 2014, http://fortune.com/2014/10/27/global-gender-gap-america/; and the Klaus Schwab quotation can be found in "2095: The Year of Gender Equality in the Workplace, Maybe," *World Economic Forum News Release,* October 28, 2014, http://www.weforum.org/news /2095-year-gender-equality-workplace-maybe.

16. Judith G. Kelley and Beth A. Simmons, "Politics by Number: Indicators as Social Pressure in International Relations," *American Journal of Political Science* 59, no. 1 (2015): 55–70; Aaron K. Chatterji and Michael W. Toffel, "How Firms Respond to Being Rated," *Strategic Management Journal* 31 (2010): 917–945; Joseph S. Nye Jr., *Soft Power: The Means to Success in World Politics* (New York: Public Affairs, 2005).

17. For the impact of college rankings on applications, see Michael Luca and Jonathan Smith, "Salience in Quality Disclosure: Evidence from the *US News* College Rankings," *Journal of Economics & Management Strategy* 22 (2013): 58–77; for the negative impacts of rankings, see Benjamin Edelman and Ian Larkin, "Social Comparisons and Deception across Workplace Hierarchies: Field and Experimental Evidence," *Organization Science* 26, no. 1 (2014): 78–98; Gary Charness, David Masclet, and Marie Claire Villeval, "The Dark Side of Competition for Status," *Management Science* 60, no. 1 (2013): 38–55.

18. See Robert Cooter, "Expressive Law and Economics," *Journal of Legal Studies* 27, no. 2 (1998): 585–608; Richard McAdams, "An Attitudinal Theory of Expressive Law," *Oregon Law Review* 79 (2000): 339–390; Cass Sunstein, "On the Expressive Function of Law," *University of Pennsylvania Law Review* 144 (1996): 2021; Robert D. Cooter and Iris Bohnet, "Expressive Law: Framing or Equilibrium Selection?" (Boalt Working Papers in Public Law, November 1, 2003), http:// escholarship.org/uc/item/65z2m533; for a methodology on how to measure descriptive and injunctive norms in organizations, see Erin L. Krupka and Roberto A. Weber, "Identifying Social Norms Using Coordination Games: Why Does Dictator Game Sharing Vary?" *Journal of the European Economic Association* 11, no. 3 (2013): 495–524; for a detailed exploration of social meaning and the National Hockey League example, see Lawrence Lessig, "The Regulation of Social Meaning," *University of Chicago Law Review* 62 (1995): 943–1045.

19. "Title IX of the Education Amendments of 1972," US Department of Justice, http://www.justice.gov/crt/about/cor/coord/titleix.php; Jake Simpson, "How Title IX Sneakily Revolutionized Women's Sports," *Atlantic Monthly,* June 21, 2012, http://www.theatlantic.com

/entertainment/archive/2012/06/how-title-ix-sneakily
-revolutionized-womens-sports/258708/; "NCAA® to Debut Title
IX Anniversary Documentary Sporting Chance" presented by
Northwestern Mutual on ESPN2, Northwestern Mutual, http://www
.multivu.com/mnr/53644-northwestern-mutual-and-ncaa-title-ix
-40th-anniversary-documentary-espn2.
20. Douglas Birsch and John Fielder, eds., *The Ford Pinto Case: A Study in
Applied Ethics, Business, and Technology* (Binghamton, NY: SUNY Press,
1994).

13. Increasing Transparency

1. Carlos Jensen, Colin Potts, and Christian Jensen, "Privacy Practices of
Internet Users: Self-Reports Versus Observed Behavior," *International
Journal of Human-Computer Studies* 63 (2005): 203–227; Roger L.
McCarthy, James P. Finnegan, Susan Krumm-Scott, and Gail E.
McCarthy, "Product Information Presentation, User Behavior, and
Safety," *Proceedings of the Human Factors and Ergonomics Society Annual
Meeting* 28 (1984): 81–85.
2. For the spotlight effect, see Thomas Gilovich, Victoria Husted
Medvec, and Kenneth Savitsky, "The Spotlight Effect in Social
Judgment: An Egocentric Bias in Estimates of the Salience of One's
Own Actions and Appearance," *Journal of Personality and Social
Psychology* 78 (2000): 211–222; for a discussion of producer versus
consumer responses to disclosure, see George Loewenstein, Cass R.
Sunstein, and Russell Golman, "Disclosure: Psychology Changes
Everything," *Annual Review of Economics* 6 (2014): 391–419; "Energy
Efficient Products," Energy-European Commission, https://ec.europa
.eu/energy/en/topics/energy-efficiency/energy-efficient-products;
"Energy Labeling Rule," Federal Register, https://www.federalregister
.gov/articles/2014/08/12/2014-18501/energy-labeling-rule.
3. "Compare Side-by-Side: 2015 Toyota Prius," US Department of
Energy: Energy Efficiency and Renewable Energy, http://www
.fueleconomy.gov/feg/Find.do?action=sbs&id=35556.

4. Cass R. Sunstein, *Simpler: The Future of Government* (New York: Simon and Schuster, 2013), quotation on p. 10; Michael Luca and Chelsea Burkett, "The Digital Opportunity Staring Credit Cards in the Face," *Harvard Business Review,* https://hbr.org/2014/06/the -digital-opportunity-staring-credit-cards-in-the-face.

5. "Choose My Plate: Frequently Asked Questions" (USDA, April 24, 2013), http://www.choosemyplate.gov/downloads/PermissionsFAQs .pdf; Richard P. Larrick and Jack B. Soll, "The MPG Illusion," *Science* 32 (2008): 1593–1594; Sunstein, *Simpler*; Chip Heath and Dan Heath, *Switch: How to Change Things When Change Is Hard* (New York: Crown Business, 2010), quotation on pp. 61–62.

6. Ginger Zhe Jin and Phillip Leslie, "The Effect of Information on Product Quality: Evidence from Restaurant Hygiene Grade Cards," *Quarterly Journal of Economics* 118 (2003): 409–551; Jun Seok Kang, Polina Kuznetsova, Yejin Choi, and Michael Luca, "Where Not to Eat? Improving Public Policy by Predicting Hygiene Inspections Using Online Reviews" (Proceedings of the Conference on Empirical Methods in Natural Language Processing, 2013), http://www.hbs.edu /faculty/Pages/item.aspx?num=45649.

7. Brigitte C. Madrian and Dennis F. Shea, "The Power of Suggestion: Inertia in 401(k) Participation and Savings Behavior," *Quarterly Journal of Economics* 116 (2001): 1149–1187; for a discussion of the advantages and disadvantages of defaults, see N. Craig Smith, Daniel G. Goldstein, and Eric J. Johnson, "Choice Without Awareness: Ethical and Policy Implications of Defaults," *Journal of Public Policy & Marketing* 32 (2013): 159–172.

8. "Australian Securities and Investments Commission," http://asic.gov.au/; "Canadian Securities Exchange Home," http://www.cnsx.ca/CNSX /Home.aspx; "Financial Conduct Authority," http://www.fca.org.uk/; "Autoriteit Financiële Markten (The Netherlands Authority for the Financial Markets)," http://www.afm.nl/en; "US Securities and Exchange Commission," http://www.sec.gov/; "Board of Director Gender Diversity 'Comply or Explain' Disclosure a New Reality for Canadian Reporting Issuers" (LaBarge Weinstein LLP), http://www

.lwlaw.com/board-of-director-gender-diversity-comply-or-explain
-disclosure-a-new-reality-for-canadian-reporting-issuers/; "Women
on Boards 2011" (UK Government, February 2011), https://www.gov
.uk/government/uploads/system/uploads/attachment_data/file/31480
/11-745-women-on-boards.pdf; "Women on Boards 2015: Fourth
Annual Review" (UK Government, March 2015), https://www.gov
.uk/government/publications/women-on-boards-2015-fourth-annual
-review.

9. For data on women on boards in the United States, see "2011 Catalyst
Census: Fortune 500 Women Board Directors," *Catalyst,*
December 13, 2011, http://www.catalyst.org/system/files/2011
_Fortune_500_Census_WBD.pdf; "2014 Catalyst Census: Women
Board Directors," *Catalyst,* January 13, 2015, http://www.catalyst.org
/knowledge/2014-catalyst-census-women-board-directors.

10. Jason P. Block and Christina A. Roberto, "Potential Benefits of
Calorie Labeling in Restaurants," *JAMA* 312 (2014): 887–888; Alexa
Namba, Amy Auchincloss, Beth Leonberg, and Margo G. Wootan,
"Exploratory Analysis of Fast-Food Chain Restaurant Menus Before
and After Implementation of Local Calorie-Labeling Policies,
2005–2011," *Preventing Chronic Disease* 10 (2013): 1545–1151; Jonas J.
Swartz, Danielle Braxton, and Anthony J. Viera, "Calorie Menu
Labeling on Quick-Service Restaurant Menus: An Updated
Systematic Review of the Literature," *The International Journal of
Behavioral Nutrition and Physical Activity* 8 (2011): 135. For design
features, see: Susan E. Sinclair, Marcia Cooper, and Elizabeth D.
Mansfield, "The Influence of Menu Labeling on Calories Selected or
Consumed: A Systematic Review and Meta-Analysis," *Journal of the
Academy of Nutrition and Dietetics* 114 (2014): 1375–1388. For a
discussion and review of the evidence, see George Loewenstein,
"Confronting Reality: Pitfalls of Calorie Posting," *American Journal
of Clinical Nutrition* 93 (2011): 679–680; Julie S. Downs, George
Loewenstein, and Jessica Wisdom, "Strategies for Promoting
Healthier Food Choices," *American Economic Review* 99 (2009):
159–164; Bryan Bollinger, Phillip Leslie, and Alan Sorensen, "Calorie

Posting in Chain Restaurants," *American Economic Journal: Economic Policy* 3 (2011): 91–128.

11. "Executive Order—Non-Retaliation for Disclosure of Compensation Information" (The White House, Office of the Press Secretary, April 8, 2014), https://www.whitehouse.gov/the-press-office/2014/04/08 /executive-order-non-retaliation-disclosure-compensation -information; "Presidential Memorandum—Advancing Pay Equality Through Compensation Data Collection" (Office of the Press Secretary, The White House, April 8, 2014), https://www.whitehouse .gov/the-press-office/2014/04/08/presidential-memorandum -advancing-pay-equality-through-compensation-data; "Valerie Jarrett: Wage 'Transparency' Will Help Employers 'Avoid Lawsuits'" (CNS News, April 8, 2014), http://www.cnsnews.com/news/article/susan -jones/valerie-jarrett-wage-transparency-will-help-employers-avoid -lawsuits.

12. Duncan Gilchrist, Michael Luca, and Deepak Malhotra, "When 3+1>4: Gift Structure and Reciprocity in the Field," *Management Science* (April 2015), http://www.hbs.edu/faculty/Pages /item.aspx?num=45668.

13. Negotiation and aspiration: see Leigh Thompson, *The Mind and Heart of the Negotiator*, 5th edition (Boston: Prentice Hall, 2011); on women's response to targets, see Madeline E. Heilman and Victoria Barocas Alcott, "What I Think You Think of Me: Women's Reactions to Being Viewed as Beneficiaries of Preferential Selection," *Journal of Applied Psychology* 86 (2001): 574–582; Jennifer Whelan and Robert Wood, "Targets and Quotas for Women in Leadership" (Gender Equality Project, Center for Ethical Leadership, Ormond College, University of Melbourne, August 5, 2014), https://cel.edu.au/our -research/targets-and-quotas-for-women-in-leadership.

14. For the importance of having a single goal, see Dilip Soman and Min Zhao, "The Fewer the Better: Number of Goals and Savings Be-havior," *Journal of Marketing Research* 48 (2011): 944–957; for the importance of subgoals in saving, see Helen Colby and Gretchen B. Chapman, "Savings, Subgoals, and Reference Points," *Judgment &*

Decision Making 8 (2013): 16–24; for subgoals and proofreading, see Dan Ariely and Klaus Wertenbroch, "Procrastination, Deadlines, and Performance: Self-Control by Precommitment," *Psychological Science* 13 (2002): 219–224.

15. For the study on accountability and stereotyping in Israel, see Arie W. Kruglanski and Tallie Freund, "The Freezing and Unfreezing of Lay-Inferences: Effects on Impressional Primacy, Ethnic Stereotyping, and Numerical Anchoring," *Journal of Experimental Social Psychology* 19 (1983): 448–468; for related evidence, see Louis A. Boudreau, Reuben M. Baron, and Peter V. Oliver, "Effects of Expected Communication Target Expertise and Timing of Set on Trait Use in Person Description," *Personality and Social Psychology Bulletin* 18 (1992): 447–451; Louise F. Pendry and C. Neil Macrae, "What the Disinterested Perceiver Overlooks: Goal-Directed Social Categorization," *Personality and Social Psychology Bulletin* 22 (1996): 249–256; for a review of the literature, see Jennifer S. Lerner and Philip E. Tetlock, "Accounting for the Effects of Accountability," *Psychological Bulletin* 125 (1999): 255–275; and Elizabeth Levy Paluck and Donald P. Green, "Prejudice Reduction: What Works? A Review and Assessment of Research and Practice," *Annual Review of Psychology* 60 (2009): 339–367.

16. Alexandra Kalev, Frank Dobbin, and Erin Kelly, "Best Practices or Best Guesses? Assessing the Efficacy of Corporate Affirmative Action and Diversity Policies," *American Sociological Review* 71 (2006): 589–617.

17. Stefano DellaVigna, John A. List, Ulrike Malmendier, and Gautam Rao, "Voting to Tell Others" (NBER Working Paper, Cambridge, MA, January 2014), http://www.nber.org/papers/w19832.pdf.

Designing Change

1. Michael Luca, "Were OkCupid's and Facebook's Experiments Unethical?" *Harvard Business Review,* https://hbr.org/2014/07/were-okcupids-and-facebooks-experiments-unethical.

2. David Halpern, *Inside the Nudge Unit: How Small Changes Can Make a Big Difference* (London: W.H. Allen, 2015); Gabriel D. Carroll, James J. Choi, David Laibson, Brigitte C. Madrian, and Andrew Metrick, "Optimal Defaults and Active Decisions," *Quarterly Journal of Economics* 124 (2009): 1639–1674; Richard H. Thaler and Shlomo Benartzi, "Save More Tomorrow™: Using Behavioral Economics to Increase Employee Saving," *Journal of Political Economy* 112 (2004): 164–187; Richard H. Thaler, *Misbehaving: The Making of Behavioral Economics* (New York: W.W. Norton & Company, 2015).

3. World Bank Group, *World Development Report 2015* (Washington, DC: World Bank, 2015), https://openknowledge.worldbank.org/handle/10986/20597; Behavioral Insights Group, Harvard Kennedy School Center for Public Leadership, http://cpl.hks.harvard.edu/behavioral-insights-group. John Beshears and Francesca Gino, "Leaders as Decision Architects," *Harvard Business Review,* https://hbr.org/2015/05/leaders-as-decision-architects.

4. David W. Nickerson and Todd Rogers, "Do You Have a Voting Plan? Implementation Intentions, Voter Turnout, and Organic Plan Making," *Psychological Science* 21 (2010): 194–199; Neil Malhotra, Melissa R. Michelson, Todd Rogers, and Ali Adam Valenzuela, "Text Messages as Mobilization Tools: The Conditional Effect of Habitual Voting and Election Salience," *American Politics Research* 39 (2011): 664–681; Christopher J. Bryan, Gregory M. Walton, Todd Rogers, and Carol S. Dweck, "Motivating Voter Turnout by Invoking the Self," *Proceedings of the National Academy of Sciences USA* 108 (2011): 12653–12656.

5. Halpern, *Inside the Nudge Unit*; Scott S. Wiltermuth and Francesca Gino, "'I'll Have One of Each': How Separating Rewards into (Meaningless) Categories Increases Motivation," *Journal of Personality and Social Psychology* 104 (2013): 1–13; Todd Rogers and Max H. Bazerman, "Future Lock-in: Future Implementation Increases Selection of 'Should' Choices," *Organizational Behavior and Human Decision Processes* 106 (2008): 1–20; Max H. Bazerman and Ann E. Tenbrunsel, *Blind Spots: Why We Fail to Do What's Right and What to Do About It* (Princeton: Princeton University Press, 2012); Dan Ariely,

The Honest Truth About Dishonesty: How We Lie to Everyone—Especially Ourselves (New York: Harper Perennial, 2012); Francesca Gino, *Sidetracked: Why Our Decisions Get Derailed, and How We Can Stick to the Plan* (Boston: Harvard Business Review Press, 2013).

6. Farhad Manjoo, "Exposing Hidden Bias at Google," *New York Times*, September 24, 2014, http://www.nytimes.com/2014/09/25/technology /exposing-hidden-biases-at-google-to-improve-diversity.html.

7. I serve on the scientific advisory council of EDGE and have advised Applied.

8. "Boston Women's Workforce Council," City of Boston, http://www .cityofboston.gov/women/workforce/.

Credits

The Promise of Behavioral Design

Checkershadow illusion. Image © 1995, Edward H. Adelson.

Chapter 1

Stroop test. Image created by the Women and Public Policy Program at Harvard Kennedy School based on research originally conducted by J. R. Stroop, "Studies of Interference in Serial Verbal Reactions," *Journal of Experimental Psychology* 18 (1935): 643–662.

Chapter 6

Interview checklist. Image created by the Women and Public Policy Program at Harvard Kennedy School.

Chapter 10

New portraits of women leaders at Harvard Kennedy School: Ellen Johnson Sirleaf, President of Liberia. Image courtesy of Stephen Coit, reprinted with permission. All rights are reserved.

Daughter Water. Created by the Australian Workplace Gender Equality Agency in partnership with DDB. Photograph used with permission of the Workplace Gender Equality Agency.

Chapter 12

Women on Boards. February 24, 2011. Department for Business, Innovation & Skills, United Kingdom. © Crown copyright, Open Government Licence v3.0.

Gender Diversity on Corporate Boards. Image created by the Women and Public Policy Program at Harvard Kennedy School.

O-Power Personalized Home Energy Report. Data from Opower Home Energy Report, 2014, http://www.opower.com. Reprinted with permission.

Acknowledgments

This book is the result of a nearly ten-year journey that started when David Ellwood, then dean of Harvard Kennedy School, invited me to serve as faculty chair and later director of the Women and Public Policy Program (WAPPP), one of the Kennedy School's research centers. What excited me about the position was the opportunity to apply the insights and tools that I, as a behavioral economist, had used to help people and organizations make better decisions, and to help society close gender gaps. I soon realized that the two challenges were, in fact, one and the same. Making better decisions means making unbiased decisions. Much like other biases, gender biases hold us back. They affect how we think, judge, and decide, even while we may be unaware of their existence. They lead us to make suboptimal hires and promotions, conduct tests unfairly, and allow stereotypes to proliferate in our classrooms and boardrooms.

As a behavioral scientist, I had the tools to fix some of this. De-biasing the environments in which we live, learn, and work became a personal mantra informing not only my research but also how I led my team at WAPPP and, later, how I conducted myself as academic dean at the Kennedy School. Although serving as academic dean from 2011 to 2014 took me away from the book that I desperately wanted to write, working with and learning from David Ellwood and the leadership team at our school provided me with invaluable insights into the workings of an organization and the management of people. It has been an honor, David, John Haigh, Suzanne Cooper, Sarah Wald, Melodie Jackson, Matt Alper, Charlie Haight, Beth Banks, Karen Jackson-Weaver, and Janney Wilson.

In the summer of 2014, I returned to teaching, research, and the Women and Public Policy Program, and to a wonderful team. Victoria Budson, WAPPP's executive director, is an amazing translator of research findings for policy- and decisionmakers. Her organization works with the White House Council for Women and Girls, the Women in Public Service Project founded by then secretary of state Hillary Rodham Clinton, the Boston Workforce Council, and so many more organizations. Also, Anisha Asundi, Danielle Boudrow, Nicole Carter Quinn, Kerry Conley, Em Gamber, Cara Mathews, Heather McKinnon Glennon, and Lindsey Shepardson all make the world a better place for women and men every day. I owe you all so much.

Anisha, Cara, Kerry, and Nicole have taken a particular interest in my book and have offered invaluable advice and feedback. Anisha provided far more than research assistance, again and again going above and beyond—I could not have wished for a more expert and dedicated person to work with. Kerry's brilliant eye for everything "design," including communication, has made the book (as well as my presentations, web page, and more) so much better. Nicole is the person I turn to when I need level-headed advice—on everything. Thank you, Cara, for keeping me organized and for your insights. And thank you to the entire team for helping me think through particular concepts and data I was trying to communicate—and yes, what the cover of the book should look like. We discussed and voted on colors, designs, fonts, involved my family here and in Switzerland, and led by Tim Jones and Eric Mulder at Harvard University Press, came up with what you have in front of you. Thank you, Tim and Eric, for your creativity and patience!

Indeed, the title itself is the outcome of a process that involved many, inside and outside of WAPPP. I knew from the beginning that the title had to include gender equality and design, but there was a piece missing. So I reached out to a few friends with ideas and a plea for help, and they all generously offered their expertise. I learned so much in my exchanges with Max Bazerman, Jason Beckfield, Paul Bohnet, Dominik Bohnet Zürcher, Mary Brinton, Steve Frost, Jana Gallus, Claudia Goldin, Carol Hamilton, David Laibson, Michael Mauboussin, Kathleen McGinn, Felix Oberholzer-Gee, Lisa Oberholzer-Gee, Carol Schwartz, Cass Sunstein, Lara Warner, Richard Zeckhauser, and Michael Zürcher—and, again, with Anisha and Kerry. It is a surprise we can still use our white board, after all it had to endure with our notes and scribbles. My warmest thanks.

This book would not have been possible without the support of the Women's Leadership Board. These amazing women leaders believed in me before I had written anything substantive on gender, and they have accompanied me on this exciting journey of knowledge creation, implementation, and impact over many years. I learn so much from you! My special thanks for their trust and dedication to the current chair, Lara Warner, as well as her predecessors, Jeannie Minskoff Grant, Roxanne Mankin Cason, Barbara Annis, and Francine LeFrak.

I remain grateful to Abigail Disney, the Exxon Mobil Women's Empowerment Initiative, and the Weatherhead Center for International Affairs at Harvard for providing additional support for my research; to the visionaries who helped lay the groundwork on gender at the Kennedy School, Victoria Budson, Swanee Hunt, Jane Mansbridge, Joe Nye, Holly Taylor Sargent, and Shirley Williams; and to the leaders with whom WAPPP has had the pleasure of collaborating over the years, Analisa Balares of Womensphere, Laura Liswood of the Council of Women World Leaders, Robert Mnookin of the Program on Negotiation at Harvard Law School, Deborah Kolb of the Simmons School of Management, and Saadia Zahidi of the World Economic Forum.

I have learned much from my work on the Board of Directors at Credit Suisse Group and thank Urs Rohner, the chair, my colleagues on the board, as well as Tidjane Thiam, the CEO, Brady Dougan, his predecessor, and the members of the executive board for their interest in behavioral science and their commitment to gender equality. Thanks also to the many people who make Credit Suisse the great company it is and who I have had the pleasure of meeting over the years.

I am indebted to my collaborators who helped shape my thinking for this book: Mohamad Al-Issis, Nava Ashraf, Max Bazerman, Bruno S. Frey, Fiona Greig, Benedikt Herrmann, Kessely Hong, Steffen Huck, Dorothea Kübler, Stephan Meier, Felix Oberholzer-Gee, Maliheh Paryavi, Farzad Saidi, Alexandra van Geen, and Richard Zeckhauser; my colleagues at Harvard, particularly the Behavioral Insights Group that I have the pleasure of co-chairing with Max Bazerman and is so effectively run by Abigail Dalton, WAPPP's faculty advisory group, and the Weatherhead Initiative on Gender Inequality; my current and former students and fellows; the Young Global Leaders of the World Economic Forum, whom I have had the pleasure of working with; the members of the WEF's Global Agenda Councils on Behavior and on Women's Empowerment, who all do such amazing work; and to both long-standing and new friends, who have gone beyond the call of duty for this book— Candice Beaumont, David Boehmer, Deborah Borda, Beth Brooke-Marciniak, Steve Frost, Michelle Gadsden-Williams, Carol Hamilton, Pat Harris, Olivia Leland, Carolina Müller-Möhl, Melanie Richards, Mirjam Staub-Bisang, and Kelly Thompson.

I wrote much of the book while on sabbatical at the University of Sydney in Australia. I am grateful to Mike Hiscox for his generous help in making this happen and paving the way for my family to settle in beautiful Manly. My thanks go to Bates Gill and Melissa Grah-McIntosh for their hospitality at the US Study Center, and the participants of the workshop I led for many fruitful discussions that moved my book project along. Graeme Head deserves special recognition for the amazing work on behavioral insights and inclusion he is leading as the head of the New South Wales Public Service. I am also deeply grateful to Carol Schwartz for her inspiring leadership on gender equality and for opening many doors for me, to Dianne Laurance for leading the way as an entrepreneur and for her most gracious hospitality, and to the Australian Workplace Gender Equality Agency for its thought leadership.

Enormous thanks to the friends and colleagues who have read the manuscript or parts thereof: Linda Babcock, Max Bazerman, Hannah Riley Bowles, Jana Gallus, Kate Glazebrook, Cass Sunstein, and Aniela Unguresan. I benefited so much from your thoughtful feedback and wise counsel! I am also most grateful to people who were kind enough to read the page proof, for I really needed your additional insights: Dolly Chugh, Theresa Lund, and Susanne Schwarz. And of course, Anisha again provided amazing oversight throughout.

The person who had the biggest impact on my book is Thomas LeBien, my editor at Harvard University Press. Thomas exemplifies every quality that an author could want in an editor. A master in the art and science of weaving often disparate threads together and of turning research findings into actionable insights, Thomas helped me find my voice and bring my ideas to life. Thank you, Thomas! I am also grateful to Kate Brick for her discerning feedback and Amanda Peery for her diligence and support. Thanks, too, to Kimberly Giambattisto for her help as production editor. Many thanks also to Anne McGuire for her timely index. Mike Giarratano, Emilie Ferguson, and Rebekah White of Harvard University Press, and Angela Baggetta and Lynn Goldberg of Goldberg McDuffie Communications led the charge on publicity— thank you for all you have done to champion the book and help share the message. Thank you to Susan Donnelly for believing in this book from the first moment we met, and for your passion for the cause.

When I first contemplated the possibility of writing a book, my friend Max Bazerman could not have been more generous with his time, experience, and considerable expertise. A prolific author and influential thinker,

Max walked me through every stage of the process, suggested people I should talk to, and helped me avoid pitfalls along the way. You made this experience so much more enjoyable and smoother, Max, thank you for your generosity and friendship! Early on Max and Cass Sunstein introduced me to Thomas. Having both worked with him, they must have suspected that a one-hour meeting might well turn into a fruitful multiyear collaboration. I also thank Judy Singer for introducing me to Harvard University Press, Don Moore for taking the time to give me early advice, Dave Nussbaum and Cade Massey for building bridges and making introductions, and Adam Grant for his generosity and wise counsel—a true giver who lives the values of his own book.

I could not have written this book without the support of my family. My parents, Ruth and Paul, are simply the best parents in the world. Your enduring trust and support, and your unconditional love mean so much to me. My sister, Brigitte, has been an inspiration since we were small. She is one of the most graceful people I know, always considerate, always giving, always loving. It has been a privilege to be part of her beautiful family, with Hans-Ruedi and with Gabriela and Mirjam, two strong young women who are changing the world—in Murg, Switzerland, and Delhi, India.

And while in this very book I write about people's tendency to be overconfident, some of us are in fact blessed to have many "bests" in their lives. My husband, Michael, is the best husband ever. Words cannot describe how much your love and understanding mean to me. You make it seem so easy to live gender equality! Our children, Dominik and Luca, are such a gift, and yes, they are the very best children we could have. They taught me to live in the present and enjoy the moment, and they are among the best ambassadors this book and its author could ever have.

Index